Hollow

Hollow

A MEMOIR OF MY BODY IN THE MARINES

Bailey Williams

Abrams Press, New York

Library of Congress Control Number: 2024937484

ISBN: 978-1-4197-7192-7
eISBN: 979-8-88707-212-8

Printed and bound in the United States
10 9 8 7 6 5 4 3 2 1

The views expressed in this publication are those of the author and do not necessarily reflect the official policy or position of the Department of Defense or the US government. The public release clearance of this publication by the Department of Defense does not imply Department of Defense endorsement or factual accuracy of the material.

ABRAMS The Art of Books
195 Broadway, New York, NY 10007
abramsbooks.com

For my sisters.
Their mothers.
And for daughters everywhere.

Dedicated to the 5.Ladies.

Stories about running are often like this, in that they're about something else. They are tales of shape shifting, of the desire to shed one skin and step into another. One running story may be a parable on persistence or denial; another a warning.

—*Catriona Menzies-Pike,* The Long Run

The Army and Navy are run like traditional military services.
The Air Force is run like a corporation.
But the Marine Corps is a religion.

—*Attributed to an anonymous Navy admiral*

There are no women Marines. Only Marines.

—*Something we said way too often*

PART I

MAKING

CHAPTER I
ENLISTING

Alternatively, individuals at risk for eating disorders may self-select into the military.

—*Lindsay Bodell, et al., "Consequences of Making Weight"*

When I gripped my desk, the skin whitened across my knuckles. Red scars flashed across the joints.

I grabbed the phone and made the call. "Hi," I said, heart bellowing. "Do Marines need to have twenty-twenty vision?"

"They do not," said the deep voice on the other end of the line.

"Oh, okay. Great, thank you. Um . . . what about really bad? I'm blind as a bat. Figuratively, obviously, mine's actually much worse, bats use sonar . . ."

"As long as it's correctable to twenty-twenty, ma'am."

"Great, okay, great. Thank you very much for your time."

He caught me before I hung up. "Do you have any other questions I can help you with, ma'am?"

"No, thank you. Um, I would like to join now, though, please."

He paused. "Where are you? We'll have someone pick you up."

"Oh. I'm at work, sorry. I don't get off until five."

"We'll have someone pick you up at five, ma'am. Seventeen hundred."

"Oh. Okay. Thank you." The address. "How will I know you?"

"Ma'am, he'll be the one wearing the blue trousers with the red stripe."

"Oh."

And so he was, the first Marine I ever met, stepping out of a white car with government plates. His striped trousers stood out smartly on Rodeo Drive. The tall recruiter wore a white hat. The black brim shaded his face.

He opened the car door. I slid in. As he pulled into Beverly Hills traffic, he encouraged me to introduce myself. "So you're from here, California girl? Born in LA?"

"I only moved here in December, actually. I grew up in West Virginia."

"You moved out here alone? What was high school like?"

"Stereotypical. Prozac and minor existential crisis."

"Yeah? Get into anything illegal?"

"Oh! No, sir, nothing like that. Um, I think I got like one speeding ticket. I worked for a veterinarian out in the country and—"

He glanced at me. "Any problems with boys?"

Another door held open for me, at the Culver City Armed Forces Recruiting Center. Posters of service members lined the walls. Marines stood potent in high-collared dress blues, variations of chiseled white guy in front, solemn Black guy to his left, Latina woman behind, all looking hard as nails. No discrimination here, so long as you had an imposing jaw line.

We sat at his desk. My flushed confession continued. It felt almost good, talking to someone.

"I used to be bulimic. But I'm doing okay, right now."

His relaxed face exuded camaraderie. I stumbled on. I cited the only thing I had found online searching *enlisting in recovery from an eating disorder.* "So long as I'm willing and able." I met his eyes. "I am."

The recruiter nodded. "Well, and I mean. Don't most females go through an eating disorder phase?"

I hated that question. But the certificate above his desk declared his Silver Star from a firefight in Iraq, so I nodded. Who was I to correct a war hero?

He leaned back and laced his hands behind his head. He even bent his knees at right angles. "I wouldn't worry about it. You're going to be working so hard, your body will just make you eat. At a certain point, you won't be able to *have* an eating disorder in the military."

I seriously doubted this.

What I needed was help. A place wooded and gentle, where someone would press a mint-infused washcloth to my forehead and assure me it was fine if I wanted to talk about my mother every once in a while.

Joining the Marines was easier.

The recruiter made an appeasing face. "I mean, just looking at you—" a vague hand gesture "—you're obviously doing fine. You don't look like you're starving yourself."

I heard, *You could stand to lose ten pounds. Or twenty.*

"Now, about the other thing," the recruiter said. I stiffened. The other thing. The whole kill myself thing.

"Prozac. Can you keep your shit together without it?"

"Oh. Absolutely. It's better actually, without all that stuff. Luvox, Lamictal, Prozac, I think one other one. They made me blurry, like things were fading around the edges. They were part of the reason . . ." I trailed off, but I'd lost him. "Um. I actually think they were part of the reason I tried to check out early."

"Oh, right. You mean when you—"

"When I tried to kill myself, yeah." For some reason he seemed absurdly unconcerned with this. "I know, it's cliché. It was, like, super Sylvia Plath. Like if you grow up a girl in America, you'll probably consider slitting your wrists at some point."

"And it's not really, you know, a big thing."

"It's not really a big thing," I agreed, marveling at my naivety that I certainly thought it had been.

He ran his fingers over his lips. "How old were you?"

"Sixteen. I stumbled into Nietzsche."

He tapped his finger to his lips. "If you don't mind me asking, what'd you do?"

"Swallowed the medicine cabinet."

"Do you feel that way now?" he asked pointedly.

I knew something stalked me, some breathless compulsion I couldn't name. I knew I walked to class in Westwood and caught myself watching passing buses too closely. I knew I lingered over razors at Walgreens. But once I was a Marine I wouldn't spiral into these defeatist blues. Once I was a Marine, I'd matter.

"No. I want to do things differently. I want to do them right."

The recruiter shrugged. "Then I wouldn't worry about it. Marines get darkness. Just ask for help, someone will always reach out to you. You'll be in good company to deal with that kind of thing. Some Marines have been through some pretty rough stuff."

"Combat," I interrupted. He raised his eyebrows.

"No, I mean right here, where you are. Marines are tough. A lot of them enlist from rough places. I promise you, what you're going to do in the Marines will be unlike anything you have ever done, or ever will do. When you get out, in four years, ten years, twenty, you'll find yourself having a beer with another Marine, because he'll be the only one who understands."

He was not wrong.

The recruiter asked, "Why do you want to join my Marine Corps?"

I stared at a recruiting poster.

The dream was to run.

I hadn't gotten much further than that. For the last two years, the light at the end of the teenage tunnel glimmered: I could leave. I could run like hell.

I dreamed of heading West. I dreamed of landing on my feet, confident in independence, with a newfound ability to take a deep breath.

I graduated a semester early and bought a one-way ticket to the City of Angels—the city where my mother was born.

The restlessness followed me, though. In Los Angeles my skin mewled in sunlight most my body had never felt.

I'd burst into California, gotten an excellent haircut, wore dramatically low-cut black dresses. I interned at the musty Elephant Theatre, learning the mysteries of the tech board. And someone I worked with saw me, a seventeen-year-old girl with a great haircut who listened more than she spoke.

Afterward he gasped and held my hips—but they could be his hips, I didn't claim them—and said he'd never met a girl like me.

I heard it as a compliment, not being like other girls.

"No, you have to inhale," Tom, the man from the theatre, laughed. The party danced on the other side of a hedge strung with lights. The rank smell of marijuana overcame the lavender in the garden.

The joint startled me, as if he'd pulled a gun.

"Just smoke it like you would a cigarette," he said.

My Mormon family had turned our eyes from the billboard Marlboro cowboys above the Kanawha River Railroad, peeling and stained with coal dust. We shuddered and said, "Be simple concerning things that are evil."

And boy, was I. The girl raised Mormon declined the joint but tried a cigarette, and I put the wrong end in my mouth.

I did go on one date to a place called the Standard, the name hung upside down on the sign, with a man from my Shakespeare class, and read *The Sun Also Rises* by the pool when he said, "Sorry, I need to take this, just my girlfriend." Polyamory was way too advanced for me, the girl who still sat with ankles crossed because this was modest.

Los Angeles, my dashed bid for freedom, glared light into all the places I felt incomplete. I was overstimulated by the city, stunned by sunlight that turned skyscrapers into prisms of harsh mirrors. The pavement jarred me. I walked everywhere, breathless uncertainty at my ankles. I sought something to identify me, even to myself. Some cause, some containment, some self-worth that came in a neatly packaged box.

I needed it to hurt. I needed it to change me. I craved the courage to walk with confidence, alone under an open sky.

And so, the military.

As I understood it, the American military was sanctified since General George Washington prayed at Valley Forge. It was one of several interesting things I believed. I believed servicemen were justly named liberators. I believed the new gender-inclusive term "service member" was liberal PC crap. The traditional "servicemen" had been good enough to storm Normandy, thank you very much.

My brain glossed over the fact that my entire conceptualization of the military, dignified bands of brothers, did not, in fact, include, you know, me.

I would simply not be a girl. I didn't want to be a girl. The Marines seemed like a fine alternative.

I'd abandoned the clergy but couldn't so easily leave faith.

I craved a new religion. Every pore recognized one when I found it.

I believed the god I insisted I didn't believe in wanted nothing to do with me. I felt hollow somewhere deep inside. There was a Mormon painting I loved as a kid. It showed Mormon pioneers dusted in snow at the banks of the Platte River in Nebraska, in 1847. Angry mobs drove the disruptive church from the United States and martyred their prophet, so they had commenced the great exodus to the Utah Territory. Winter is not a good time to cross a river, not laden with all your possessions to start a new life in a new country, not when you are transporting children and elders, not when there is no bridge and it is Nebraska.

Three young men came forward. They were strong and willing to help. They crossed the icy river over and over again, carrying children, shouldering handcarts, creating ferries.

The cold claimed their lives. When the new prophet Brigham Young heard of their actions and deaths, he reputedly wept and prophesied, "For this action alone, these men will be delivered to the celestial kingdom."

The highest kingdom of heaven, where the Father Himself lived.

As I sat in the recruiter's office, shame ran through my veins rich as blood. I felt scarred and angry and scared. Deep down, a hollow resonance pulsed a conviction on which I coursed my direction. The only way to earn my place in the kingdom of God, or at least to be counted among the good and right, was through my physical body. I didn't really expect to be a good person in and of myself. But maybe I could *do* something honorable enough to sweep out all my shame.

I wanted to put myself on that icy river. I wanted to know if I would cross.

What I said was, "Because I was abused as a kid, like, sexually. I don't ever want to be the person that could happen to, ever again."

The recruiter, with his Combat Action Ribbon and his Operation Iraqi Freedom Ribbon and his Silver Star, nodded. This, he understood. "Don't worry. From the day you sign that dotted line, you will always have the Marines. Once a Marine, always a Marine. We will *never* leave a Marine behind.

"That's the thing about being a Marine. We don't care who you were before. Once you wear the eagle, globe, and anchor, what's behind you is irrelevant."

I couldn't sign the paperwork fast enough. My initials became a streak with repetition. How badly I wanted irrelevance. Baptism by enlistment.

"Everyone has that—*thing*, you know. Skeleton, everyone has that skeleton in the closet." The recruiter watched as I waded through stacks of paperwork. "I don't think I know a single Marine who doesn't have some shit behind him. Having the Marines, though, teaches you the discipline to take it. You're going to be part of a family. We take care of one another.

"You will learn the discipline to take care of your brothers first."

While I was in Los Angeles begging my recruiter for reassurance yet again that I wasn't too fat for boot camp, Marines surged into Iraq. It was ostensibly the final bloody sponge. Pundits preached it could be the end of the occupation if we only had the guts as a nation to see it through. I read the *LA Times* and felt very involved. On the news, men wearing American flag pins shouted we could drum up a great final blow and end this thing, finish what they started on 9/11, if only the American people could rally the courage and the guts.

Why did the Marine Corps take me? When our national strategy was guts, the requirement to enlist was a pulse.

"No, you can't be infantry."

"But . . . that's why I'm joining. That's what I want to do. I want to fight."

"Well, you can't. Females can't be in the infantry. There's health reasons, you know. The female body can't go that long without showering."

This was news to me. In an attempt to appear worldly I nodded.

"I mean, you could go weeks without a shower. You run into medical issues, for female types."

"I really want to deploy," I insisted.

Another afternoon in the recruiter's station. Somehow there was more paperwork. We were discussing my MOS, military occupational specialty, or what I would actually do for the next four years.

"You'll still deploy without being in the infantry. There're females all over the FOBs."

"Fobs?"

Men and women became males and females in military jargon. It sounded funny initially, wrong if only grammatically. Then it became normal.

"Forward operating bases. Just not, you know, in the MOS that require males."

"Combat camera, then, please?"

"No, the Marines doesn't need you there. How about aviation ordnance? That's a pretty badass gig, for a girl."

"What is that?"

"Putting bombs on planes."

"Will I deploy?"

"You will definitely deploy."

"Okay, that sounds good then. Thank you."

The Los Angeles recruit processing center smelled industrially scoured. I finished the military intelligence test and shot a guilty glance around the computer lab. Boys ran hands over their necks as if their fresh haircuts had answers. The room was silent but for mouse clicks and the sharp footsteps of the proctor, a dour first sergeant who prowled the room in shiny Corframs. No one else moved. It had taken me more time to solemnly nod through his grim integrity lecture against cheating than it had to actually take the test.

Well, I was done. I walked out as quietly as I could. The white-haired woman at the front desk pursed her lips at me. I had the distinct impression she thought I'd given up.

I thought, *Oh, God. I'm too stupid to join the Marines.*

"You're too short for aviation ordnance."

"What?" I was so startled I fell off the pull-up bar at the recruiter's station. "I wasn't too short yesterday."

The recruiter was looking at my test score. "It's the equipment they use and stuff. There's a cut off and you're too short. Look, you did really well on the ASVAB. You can have any job in the Marine Corps you want. How does cryptologic linguist sound? It's in intel."

Instant alarm bells. My stomach dropped realizing he was serious: he wanted me to go learn a foreign language. I would prefer the bombs.

"I do not think I'm particularly good at learning languages."

"Look, when I say you did really well on the ASVAB, I mean you did even better than me. You got the highest score I've ever seen. People with lower scores go into this field and they do fine."

"I really want to go to Iraq." I didn't want to while away an entire year studying Russian. The war might be over by the time I got there.

"You'll get the highest security clearance in America. It'll be great for jobs afterward."

"I really, really don't think I'm very good at learning languages."

"You'll learn. This is where the Marine Corps needs you. Military occupational specialty twenty-six hundred: cryptologic linguist."

I tried one last time. "Um, I think I might have like, an obstacle to learning languages. Um. I hear in color. Days of the week, numbers. February is maroon. Um . . ."

He interrupted. "Look. If you want to be a Marine, you're going to have to learn to think of others first. You're smart. This is a hard field to get into. You will learn because you'll *have* to."

I quailed. "Okay." And rallied. "Thank you."

I couldn't find my Social Security card and thought I might've left it with my dad. I paced in circles and called.

I tried to casually mention I'd be moving to South Carolina in the next week or so.

Dad sounded confused. "What's in South Carolina?"

"Parris Island."

"As in the military base? Are you dating a Marine?"

Not quite.

The next day Dad called back. "Don't get me wrong, Bailey. The US military is the best in the world. You could do a lot of good. You'd have access to amazing resources you'd get nowhere else, and I'm sure you'd get a profound education in its own right."

He was not wrong.

"But you have to play to your strengths. We had hundreds of thousands of guys invading Europe in World War II. We had something like eighty scientists working on the Manhattan Project. It takes a lot of bodies to fight wars, but brains end them. What if Einstein had parachuted into France?"

"Dad."

"Why not finish college, then if you must do this crazy thing, become an officer?"

"There's a war going on."

"Then there is the small, infinitesimal fact you have never shown the slightest interest in anything martial, whatsoever. On our family vacations to every American aircraft carrier, submarine, and radio installation to survive World War II, I always found you curled up reading somewhere. Your brothers were crawling all over the anti-aircraft guns on the USS *Alabama*, and you were under the torpedo tubes reading *Black Beauty*. So I have to wonder," Dad laughed, not mocking but baffled, "Why my Shakespeare-enthralled daughter would seriously want to join the Marines."

"It's a good book. *Black Beauty* inspired animal rights policies."

"Is it a Hemingway thing? Are you aspiring to be the Wilfred Owen of Iraq?"

"Dad!"

We were both quiet. "I just have to."

He was right. I cringe to admit it, but I envisioned myself canonized in Facebook photos wearing battle-dirty cammies and a keffiyeh for some reason, holding an Iraqi child outside of a newly safe school. Coming home world-weary at the wizened age of twenty and putting it down how it really *was* over there.

I *didn't* actually care about ships or planes or projectiles. I wasn't *remotely* interested in guns or cybersecurity or ground-shaking explosions. I didn't give a blistering *damn* about any of the metal trappings of the United States military's destructive shock-and-awe might.

But I did care, deeply, that my family had cared enough to visit every American aircraft carrier, submarine, and radio installation to survive World War II.

Dad was baffled by my insistence. Over the phone, he advised me sadly, "Well, please don't get into the whole culture of . . . tattoos."

I was so surprised I stopped pacing. Dad didn't know it, but on my left wrist my first tattoo was still healing, a tiny Star of David. Tattoos were haram in Mormonland, because they harm the temple that is the body.

My forearms were crisscrossed. Some scars were round and purple, others white and raised, match heads and razors. But tattoos would displease God.

On the last bus across campus in Westwood, I pored over a copy of *The Sun Also Rises*. I sensed a familiar darkness at my feet. I refused to look away from the yellowed paperback. I knew—my heart pounded painfully—that on the other side of my book, every human on the bus stared at me. Stared at this strange, pale, dark-haired, kinda-pretty-if-she-weren't-so-fat girl, a black phantom scuttling around her feet like a crab. I am joining the United States Marine Corps, I protested against my shaking. I am going to make me right.

And as for you, I thought fiercely, to the shadow that moved independently of me, I will grind you into an Iraqi desert.

And that was it, enlisting. The recruiter laughed when someone slammed the door and I jumped out of my marred skin. He ignored the scars at my wrists. He didn't ask so I hadn't told my maddening attraction to other girls. All of it irrelevant. I signed the dotted line.

Something wasn't right under my skin. Something about mirrors confounded me, and sometimes I heard things other people didn't, laughter and cracked voices. Sometimes, walking down the street, great shivers of fear trembled down my spine so breathtakingly I thought I was going to explode, spontaneously combust right on the pavement, RIP.

Something wasn't right, and I knew it, and my recruiter knew it, and we both nodded and beamed, like the Marine Corps was the best place in the world for me.

We Marines like a little crazy, we agreed conspiratorially, like I had any idea.

Something I didn't know. If the Marines stopped every hungry kid from enlisting, told every anxious teenager to go home and get themselves and their families right, there'd be whole bases deserted. Camp Lejeune would fall into the swamp. Joshua trees would reclaim 29 Palms.

The recruiters had their quotas.

We had our guts.

CHAPTER 2

BOOT

Histories of eating disorders start with the saints.
Personal histories start with first diets.

—*Susan Burton,* Empty

I began fasting when I was seven. Dad was pleased. "Precocious," he beamed the first time I said no dinner for me, thanks.

"Well, I turn eight soon, and I want to practice before I reach the age of accountability," I said primly. In Mormonland, children were baptized at eight. After that I'd be held accountable for sins I committed. I had a strange feeling I was going to commit an awful lot of them.

It was a Mormon covenant, a once-monthly fast. To go without food or water softened the body's animal grip on the spirit. To deny bodily hungers was to move closer to the spiritual world. We fasted when we needed to feel closer to God. We fasted to ask for help. We fasted to repent. Through adolescence, fasting held my own body, with all its wrongness, at an increasingly bony arm's distance.

I slammed the door on the Mormon church when I was sixteen. That was the year the patriarch's son told me he'd prayed and the priesthood revealed me to him, to put his tongue in my mouth. The final straw.

The door made no sound behind me. But fasting burrowed into my bones.

I arrived at Parris Island at midnight with other nervous recruits. The bus slowed under the ominous gates of the Marine Corps Recruit Depot. We had barely rolled to a stop when a growling Marine barreled up the steps yelling to move, move now. We dove off the bus in flailing civilian inefficiency and sprinted to the yellow footprints. The girl next to me, a bat tattooed across her chest, barked a laugh. Instantly the Marines dove on her. "You won't be laughing long, recruit."

With glass-shattering howls a Latina sergeant roped us females from the men. We stumbled through warehouses, the shuffling of cardboard. We changed into stiff cammies, utilitarian uniforms printed with desert camouflage, and handed over our civilian clothes—henceforth, civvies—to be tagged, bagged, carted away.

Uniformed, we funneled back with the men for a sterilized whirl through medical. As the sun rose, recruits began to fall asleep standing, dozing against cinderblock walls. Our Marine herders startled them awake. "SLEEP? Does this look like a sleepover to you, recruit? Did you think you were joining the goddamn GIRL SCOUTS?"

Doctors, mercifully not yelling, patted us down. I peered helplessly at an eye chart. Medical issued me glasses designed to survive jumping out of a plane or a punch to the face. Thick and owlish, military-issued glasses were called BCGs: birth control glasses.

We ran through a gauntlet of nurses who flicked shots into our triceps, jabs on each side. I asked a nurse what the vial entering my arm was. Surprised I talked, she said, "It's a shot," and pushed me forward. Well, wherever we were going, we were vaccinated.

The smell of the armory underlined the humid morning with a metallic edge. I marveled, holding the M16 in my hands. I'd never held a firearm.

We were uniformed, medically verified alive, and armed. Their work complete, screaming Marines divided us. Buses vacuumed bald-headed males away. We females pressed into beige buses that smelled like ammunition, squeezed tight with all our gear, knocking our packs into one another. Another wide-eyed recruit and I rode so nearly face to face, our sweaty skin brushed as we rattled to fourth battalion.

It disappointed me they didn't make us march. This didn't seem all that hardcore.

We fell out of the bus and tumbled up the stairs, a little breathless, to the squad bay of our first-ever barracks, a squat brick building under draping willows. It smelled clean, open, as day broke fully.

Down the long squad bay, metal bunks we would now know as racks stood in perfect alignment perpendicular to two painted lines that ran the length of the cement floor, which we would henceforth know as the deck. We too were expected to align. Awkwardly, we stood in our newly acquired positions of attention. Heels together, feet at forty-five-degree angles, fists along the seams of our trousers. A few sleep-deprived girls swayed on their feet. We snuck glances at one another. Futilely I wished away my flyaway hair.

We sized each other up as surely our male counterparts did across the island, but in a thought probably not reflected among the men, as I eyed my cohort, I felt reassurance I was among the smallest. It wasn't that I thought visible collar bones made me good, but I'd surely gotten the message that skinniness carried power. Power of concealment, of latent approval, even envy, from other women.

I bid silent farewell to the Latina Marine who'd screamed us from yellow footprints to squad bay with admirable verbal virulence. As a parting screw-you she threw open a floodgate. Our drill instructors tore in the door.

They surged in a ferocious pack, frenzied wolves springing, howling in our faces, bobbing explosions, circling the line, viciously loud. Veins throbbed in their temples and sweat slicked their jaws. They slammed the metal racks above our heads, sending startling percussion down the squad bay. Recruits' eyebrows shot up. Shrieking back our only lines: Yes, ma'am. No, ma'am. Aye, ma'am.

The window across the squad bay showcased a bowing tree. I fixed my gaze on the golden sunlight in its boughs, the shifting mandala of light.

Then something magical happened. A drill instructor bore down on me, seized my wrist, and pushed my fist back. Her grip swallowed my pulse. "Thumb along the seam, recruit!" she death-growled, her voice wind-tunnel hoarse, "If you want to stand in MY Marine Corps uniform."

A savage burst of joy. Golden warmth erupted beneath my sternum.

I knew exactly who I was in that moment, exactly who my drill instructor was. We were in a relationship I understood better than any.

Marine Corps boot camp suddenly felt a whole hell of a lot like home. I guessed it was all the shouting.

We renounced the personal pronoun. I was this recruit. We were these recruits. These recruits required permission to speak. To pee, we screamed, "Good morning, ladies! Recruit Williams requests permission to speak to Drill Instructor Staff Sergeant Hernandez!"

Nerve-racking, summoning a demon. Staff Sergeant Hernandez leaned close, black eyes flashing, yelling hot breath on our faces, "You speaking to me, recruit? You speaking to me like that with those IPs"—Irish pennants, or loose threads, implying poverty, because only in the Marine Corps is picking on Irish immigrants like it's 1852 a fine family tradition—"hanging off your goddamn uniform?" or "With that excuse for hair, all jacked the fuck up?" Whatever our current wrong was. Once we squared it away, we could try again.

Not a girl among us was surprised to learn appearance mattered, earned our right to speak.

That staff sergeant loved the Marines with a ferocity that dared us to contradict how much fun we were having. I called her the Angry One.

The crop-haired drill instructor, the one who reminded me of home, roared hoarse. She screamed anyway in a high and horrifying whistle that raised blue webs of veins across her face. I named her the Drill Instructor I Love.

Fierce drill instructors, the senior fiercer still. Tall and Black and beautiful and collected, preternaturally calm as a moonlit lake. She spoke quietly. To anger her provoked rare and awe-inspiring, squad-bay-overturning, Shiva-destroyer-of-worlds cataclysms.

She, we all called the Senior.

I loved my drill instructors. I loved them like iron. I loved that something about them that screamed, "Go ahead and fucking try me," even when they weren't actually, literally screaming, "Go ahead and fucking try me."

If I had to be a girl, I could get behind being like that.

The Drill Instructor I Loved yelled in the face of a platoon mate: "So you're going to be the one who makes us all look bad?"

The recruit under fire, Brite, possessed the unfortunate tendency when flustered to jettison small details like the distinction between left and right. Perpetually flustered, she created bodily collisions as we learned drill commands like column right, echelon left.

"Another unsquared away BCP female? You just gonna get us knocked up?"

Brite had a round belly, and drill instructors nipped.

Overweight Marines were banished to Body Composition Program (BCP), a diet and exercise regimen, or, in our terms, rations and physical training (PT). An insult, even dishonor, to be overweight in uniform.

We'd hear this warning repeatedly. If we somehow scraped through, genuinely became, God forbid, Marines, we would move into a world where there'd be female Marines, bad ones, who joined only to get fat and pregnant. Immediately. Perhaps simultaneously. Discipline alone prevented our natural state, slothful and impregnated. Food and sex equaled bodily appetites to bridle in order to achieve the ever-sought squared away.

Squared away meant a lot of things. Decent. Competent. With the program. Certainly not fat. All imperfect femininity was tucked into it, too; no stray hair falling out of sleeked buns.

Parris Island meted punishment through the body. We called it incentivizing.

Somewhere over our heads as we flailed in squad bay calisthenics, our drill instructors screamed, "When the mind fails to comprehend, the body must pay."

I nodded. I knew. I knew.

We stood nearly naked on the line, awaiting body inspection. A curt captain with a blond bob surveyed us. The Senior warned us in no uncertain terms to stand up straightest for our officer. She Had Been to College, and Had More Real World Experience. We somehow said it in capitals.

One by one, the blond captain examined us. Suddenly she stood in front of me. She gazed with cold blue eyes as I turned in a circle, arms above my head, praying I didn't look so fat she'd just throw me out immediately.

No one had ever seen me so naked.

She peered at my forearms. "What are all these scars, recruit?"

I'd worked for a veterinarian in high school, which was remarkably convenient.

"From working with animals, ma'am," I shouted. Some of them even were.

"Hmm." She pointed to the minuscule tattoo on my left wrist, the Star of David. "Are you Jewish?"

"This recruit's mother was Jewish, ma'am."

"I didn't ask you for all that, recruit," snapped the blond officer, but she passed by.

We marched to the track for the initial strength test. Clumsily we stacked rifles and lined up at the marker.

I shook like a wind-whipped power line. I feared failure. More than failure: I was sure I'd putter in dead last. I was terrified of banishment to Preparatory Conditioning Platoon. Fatty boot camp, Marines warned us. Recruits assigned extra PT to lose weight in order to continue.

I'd always been a back-of-the-pack runner. At thirteen I joined cross-country, alarmed dieting alone hadn't whittled me two-dimensional. My eyes bulged when I realized Coach was serious about the warm-up being a mile. A mile rendered me red and huffing. I begged for a swift death. Still I kept running. By every measurable account I sucked. For four years of cross-country I finished dead last every morning, doggedly trailing a pack of thinner and leggier girls. Teammates on the girls' high school cross-country team went to state and took it by storm. I went to throw up in the locker room.

A pistol fired. I ran, fists clenched.

An impossibly athletic woman in our sister platoon, a former gymnast, ran a powerful time, sliding in first. A tall redhead slammed in behind her.

And then, gracelessly smashing in behind her, was . . . me.

Irrelevant, whatever grit it took to keep running for years finishing last. I attributed it entirely to the weight I'd lost so far.

No matter what we did, we were wrong and kind of worthless. That was the simple nature of boot camp. We all responded to constant wrongness in our own ways. Most girls stressed over it, assigned moral value. They used our quiet hour at the end of the day to do push-ups, sit-ups, pull-ups. Do better, be better. Get Motivated. Some shrugged it off. It was all an act, a little harmless hazing. They used our quiet hour to form friendships.

Some girls protested. They refused to spring out of bed or speak in the third person, or insisted on making eye contact with Marines, like we rated. They spent the quiet hour venting this wasn't what they were *here* for, they had self-*esteem*. One by one they went away. My cycle spit out half its recruits, forty-something of us becoming twenty.

As for me, I dove in. I stopped eating. I knew this one. I used our quiet hour to do sit-ups until I got so bony my spine jutted like a stegosaurus and bruised against the cement deck. Then I read the Book of Mormon.

In case anyone ever wondered, it is very much possible to make it through United States Marine Corps boot camp on well under six hundred calories a day.

Strange things happen, though.

Boot camp just wasn't that damn hard.

There were a handful of us. A slender brown girl with pockmarked skin. A stout woman from the South. We kept our heads low. We looked at each other and knew.

This . . . ? This was not that bad.

The mindfuck, that is. Boot camp's job was to condition this into our souls: You. Don't. Know. Shit. *So listen to me.*

I already got that. I accepted the premise of boot camp: you're quite correct, ma'am, I am nobody. I had been trained in masochism. When drill instructors screamed in my face, I went to a still, quiet place. I knew how to hunker in plain sight. To lean *into* the shouting, to absorb it, let it tingle through you. Swallow the charge. Savor it. Find pleasure in the burning, the stab of accusation, the blunt edge of judgment. If you let it fill you, it couldn't hurt you.

That had been my childhood. Hell, I was eighteen. That had been my life.

Week by week, I slipped further underground, dredging the cold tunnel to anorexia. Every few nights I took my turn on fire watch. When I stood duty, I didn't walk up and down the deck. I ran, high knees in combat boots, looping circles around the sleeping squad bay.

One morning the Senior ordered me out of hand-to-hand grappling and into a truck with government plates. To my delight a tall redhead, Artigas, bumped my elbow sliding into the truck next to me.

I'd noticed this girl immediately. I wanted to stand up straighter when I saw her. Even the company commander, the officer with the blond bob, deigned a curt nod when Artigas spoke. Artigas, too, had Gone to College and had Real World Experience. She towered about six feet tall and shouted so loudly you could hear it clear across the drill field.

I suspected Artigas was in a furtive camp with me, the one the military decided wouldn't exist if we didn't talk about it. We'd been asked to shed a minor part of our lives, but it tracked our military careers like encampments following railroad workers westward as they built the transcontinental railroad. In dark, unlit shanty camps lived our disowned sexual orientations, what we couldn't leave behind but couldn't invite into public light.

In the truck we sat together with heads down. We weren't allowed to look out windows at boot camp because screw you, that's why. Drill instructors snapped we didn't rate to look at shit. We sympathized. We bowed our heads and jostled around base piously, heads knocking together.

My eyes fell on our arms. Hers: solid, freckled red, muscled, tanned brown. Mine: startlingly pale. Blue veins laced the soft skin. My elbows had begun to protrude where hers were roped with sinew. We looked like two different species. There was going to be a whole different kind of female Marine, and I loved her immediately.

Artigas and I bounced along as a drill instructor in Artigas' platoon drove without explanation. This drill instructor was a Lioness, a Marine in the female engagement teams (FET) in Iraq. We'd seen her in a book about women serving in the war, which we whispered over and passed around after lights out.

We rolled to a stop at a low building under draping willows. We were on a part of Parris Island we hadn't seen before, and still hadn't, as we studied our laps. The Lioness growled at us to sit, stay, while she figured out what to do with us.

The keys dangled invitingly in the ignition. Artigas nudged me. "We should make a break for it," she whispered. I was shocked she'd even joke about going AWOL, but I wanted to be her friend so I smiled tightly.

The Lioness violently swung open the truck door, ordered us out, and explained our mysterious errand. We were here for the first of our security clearance interviews. Artigas, too, was bound for the 2600 cryptologic linguist field. We were candidates for the highest security clearances in the United States, and as active duty military, top priority.

At news of an interview my neck burned. To the Saints, three sins stain worse than any others. Killing, sex before marriage, and apostasy—leaving the faith. I'd committed two of the three sins, including the one called unforgivable, and I'd tried my damnedest to commit all three. I very much doubted the federal government cared about sex or apostasy, and I knew to obfuscate the suicide thing. Still I felt corrosive shame.

We waited. Parris Island dripped under the humid heat. A swamp cooler blasted the hovel. If this process went through lunch, maybe I wouldn't have to eat at all.

A voice called me into an office.

The gentleman interviewing me wore civilian clothes, so I had no idea his rank or role. Sleepy red eyes surveyed me, bags of skin under them like a bloodhound. We faced each other across the desk.

"Do you drink?"

No, sir.

"Do you smoke?"

No, sir.

"How many sexual partners have you had?"

One, sir.

"You're very young."

Yes, sir.

"You're very pretty."

Thank you, sir.

"Unusually pretty."

Thanks. Sir.

"And how many sexual partners have you had?"

Still just the one, sir.

"Are you sure?"

Yes, sir.

"Okay. And what did you do with him that you're ashamed of that can be used against you?"

Not a damn thing, sir.

"This one sexual partner was a man?"

Yes, sir.

"Are you sure?"

Yes, I checked thoroughly. Sir.

"Why have you never smoked marijuana?"

I cited not wanting to get kicked off the cross-country team. I did not mention that, raised Mormon, I had no clue how one went about acquiring The Marijuanas.

He pointed at my wrist, my tiny shield, the Star of David just left of the pulsing blue vein. "Why *that* tattoo?"

The Star of David is what it's normally called in English. But in Hebrew, *Magen David* means shield.

Well, sir, because when I put my thumb on that star, I feel my pulse, and for a moment I remember—no matter what, no matter how dark things seem—a flickering sense of my own being. I recall I came from somewhere, that I am the daughter of someone I don't remember.

On my eighteenth birthday, my first alone back in Los Angeles, I took the fifty dollars my father sent in his card and translated it into something I would never, no matter what, not carry with me.

"This recruit's mother was Jewish."

"Are you Jewish?"

"Nominally, this recruit supposes."

"You can answer yes or no to direct questions," the bloodhound reminded me quietly. "In the Marines you may deploy to lands where that tattoo won't be welcome. What will you do?"

"Wear a watch, sir."

I thought I saw a flicker of approval. "Are you religious?"

"Yes, sir, I am."

His voice warmed then. He told me when It began, people would start disappearing, and then, "You'll know." I believed he was talking about the Rapture, but I wasn't in a position to ask questions. I nodded politely and said thank you for your time, sir, and then I was dismissed.

I walked out shaking. Well, I'd be. Guess Uncle Sam did care about sex and apostasy. Good thing I hadn't killed anyone.

After eight weeks, Cassie, a buzzcut recruit with a Kentucky drawl, whispered as we scrubbed the deck, "You know, if we were Navy, we'd be done by now."

Ah, but then we would have missed the fun that was swimming in combat boots. We floundered in awkward calisthenics in the pool, rifles held aloft, choked down enough chlorine to pass, and tromped back to Fourth Battalion cheerful and dripping.

Swim qualifications were weird because the men were there. Male-female relations on Parris Island were strange. Looking at male recruits was an integrity violation, as it might provoke them to look back at us. We brushed shoulders with them on co-ed shuttles, where male and female recruits sat together on gravest orders not to dare mess around, as in, see each other. Warnings against the "nastiness" of male Marines came early and consistently.

What our drill instructors thought of the controversy of gender-segregated Marine boot camp, the last military branch holding out, they didn't say. Mostly drill instructors fought hard to pretend there were no men on the island. Maybe they knew what we couldn't—that we would never again exist in a Marine space exempt from male eyes. Maybe they wanted us to see what women could look like as a team. Probably they were just following orders.

The rifle ranges sprawled across male territory, so while studying marksmanship we ate at the males' chow hall. When we marched in after a morning firing rifles, a few female recruits caught it hot for peering across the partition to where male recruits ate. Later they rolled their eyes. We'd heard tantalizing rumors males got dessert at boot camp, that the chocolate wasn't removed from their MREs. Though our training was otherwise identical, we were denied sweet things on the agreed assumption that as females, we should always be watching our weight.

We females weren't interested in the males. We lusted after their *food.*

"You know, if we'd joined the Air Force," Brown Bull, the Dakota recruit, whispered after nine weeks, "We'd be done by now."

Then I would have missed the pleasure of softly losing my mind.

Two fears, going into boot camp: I would fail everything, and I wasn't allowed books. I braced for Parris Island by running to a Los Angeles gym, and smuggling in reading material by rote memorization. I memorized tracts of Shakespeare. I memorized things to boost motivation: the Gettysburg Address, the preamble to the Constitution of the United States, Charlie Chaplin's speech from *The Great Dictator*, Winston Churchill's We Shall Fight on the Beaches speech. When we marched or cleaned or pulled rifles apart, I read Lincoln in my head. If anyone wondered, mentally reciting two Shakespearean sonnets while holding the flexed arm hang timed out the perfect score.

But after weeks of stage eating my tray of lettuce, a cavernous worm gnawed its way through my cerebral library. Words vaporized. In misty still-cool mornings at the rifle range, I cradled my rifle and tried to call up something to read behind my eyelids. There were missing words, paragraphs expunged. Whole passages evaporated. Instead I stood staring, fixated downrange with lightheaded blankness. *I like the rifle range* was the extent of thought my brain stitched together. *It smells like the Fourth of July.*

It was strangely peaceful, that quiet.

At ten weeks, and staring down the barrel of another twenty-one days, Janis, a Black platoon mate, a mother, gloomily whispered, "You know, if we'd joined the Army, we'd be done by now."

Then I wouldn't have known the still weeks.

Hunger forced internal triage. Heart kept beating. Muscles kept moving. Thought dimmed. Behind a blank face of military bearing, hanger prodded me into a reactive, impotently weeping cell. All that stilled disintegration was forging through another chow, another day, seeing how little I could eat. Around my waist, the tail of my issued belt, initially a uniform three inches, now wrapped around to my kidney.

I didn't question my zealotry and would've offered to fight you if you suggested I should. I didn't raise an eyebrow at marksmanship instructors snickering at "winning hearts and minds" of Iraqi civilians, evoking that public relations rhetoric at the rifle range as directive on where to aim. "Two in the heart, one in the mind."

I didn't think about violence or imperialism. I didn't think about the gradual slipping away of my inner language.

I thought about salt.

At the end of July my body fell off. It was gradual and then all at once. I was curved when I went in, then bolt thin, then abruptly angular. I woke up one morning knobby. Veins protruded from shoulders to elbows, round and raised, long blue mounds.

Bones in my neck rose like a briny sea creature when I bowed my head. Each time we went to be measured for uniforms, wordless civilian seamstresses took in my trousers or skirts another few inches. Closer.

What was in those pounds? I wondered, arms aloft, as the seamstress slid in pins.

The curt blond officer noted me as I pulled targets at the rifle range. "Are you a recycle?" she asked, confused. She thought I was new to her company. She who had seen me circling naked didn't recognize me; my face had sunk into my bones.

I was delighted. I hoped not to be recognized ever again.

In class I ran fingers over text on the Frozen Chosin, Marine legends of the Korean War, while my clavicles rose in ridges.

I took notes. Marine Corps history: "If you're ever in doubt, ask yourself what he would do." He, the war hero. *Lunch: ½ slice bread, 40. Salad: Lettuce, 30, tomatoes, 30, fat free dressing, 40.* Combat first aid: "Stop the bleeding, keep them calm, and yell your fool head off for someone with better training." *Dinner: 1 slice bread, 80. Salad: Lettuce, 30, tomatoes, 30, fat free dressing, 40.* Rules and regulations. "You can date anarchist punks for all the Marine Corps cares, but do not date your damn NCOs." *Total today: 432 calories.*

I wanted to lose all of me that was not Marine, burn every bit that wasn't as tough as Marines facing kamikaze Japanese or insurgents in Iraq. There was so little of me worth keeping. Maybe the tiniest pockets of self-discipline hid beneath my sternum, if I could muck out the fat.

Other recruits tried to talk to me. Kindly, angrily, in exasperation, in concern. Forbidden notes, illicit whispers after lights out.

Williams. Eat. You're going to break.

Break, no. Not yet. Freeze, yes. When temperatures scorched Parris Island, the battalion raised a black flag over the drill field. When Marines saw the black flag, they ordered us inside. The panting platoon whispered relief.

I wished they wouldn't march us in. It felt pansy. And I felt cold even on black flag days.

Boots crushed pine needles underfoot. We marched to the male side of base, to their bigger, nicer obstacle course.

I poised on an elevated log, bracing to jump to the next. Beside me a recruit who wouldn't graduate shook. The Angry One motivated her.

"This shouldn't be hard for you, Diaz!" the Angry One screamed, hands on her hips. She narrowed her eyes at the recruit's midsection. A roll of flesh quivered over her web belt.

"Looks like all this PT has really improved you," growled the Angry One sarcastically. "Looks like you really learned self-discipline here. Glad we taught you something. Jump!" Diaz wavered.

I leapt, wrapped the log with my skeleton. I bear-hugged, rolled, landed on my feet, drunk with pleasure at the solid clunk my hip bones sounded against the log.

"There you go, Williams," shouted the Angry One as I sprinted forward. "Diaz, maybe you should have followed Williams' example with chow. Disciplined."

I levitated. I felt bad for Diaz, though. I was perfectly aware my particular strain of discipline was classified as anorexia nervosa, and I wouldn't wish its cage of numbered walls on anyone.

Every morning fire watch screamed, "LIGHTS, LIGHTS, LIGHTS," and threw the switch. We rushed the line. Standing up quickly was a fun experiment in how low my blood pressure would drop that day. I'd stand on the line blinded and lightheaded, feeling like I was plummeting down a coal mine shaft.

Preparation for final drill turned the squad bay into a starched flurry of ironing boards and Q-tips darkened from hours cleaning rifles. We marched to orders from a woman I couldn't see. The asphalt radiated tropical sun upward. Black spots shuffled hazily across my vision.

"About. FACE!" the Senior roared.

We spun on our heels. Black ink spilled into my eyes. Still I marched, aligned with my platoon. I couldn't see but didn't need to. I knew the bodies of the recruits around me, knew their breath and stride, knew the sharp spacing of our rifles, knew how I fit into formation like part of a larger body.

The open secret of fanaticism: it does just fine blind.

The road through Parris Island anorexia style passed one last strange landmark. The platoon marched to our final martial arts test in shimmering heat. I didn't sweat like the women around me; still, in the sun, I thawed. Gladness, this rising, this basic physiological need satiated. Finally, finally warm. Ah, and then a breeze. Palm trees rustled. I felt ecstatic. I loved the wind. A lift, a buoyancy, the faith that all Icarus had needed to do was listen to his father.

Then for one cracked-open second, I heard a voice as clear as my own say, *God is in the wind.*

This mystical, hunger-drunk place held me as we packed for the Crucible. The Crucible was the final stage of boot camp. Marines intimated it would be a few strenuous days, a do-or-die sufferfest. We had first aid kits and MREs laid out for days, rifles at the ready.

For years I'd squeeze my eyes shut and think, if there was one time, one place, where I could go back and try again, reset to one moment knowing what I know now, I'd give anything to go back to that morning before sunrise when I marched with my platoon to the Crucible. The last moments I lived in a shell so small.

That was when it all started going to hell.

That morning I did a strange thing. We woke at zero dark thirty and broke into the boxed chow laid out for breakfast. All summer I'd eaten the apple and tossed the rest.

That morning I ate the apple. I ate the peanut butter. I ate the granola bars.

As I said. Everything going to hell.

As we marched toward the woods, I felt the disturbing surge of sugar. I felt a little more active, a little more alive. A little less removed from my body. I stomped as hard as I could, trying to burn out not only those extra calories but whatever feral creature leapt into my skin and ate them.

At dawn my squad sat on our packs under pine trees. I sat with the Drill Instructor I Loved. I remember nothing of what she said that morning, her motivation at the cusp of our grand finale of basic training. Never mind this was where we made it, or we didn't.

I was opening my MRE. I was tearing open a flat bread. I was swallowing it without breathing.

Unaccustomed to any reasonable amount of glucose, I shot into the stratosphere. A rocket, this surge of energy erupting through me. Artigas and I received permission to use the head. We ran to it, not because we'd been ordered to, but from pure joy, sprinting in the sun through the trees. Some consciousness clicked differently than it had the last blurry few weeks. I abruptly felt what we were: athletic and young, driven and promising, two young women running in dazzling woods. I felt dizzy and gleeful and senseless.

"WHOOOOHOOO!" I shrieked. I turned a cartwheel, the pine needles friendly and inviting under my palms, then another, and another, suddenly agile, suddenly glad, my body responding in unspeakable joy to breakfast, lopsided in relief, very much, all at once, no cold starving would-be samurai but a giggling teenager stoked to play in the woods.

"Yeah," said my friend, "That's what happens when you eat something, Williams."

Alarm. Shame. I folded my arms around my belly. Shut it down.

The O course. Suspended on much higher obstacles, crawling over monkey bars, I fell. I hooked my knee over a bar and probably could have saved the whole shit show but panicked and groped wildly. I ended cradled like crab.

Mortification hammered. Fat fuck.

The MRE wasn't an MRE. To someone with an eating disorder, food is never only food. It is a moral system. By eating I'd gone and ruined everything.

To my horror, I began to sob.

It wasn't the flat bread or the granola bar. It was that even after twelve weeks of trying to be a Marine, I'd eaten them. It didn't matter that my ribs protruded in a bony ladder. Underneath them I was still the same fat-ass. I still wasn't pure or decent or clean. I hadn't transcended shit. I was still FUBAR and lazy and—

Ah, fuck a duck. I'm crying at boot camp.

The Drill Instructor I Loved stared at me, less angry than bemused, as I wept upside down on the monkey bars.

"Recruit," she said, not unkindly. I lost it then. I braced for her to yeet me across the Atlantic. Instead she said something so surprising I let go into the somersault that untwisted me.

"Recruit," the Drill Instructor I Loved repeated, "As seriously as you're taking this . . . ? This is really not that important."

The first night of the Crucible we dropped uniforms and stepped through the shower blocks. I tried to shimmy past the Senior with my towel shielding me.

"Williams."

"Aye, ma'am." I shot to attention, gripping the towel at my heart.

"What's that on your hips, recruit?"

I lowered my towel, resigned.

Pelvic bones jutted, the bones of a much larger animal. My stomach concaved at the pubis. I'd run all day with a bulky green utility belt cinched around my waist that jangled up and down my sides: my whole skinny waist situation couldn't hold up a belt. Treated to the metallic tambourine of thudding canteens, each hip bone bruised eggplant in color and size. Under industrial shower lights they were particularly garish.

The Senior murmured, "Don't let anyone see that, Williams."

We fired our final rounds the next day. I sprinted and dropped to a kneeling position, rifle to my cheek. A rush of blood to the head obscured my vision. I shot into the dark. Still the dirt *pffed* behind the target. Marines knew some things. I could shoot even blind.

After the Crucible we marched back to Fourth Battalion and stood in formation. Here it was: we were to become Marines after all. It was all early morning light and patriotism and solemnity. Most of the girls teared up.

I didn't. I didn't feel like I'd earned shit.

The Senior ceremonially placed the eagle, globe, and anchor carried by Marines into my palm.

"Ah, Williams," she said, crisply. "You know what I better see on your chow tray."

"Aye, ma'am."

"You better start eating," the beautiful woman whispered. She passed down the line.

With that I was a Marine.

The last few days I managed to weigh myself. I slipped into the supply closet, slid scales on the balancing bar. I crested 104 pounds.

I loved this math. Thirty-two pounds in three months. At this rate I'd be thin by October.

Family Day. We fell out into families rushing the gymnasium. Dad walked over to me beaming. My brother Sam pounded me on the back, the divot between shoulder blades. He asked if I was sure I'd been in boot camp and not a concentration camp and for goodness' sake, here, eat a Pop-Tart.

When Dad hugged me, he ran a hand down the bumpy roller coaster of my spine. Characteristically he chose not to mention it.

I took them on a tour of Parris Island. Dad loved the museum, the buses, the barracks, the marching formations. He particularly loved the rifle range, watching male recruits siting in, holding firing postures, motionless in long lines across the field.

"I can't believe they can hold so still," he said. "Did you do that?"

"Discipline," I said coolly, like I had any claim to it. I'd all but inhaled that Pop-Tart.

Dad and I walked next to each other in the sun, the first time I'd seen him since I high tailed it to California. I felt there was something I needed to tell him, something I badly needed him to know.

"We get pretty awesome life insurance in the military. I signed mine out to my brother Sam," I said grandly, which wasn't it.

Then we arrived, the golden banner at the end of thirteen weeks, a graduation ceremony as splendid and crisp as we'd hoped. The women in my platoon wore their hair softer and smiled. They somehow filled their uniforms differently, the fullness of something like pride. They looked ready to go. I wasn't sure I was.

Something gnawed my stomach leaving Parris Island. I pressed my forehead against the window of the rental car as Dad drove us off base, toward the airport. I didn't thank my drill instructors. I wished I'd taken the time to mill through the jubilant mob of new Marines and civilian families and said thank you. For their fervor. Their sincerity. For showing me something that could have been valuable, if I wasn't so convinced I didn't deserve it. They proved how powerful it was to stand and plant and deliver. To throw into their weight. To claim we, too, could have authority.

When I was thin—when my body stood visible testament to discipline—I could claim what I had seen possible. I'd seen what female Marines—what women—could be.

Furious.

CHAPTER 3
COMBAT TRAINING

The Marines I have seen around the world have the cleanest bodies, the filthiest minds, the highest morale, and the lowest morals of any group of animals I have ever seen.

—Attributed to Eleanor Roosevelt

Orders gripped against my thigh, I marched under towering pines to check into Camp Geiger, North Carolina. My green Alphas were starched to high heaven, puny one ribbon pinned to the breast—like all service members, I wore a National Defense ribbon for apparent courage in enlisting during a time of war.

I reported with confidence I didn't feel. I wondered if I should smile or not. The captain seated behind the desk glanced up and stared when I walked in. He stared as he took my orders, stared until my ears burned. Finally he dropped his gaze. "Hasn't been that long since boot camp, devil dog," he scoffed, shuffling open my file.

I clamped the tiny smile that tightened the corners of my mouth.

Orders duly received, the officer looked up at me. "Okay."

He gave me the rundown. Sex. Sex at combat training was strictly forbidden. For the next twenty-nine days I was on duty. I would be surrounded by men. Sex was an integrity violation. Any sexual behavior could and would be used against me.

"Aye, sir."

"*Any* sexual act."

Jesus. How many were there? "Aye, sir."

"You haven't been in long enough to rate," he ordered. "Unsavory sexual conduct can and will result in your discharge from the military under Other Than Honorable conditions. Do you understand?"

"Yes, sir."

"That isn't what you're here for."

"Aye, sir," I said, and blushed red to my hair. Did I *look* like that's what I was there for?

Dismissed.

Two men checked in after me, one after another. Like me, they handed over orders. Said aye, sir and yes, sir and no, sir. Like me, they were boot privates fresh from Parris Island.

I assumed sex was also forbidden for them, but for some reason the captain didn't mention it.

Them, he told to listen to their NCOs—"They're good men." Them, he told, "You'll learn things here you're going to need. You'll be doing this in country before you know it."

In country. Deployed. Where he saw them going.

While I was Other than Honorable.

I bowed my head. The captain must've singled me out because he saw my shame, the tightness of sleeves around my upper arms. Since leaving Parris Island I hadn't stopped eating.

Had it really only been ten days? Ten days since I woke up in Santa Monica on my first day of leave, stomach knotted from inhaling and straining to hurl an entire pizza before I'd even showered off Parris Island? I rolled out of bed and laced running shoes tight. At boot camp

I'd dreamed of running in Venice Beach, unsupervised freedom to traverse seventeen miles of California sunlight.

Instead I ran out the door and half a mile down the street into a Walgreens. I vomited pizza and bile.

I wiped my mouth. I ran water over my face.

I ran directly into a discount grocery. Knobby legs ran me to food like a guided missile. Zero consultation with my eating disorder, which screamed mayday. Okay, fine. Maybe I would eat something. A chocolatey something, something solid and full of protein. Just—something. But then I would be *done*. I would not eat again until Thursday. I bought three Balance bars, chocolate mint, ran to the register, ran out, one already half eaten. Another downed before I turned the corner, wrapper licked. I ducked into an alley and threw the third in a dumpster, then pressed myself up to go in after it. I balanced on the lip of the dumpster, metal jutting into my hip bones. I yanked my hand back, repelled by a noxious smell, then pounced on the bar and shoved it down my mouth. I spied torn packaging of mottled Reese's, flicked them out, ate them too. I poked experimentally at a Styrofoam, but it held only soggy croutons and wilted lettuce. I dropped to my feet. I ran three blocks to a Peet's, ordered a chocolate chip cookie and a lemonade, and threw up in the bathroom until my ears pounded.

Nothing stronger than the desire to eat. Nothing stronger than the desire to never eat again.

I don't know how far I ran that day, only that I ran and ate and ran and threw up and ran more or less without stopping for the next ten days.

Then I reported to combat training, mortified. My skin had begun to touch the insides of my clothes.

At Marine combat training (MCT), our tightly knit female platoon dispersed into the men. We stood scattered through much larger formations. I was suddenly short.

If you'd asked, I would've said it was a relief, joining them. I grew up with boys. I figured boys were better at taking it easy, at not always being wound up about something all the time. I relaxed as much as I could given the sweltering panic I was getting fatter by the minute. Preoccupied with driving the narrowing gap between my thighs back apart, I remained unaware of the bombardment of furtive glances at us girls. At first.

Had you caught eighteen-year-old Private Williams as she charged across base, head bowed, she would've thrown herself into parade rest. She was still so skinny her head looked too big for her body. Had you looked carefully, you'd've seen bite marks on her swollen knuckles, red diamonds chewed open, the fists of an angry little boxer who punched her own face. Had she met your eyes—she would, sometimes, look directly at you—you'd've noticed a watery sheen to them, a faint webbing of red. Had you spoken slowly, told her to be careful of men around her, to pay attention, that not all of them were fated to be heroes; had you told her that in fact she, and every female Marine, ran an exponentially higher risk of being sexually assaulted by a fellow Marine than being harmed by a foreign enemy, Private Williams would've stiffened. She would've forced loud laughter. If you didn't outrank her, she would've insisted, "That's liberal bullshit. They're the *Marines*. If you can't trust them, who can you trust?"

What she would have thought was, *I am fat. No one's assaulting me.*

Privates and privates first class (PFCs) peeled out of formation to smoke cigarettes as we waited to meet our combat instructors. Yes, we were now Marines, but we hadn't done shit yet and anyhow, any idiot can get through boot camp, we scoffed across smoke trails. The newly reintroduced *I* still stuck awkwardly in our mouths.

Then a soft voice. "Fifth platoon."

Half of us snapped to parade rest, half of us to attention. A god-help-us dance ensued, parade resters springing their heels together, those at attention popping to parade rest.

A gangly man strolled through our shit show. "'Kay, devil dogs, at ease."

The soft-spoken sergeant, Sergeant Moulten, wore a CamelBak. He sucked on the straw and squinted at us. We peered back.

Sergeant Moulten's hair was so light it was white. His eyes permanently squinted, an imprint of time in Iraq. It was as if he forever stood with the sun directly in his eyes, despite the cloudy gray sky. Sergeant Moulten had two facial expressions. One screwed his face between zen and slightly annoyed, like a camel. In the second, his face screwed up slightly tighter. He'd been working in a kitchen in New York when the towers fell. He enlisted the next day. Like every infantryman who joined on or damn near September 11, 2001, his enlistment date bore an unassailable mark of courage. We were Marines. We valued that which runs toward gunfire. Whatever the hell this guy said, we were going to believe.

He was joined by our senior NCO. Staff Sergeant Ledger laughed constantly, screaming laughter like a train engine. He spoke in shouted hilarity. He told us his favorite Christmas was in Iraq, that he was damned happier now he was divorced, that the Marine Corps would give us far more than we could ever give it. When he called us to fall in, he threw his arms wide and bellowed, "Come, my bastard children," or "Fall in, my little bastard baby birds." We loved him.

Our final NCO, Corporal Tawney, was perpetually hungover. He did not speak to me, or any female.

We did have one female combat instructor who ran logistics, supplying us with MREs and ammo boxes, which meant we didn't see her as much. The platoon murmured the hell she knew about combat, anyway.

We watched our male NCOs closely. They were among the first 0311 Marines we'd seen, infantry riflemen, which meant they were legends. Rumor whispered one of them killed an insurgent with his bare hands in Fallujah. I didn't know if it was true, but I sure as shit wasn't voicing doubt.

They rarely screamed. Instead our combat instructors terrified me in another way altogether. They laughed at us.

I rolled into combat training like a bear emerging from hibernation. In the five months since I sat in the recruiter's office, I'd lost almost a third of my body weight.

I was hungry.

We set defensive perimeters in the woods. I sighted in over my rifle, lying on my belly. I glanced at the muddy grass by my elbow. My cheekbone loosened its press into my rifle. My teeth broke cold blades from the mud. I ate the grass.

We dug foxholes with collapsible utility shovels, a futile endeavor in the rain. I turned my back to Artigas, my foxhole buddy, a scoop of dirt in my hand. I shoveled the handful of earth into my mouth. The grit exploded in my molars.

Hunched under the weight of my pack, I stared at mud splattering the heels of Marines marching in front of me. My mouth watered. Boots sank into the mire, and I physically shook, trying to refrain from throwing myself down on the ground. I longed to drop to my knees and press my mouth to the mud like a catfish.

Later I'd learn my febrile hunger for the earth herself was called geophagia, a byproduct of malnutrition. Sufficiently starved of minor details like iron, potassium, and zinc, the earth's body, with her promise of trace minerals, made my bones howl.

I was hungry in a way I did not know it was possible to be hungry.

In cold hours of the morning we sat on our packs in sheets of rain. Sergeant Moulten paced over us, waiting to move. His words formed white clouds in the splintering rain. "Eat 'em while you've got 'em. You won't always have time."

Groggy, the men around me hazarded disinterested bites of flatbread.

The man next to me saw me stuffing away an empty MRE. The deluge pinged off the plastic packaging. He nudged me. The elbow lingered, pressing into my flak jacket. I'd get so used to it, the press of elbows and hands, the friendly pull, the reason to touch. I said nothing. Didn't I want to be one of the guys?

"You ate all that?"

I choked. "Ha ha, no, this is an old one."

An enviably skinny Black girl grinned proudly. "Eat all three every day, and I've never gained a pound."

"Devil dog, you're going to make yourself sick," said our sole female combat instructor in wonder. Marines in earshot giggled.

We were each issued three MREs per day. Each packed a dense, stick-to-your-gut punch. It was rumored they were intentionally made with little fiber to "stop you up." All day, out in the field, working hard—we speculated—it made sense to not need to . . . Well, you know. To counter this engineered constipation, or so the rumor went, there were laxatives in the gum.

Amid the giggling, I ducked my head, keeping my eyes on the manufacturer's logo etched into my M16, a rearing horse. I kept my eyes on that horse frequently. It was the prettiest thing around me, in the mud and sweat. I prayed for invisibility, at least for the way I devoured all three MREs by the time other Marines expressed interest in breakfast.

Sergeant Moulten called me the most sensitive damn Marine he'd ever met. In the classroom, a low bunker squatting in the woods, Corporal Tawney threw a YouTube video on the projector for a bit of levity between slideshows depicting hollow points and ballistics principles. The video was a compilation of skate boarders hurting themselves in unimaginative ways. I didn't understand the humor at all. They were just slamming into walls or smashing their junk onto metal shit. The camera zoomed shakily in on each boy's agonized expression while the bunker laughed uproariously. After about the eighth kid fell on his groin, I turned to watch the wind stir the pines outside. Sergeant Moulten noticed me turn my gaze.

"What's wrong with you?"

I looked up from the trees. I felt like I stood at an unmarked crossroads. My vocabulary was yes, sergeant, no, sergeant, and aye, sergeant. I tried, "Aye, Sergeant."

"No, really. What's—" the bunker erupted in explosive laughter; shockingly, another skateboarder had smashed into a railing. "We'll come back to this."

Sergeant Moulten kicked my boot while we unrolled poncho liners in a field. I leapt to parade rest. He waved me down. "Are you religious?" he demanded.

"Not anymore, Sergeant." Now I eat dirt.

"Huh," he squinted, and gazed off.

Across the marshy field the platoon wearily emptied ALICE packs for the third time. Staff Sergeant Ledger shouted and sang as he pranced up and down the soggy field. We were doing inventory, as someone had lost a Gore-Tex and his temper, accused another Marine of theft to our NCOs. They were teaching us to deal with such domestics ourselves. Rain fell and our gear was soon soaked.

"Only one thief in the whole wide Marine Corps," Staff Sergeant Ledger screamed. "Everyone else just trying to get his shit back."

Sergeant Moulten's eyes zoomed back into focus. "You know what I'm going to do for this Marine Corps birthday, devil dog?"

"No, Sergeant."

"I'm gonna do something to celebrate it proper, 'cause I've been in Iraq or pre-deployment every damn November tenth, but not this year." He placed his CamelBak straw in his mouth. "This year, devil dog, I'm gonna get ass-naked and sit in a bathtub full of tequila." His eyes misted.

"Call the paramedics and just *go*. Couple handles of tequila. One straw." He sucked on his CamelBak. "Happy birthday." He walked off, smiling serenely.

God, he made me proud to be a Marine.

Pouring rain rattled the bunker. The company wedged together on narrow wooden pews. I surreptitiously huddled into the man beside me through our soaked cammies for body heat. He didn't seem to mind and pressed back into me. Indeed when I inched closer toward the man on the other side, the first scooched closer. Within ten minutes I'd magnetized two men to press into my sides. My shivering eased.

The company was in a giggly mood. This evening's regulations briefing was sex. I wasn't the only teenage Marine whose sex education had been a few unfortunately vague 1980s films in health class, embarrassed gym coaches preaching abstinence. Now that we were Marines, we required remedial sex ed.

I don't know what fool put Staff Sergeant Ledger in charge of explaining the birds and the bees, but it certainly made for a memorable briefing. He laughed as he informed us that, at least according to the regs, the only Authorized Form of Sexual Intercourse for active duty personnel was the missionary position.

"Look, nobody gives a flying fuck, but for your edification, Uncle Sam believes anything other than heterosexual missionary is vaguely threatening," shouted the beaming staff sergeant. "They're not going to like, bust into your house and scream, 'OMG, BJ!' But don't be stupid. And if you break your head, or break her head, getting into some weird Kama Sutra shit, for god's sake tell Medical it was PT."

I stifled laughter until my ribs hurt. A row down, Artigas ground her jaw.

"When you have sex in the barracks—I'm not even going to say *if* because I was a private once too—*when* you disgusting animals have sex in the barracks, do yourself a favor and *don't* get fucking caught."

He clicked the slide show. A fascinating blistered pus-filled maw of a vagina filled the front projector. The bunker gasped in collective horror. I thought my eyes would fall out of my head. I'd never seen a vagina, absolutely including my own. "Which fucking brings us to VD. Don't get caught, and don't catch gonorrhea or some shit. Clean clams save lives, good to go?"

As a closet Mormon apostate, I was astonished by this whole new vocabulary of Marine-style sex ed. I had no idea what a clam was. I did think about it, then felt relieved I hadn't asked the guy next to me what a BJ was.

Best, in this and always, to keep my ignorance to myself.

As we humped to the range Staff Sergeant Ledger surged ahead, screaming increasingly hysterical cadences. His cadences were the dirtiest, most vulgar things I'd ever heard.

I loved it. Damn censorship. Damn propriety.

At the beginning I found our gutter humor genius. We had usurped the gilded, we had shouldered the ornamental, we had done what my seminary teacher taught Christ did to the Pharisees: we had cut away rules and protocol and hypocrisy. Service rendered us closer to the spirit of the law. We were reminded constantly we had signed the dotted line, a blank check that could be cashed for everything we had, up to and including the warmth of our bodies. Thus sanctified by commitment to honor this claim to our lives, we were free to eschew the letter of the law, the bourgeois bullshit, the bleeding liberal heart political correctness. We could march into cathedrals in our filthy boots.

We said, we're not here to be politically correct.

We said, we're not here to make you feel good about yourself.

We said, we're here to win wars.

We said, fuck you.

We marched to cadences that defied what I had been taught was sacred. Sex unhallowed was such relief. Maybe we could chill out. Talk about sex like a thing humans do and move on with our lives. Maybe sex wasn't the most shameful thing you could do, ever. I thought the rancid humor stepped in the right direction. At first.

That's back when I still thought I was one of the guys.

There were no female Marines, we were reminded sarcastically, when a Marine requested our female instructor after she snared herself low-crawling under concertina wire and pulled something yanking herself free: only Marines. Surely the skirt—the woman—chased

and smashed
and slammed
and banged
and hit
and screwed
and hammered
and nailed
and pounded
—in the cadences to which we marched wasn't. You know. *Us.*

Rain rendered obstacle courses squishy. Rifles rusted purple. We spent a superb amount of time cleaning M16s, though more than once I considered, shivering, it might make more sense to move the party inside. ("Principle of the thing, devil pups.") We practiced patrols, keeping the wet North Carolina woods particularly free of Taliban. We shot AT4s at a derelict tank and crawled muddy fields under concertina wire.

Through the monsoon and concertina wire I continued to maul three MREs a day. I rifled through trash bins for more. At night I rooted around in dumpsters like a demented raccoon, digging up sealed MRE gum, praying it really did have a laxative effect.

Behind the same dumpsters, pairs of platoon mates engaged in more social behavior—at least I heard ad-hoc rifle watches arranged so couples could slip off into the woods. Crouched over my malodorous flak jacket, desperately ashamed of a belly deformed with perpetual bloat from bingeing MREs, the idea of unclothing for muddy sex made me want to puke more desperately than I already did.

There was rarely privacy—may you never feel compelled to put your hand down your mouth amid rejoicing flies as you face a port-a-shitter with a battalion's worth of shit drooling down the filthy hole; I'm genuinely amazed I didn't catch cholera—and never time to vomit, as combat instructors moaned females took too damn long to pee. "*Sooo* long," Corporal Tawney sighed as we scrambled back into ill-fitting gear, male colleagues waiting, as if we were being prissy for needing to rip off flak jackets so big they kept us from our belts.

"Hope you weren't at my artillery in a firefight," Corporal Tawney grumbled. He submitted female "plumbing" as incontestable anatomical proof we didn't belong in the infantry. I embarrassed myself musing if that was indeed the prominent issue preventing female combat readiness, we could resolve it with a well-engineered funnel. Also gear that fit.

Corporal Tawney pronounced me a goddamn genius. "Think you'll have that luxury when you're in a firefight? Pull out your damn funnel?" I blushed scarlet.

Artigas leaned into me and muttered if she was ever at the artillery in a firefight and had to go that badly, she'd piss her fucking trousers and get on with it. She always knew how to cheer me up.

We practiced checkpoints. Corporal Tawney warned us we'd do these for real in Iraq so stop dicking off and pay attention.

"'Kay, one of you, be the hajji; one of you, pat 'em down. Remember, Iraqis wear the man-dresses, so pat 'em down thorough as fuck or you're gonna get someone fucking killed. But be professional. Don't be like the fucking Lionesses who just hold a gun to everybody's head. I walked in once, and this fuckin' Lioness was standing there with her sidearm at a hajji woman's head." The young corporal imitated the stance, shook his head disdainfully. "Thought she was such a fucking badass, posing for her profile picture or some shit. When really she was *kinda* pissing off their men. Guess who got to deal with them?" He sighed heavily, pointing to his chest. "Yeah. *Us*."

"Dumb cunt," snickered a private behind me.

What happened to the Iraqi woman? The corporal didn't say.

Corporal Tawney pulled a volunteer and showed us how to slide a hand past a "hajji ass" to check for explosives. Men laughed and jeered. "Ha ha, Davis likes it!" Original. I'd been in a co-ed platoon ten minutes and already learned homoerotic teasing never stopped.

We practiced pinning each other into the mud and zip-tying each other's wrists. The corporal pointedly paired us girls together. He snarled we had to do it that way, "'Cause otherwise there's always that one female who'll get butthurt and complain about sexual assault." Same, firing machine guns. Two Marines lie close together, one firing, the other feeding the belt. Again, he shouted females together. "So no one gets butthurt."

I got it. Shut up, these warnings said. Shut up, because your female discomfort at made-up sexual attention is irrelevant, when there are Marine bodies being cracked open, when IED wounds are called blossoms. To complain is to require attention. As if you're worth as much as men on the front line, as if during real war your little sexual harassment complaints matter for shit. When no one wants to sleep with you, no one's *looking* at you that way, you're not special. So shut up, shut up, shut up.

We marched to a rifle range. I trailed along, my chest roughly parallel to the trail under the weight of my pack. I caught a rock and lost my balance. I held on to my rifle so smashed down onto one knee. Scrambling upright, I flung forward in a shamefaced jog.

Over the next few days the smashed knee swelled to twice the size of the other. Ever an optimist, I decided to ignore it.

A rare sunny lull. We sat on our packs under shifting evergreens in Camp Geiger's hybrid brume of cordite and DEET. The platoon changed boot socks and picked through MREs, bartered plastic-encased entrees and argued over dip. One guy brushed his teeth, spitting onto the grass. A few read letters.

I took off my cover. Rifle cradled into my shoulder, I frisked a TSA-sized bottle of gel from my hygiene kit. I reached up and released my bun. My dark hair fell down my back in a tangled, gel-knotted ponytail. I twisted it tightly, my grim counterattack against the humidity.

Sergeant Moulten noticed immediately. He stood over me, sidearm on his thigh and CamelBak in his mouth. "What the fuck, devil dog?"

"Aye, Sergeant?" I moved to rise to my feet but he held out his hand.

"Hell you doing, Williams?"

"Squaring my hair away, Sergeant. My bun was coming undone."

He crouched in front of me. He spoke pleasantly. "Williams, these men haven't seen a woman in weeks. You think that's a good idea?"

I had no idea what to say. I was mildly surprised to hear I wasn't a woman. I guessed, "No, Sergeant."

"Yeah. You know what I'm talking about." He leaned closer. "Your hair smells nice. You can't be waving that sort of . . . prettiness all over the place, good to go?"

"Aye, Sergeant." The hair tie snapped over my fingers.

He stood up. "You can't go displaying soft things like that, Williams. Male Marines are nasty, good to go, they notice that shit."

"Aye, Sergeant."

The scent of weapons ranges lingered in my hair. Mud caked my boots and calves. Sweat curved outlines around my flak jacket and streaked sunscreen and dirt across my face. Rampant MRE snarfing had compacted my digestive tract into a tight slug. I felt about as sexually appealing as the business end of my rifle. I wondered if he was mocking me, but he'd always been kind.

Sergeant Molten sucked on his CamelBak. "How many women you see here, Williams?"

Actually, maybe a fifth of the Marines around me sported a military regulation bun. The all-male infantry, statistically a finger of the Marine

Corps fist, had its own, much longer combat training, diluting the gender ratio. But the answer he wanted, I guessed, was zero. Best we blend in, invisible in identical camouflage. Invisible, or erased.

"Aye, Sergeant."

"Yeah. Thought so. Keep that shit tucked away. Good to go?" He smiled blissfully and wandered off.

When Sergeant Moulten charged me with too-sweet-smelling hair, I'd lost count of how many days I'd gone without a shower. Opportunities to shower were rare and brief. Most of my platoon seized every chance to storm the mildewed shower blocks, indifferently naked, scrubbing off the weapons ranges and obstacle courses under pulpy greenish water.

Disgust barred me. Mortifying, a reflection without barrel hoop ribs. Even the proud blue veins that tunneled from shoulder to elbow had receded into what I could only assume was a veneer of blubber. *Losing motivation,* one female muttered to another, a sidebar about Brite, who still kept snacks on her at all times. We all gained a few pounds after boot camp, but she hadn't stopped, they snickered. I clamped my arms around myself, grasping like if I squeezed hard enough my fingers would meet at my spine. These women had seen me naked only weeks before, when my fingertips had touched. I would not be Brite.

In front of mirrors crisscrossed with fractures and mildew, I used body wipes to address the worst of the mud on my face and neck. I pushed back my hair with water from the rusty sink. We wore Kevlar anyway.

My recruiter was wrong. Apparently a female body could in fact go weeks without showering without any particular negative health impact. If anyone noticed my fumes as I stewed in all my bodily fluids for twenty-nine days, no one mentioned it. Marines who showered were quickly befouled anyway.

At the end of those twenty-nine days we marched back to barracks with shower stalls and the relative privacy of plastic curtains. That night I finally showered.

It was the first time in my life I'd enjoyed taking off my clothes. I savored folding my trousers, the comforting solidity of the filthy green fabric. I stood, a moment, in the tolerably not-entirely-cold water, relishing the little alcove of privacy. How grand it felt, to let my skin breathe.

The water spiraled out in a black web around my feet. I felt filthy from the inside. I'd gained twenty pounds in a month. And it was a dense twenty pounds, a hard, tight shellacking of MREs and crawling through mud. Disgusting. Civilian.

The Marine on rifle watch stood outside the curtain, so I tried to gag quietly, and threw up between my feet.

The next morning Staff Sergeant Ledger noticed my swagger as the platoon rushed to fall in. "Walk like a Marine, Williams," he screamed happily.

The smashed and ignored knee had taken a nasty turn. It had a tautness to it, too turgid to fully bend. I'd waited until the end of training to deal with it. That evening I consulted the Navy corpsman who passed through the platoon bandaging double-domed blisters and splintering the occasional digit. Because I was female and had to raise my trouser leg, we conferred in a supply closet.

"Oh, fuck me," he groaned, reaching for my knee. He leaned in quickly but touched the distended joint tentatively. "Doesn't that *hurt*?"

"Umm," I said, ". . . no?"

Among the Clorox and mops, the corpsman shook his head. "Go to medical tomorrow, warrior. This one needs a doctor-type doctor."

But another female in my platoon had gone to medical earlier that week. When she peeled out of morning formation, Corporal Tawney snorted. "Yeah," he'd said with snark that carried, "Convenient how females' shit starts to hurt when going to medical gets you out of shit."

We had shit the next day too.

So that night after lights out I propped my flashlight on my rack. Fingernails tore the spongy skin off the offending knee. I rifled through my hygiene bag for nail clippers, snipped. I massaged the crude incision and squeezed. Fluid coursed out silvery in the flashlight. Fascinated, I kneaded the warm joint, pressuring out a stream that seeped down my shin, viscous like salt water. The stretched skin deflated and shriveled, mushy like fingertips in a pool.

In the morning the scarlet gash wept but my knee felt nearly back to normal. I stretched my leg experimentally. Full range of motion, if a bit tight, if with a strange internal sound, like brakes on a wet road. I declared surgery a success.

The last morning of combat training we ran disheveled, throwing gear under buses and turning the barracks inside out for errant garment bags and hat boxes, tripping over ditty bags and each other in enthusiastic chaos. We'd made it. We were finally going to the real Marine Corps.

Well, Artigas and I had long-ass training schools first. Still, finally we were divvying up into our MOSs, heading to schools that would teach us our actual jobs in the military. I was pretty vague on what linguists actually did. I spun around in the cacophony. Artigas slumped against the bus window and took a catnap, sun pouring over her freckles. Even asleep she looked angry.

I ran back. Sergeant Moulten comfortably ignored us all, sprawled on the barracks stairs, squinting at the white sky.

"Good morning, Sergeant. Um . . ."

"You finally got something to say to me, Williams?"

"Yes, Sergeant. Thank you, Sergeant."

He may or may not have narrowed his eyes. It was indiscernible.

"Err. Good morning, Sergeant." I turned to run off.

"Williams."

I pirouetted back so sharply I nearly fell over. "Aye, Sergeant."

"What in the hell for?"

What *for*? "For teaching us, Sergeant," I said stupidly.

He nodded grimly. "You're weird, Williams."

"Probably, Sergeant." I grinned. He didn't. Quickly I secured my humor. "Err. Aye, Sergeant."

"Real fuckin' weird."

"Aye, Sergeant."

"Don't change."

"Err. Aye, Sergeant."

"You just might make it."

"Aye, Sergeant."

I'll stop eating the day I leave MCT. The determined mantra had staggered me through. I ate so much at combat training I felt if it I didn't get the hell out of North Carolina I'd genuinely explode. *I'll stop eating the day I leave MCT.*

The day I left MCT I ate two Clif bars on the bus to the airport. I left my seabags with Artigas and threw up in a bathroom by our gate. Clif bars came up like slugs. Okay, once I got out of North Carolina airspace. I'd stop eating once we landed in Chicago.

On the 747 the airline attendant's voice cracked over the intercom. "We'd like to acknowledge our active duty military members who are flying with us tonight and thank them for their brave service to our country." The cabin applauded. A gray-haired gentleman leaned over and shook hands with the male PFC seated next to me. Though he was close enough to offer his hand, to me he only smiled indulgently.

The layover in Chicago divided boot Marines further. Artigas and I stopped in a bookstore. She bought *The Da Vinci Code* and I bought eight dollar walnuts, which was an eight dollar lesson that walnuts suck to puke.

California. I'd stop eating when we touched down in California. Like a protective wall bordered the state that I'd see poking through the clouds.

In San Francisco I traded a bill for a Ghirardelli bar at a terminal kiosk. I boarded at dusk, crackling the wrapper in my hands. As soon as the pilot turned off the fasten-seatbelt sign, I locked myself in the head and sank my hand down my throat. Black swirls in the tiny airplane's toilet, the lingering taste of acid and peppermint.

I sank back to my seat and peered at the Pacific fog. Monterey. I'd stop eating when we got to Monterey. A fresh start, once the airplane landed.

I let my head fall against the window, regarding the soft line of my chin reflected on the glass. Heading west. That was always the dream, wasn't it? Live out West and do something with words. Maybe this would be alright. I could be happy in California. I could still get my shit together and stop eating like a degenerate. A routine was what I needed. A nice, sensible regimen where I ate nine hundred calories and ran five miles every day. Once I lived in Monterey, I'd work back to Crucible weight. One hundred and four had been nice. Shelled out.

Next to me Artigas was passed out, dead asleep. She leaned onto me. She was so much taller her head rested not on my shoulder but on top of my head. The weight against my head reminded me of something. In the quict hum of the airplane, I tasted a bitterness in the back of my throat. I remembered again the Patriarchal Blessing I'd received a month before, on leave between boot camp and combat training.

I hadn't stopped running and eating and puking when I'd flown to visit my dad. The hour before my blessing I raided my father's kitchen. I tore apart a block of cheddar cheese, ate it smashed in barbecue sauce.

Dad drove me to the patriarch's house. I ruminated on the oily crumbles of cheese in the toilet, baroque swirls of barbecue, trying to read if I'd purged enough.

The patriarch had ten kids. The house smelled like tuna casserole, the kind with corn flakes sprinkled on top. Framed photos of the Mormon prophet Gordon B. Hinckley and the Salt Lake Temple decorated the living room, propped on little doilies. He offered me a kitchen chair. I sat stiffly in my Charlies.

I turned my garrison cover over in my hands, running my finger through its folds. I liked the garrison cover. This hat, with its traditional green style, evoked something from World War II. You could see a warrior in such a cover, and not just any warrior. There on its side, the eagle, globe, and anchor emblem of the US Marine Corps. Reassurance. A reminder that the path I'd chosen, as fucked-uply as I currently trod it, was good. Mine was the team of Iwo Jima, victors over fascism, defiers of dictators. Who was I to bow my head under such a cover?

At combat training, Marines called this hat the cunt cover.

The patriarch stepped behind me. Dad shook a drop of anointed olive oil from Jerusalem onto my hair. The two men dropped their hands on my head. I was familiar with the heaviness of men's hands on my crown. As always I fought between slouching under the compressive weight of their palms and straining to press my skull up against them. Never could I just be still and balance. I swallowed fury and bowed my head under their hands, bristling and contrite as a knight ever placed his lance before a priest.

Dear God, please send me into the Marine Corps with what I need to get my head out of the toilet.

The patriarch began.

"Sister Williams," he intoned, "By the power of the holy Melchizedek priesthood which your father and I hold, we place our hands upon your head to confer upon you your Patriarchal Blessing. Through this high priesthood, conferred to the prophet Joseph Smith by the apostles Peter, James, and John, we have been asked to offer you guidance and consolation. I exhort you."

I really thought words like intone and exhort were normal, everyday words. He exhorted me to avert my gaze from the sinfulness desired of women in these sorrowful Last Days, women who flaunted their bodies and disobeyed and scorned their sacred role as wife and mother and instead participated in all manner of wickedness. To clothe my body and countenance with modesty, so I wouldn't incite temptation. Keep myself clean and pure so I'd be worthy to face my future husband across the altar in the temple, to be sealed for time and all eternity along with the many children the patriarch generously informed me I would have—the words "fruitful womb" made me wince—if I stayed faithful in Christ.

Yup. Modesty and marriage, babies and a housebound life. Where in the shit was the way of the goddamn warrior?

Disappointment bowed my head.

Then the patriarch's voice changed. He cleared his throat, and for one startled second I thought my dad had finally spoken up.

"You are a seeker. You will lead others to truth as you continually seek it throughout your life. You carry a great light that will deliver you through many dark places.

"As you strive always to return to your Maker, your gifts will be patience, humility, and what for you will be the greatest gift of all: a grateful heart."

Then he said, "You will be protected by the sweet femininity inherent to your gender."

I gripped my femurs, feeling for bone.

Artigas softly snored against my head. I stared into the clouds and wondered anew what on earth I'd done and how the hell I was going to do it. The patriarch's blessing didn't give me much. The hell was humility going to help? I wanted savagery and fuck a grateful heart, I wanted a brave heart. Worst of all: the sweetness of women?

When I was small my stepmother had seized me and thrown me down unfinished stairs to a cement basement. She gripped me often. When she grabbed me, I didn't know where I was going. It felt like flying. I'd throw my hands out wildly. Once I watched my hand bend all the way back to my forearm when I landed on green stone tile. It swelled and it hurt and she'd screamed at me to stop being dramatic, I was always so dramatic, stop holding it like it hurts, Bailey, just *stop it*.

Twisted joints had healed. Whiplash had not.

The anticipation—the taut wiring, in my body, that at any moment angry hands could be on me; and that it was my role to comply, to go numb and hollow and brace for landing—that. That hadn't really healed.

What sweetness, the saccharine? Femininity that left lipstick on its glass and kicked you under the table?

Womanhood as I knew it was the tearful apology between bouts of rage, ice cream, bookstores, walking in the trees on days she promised she'd never do it again. Emotion trembled her voice when she promised it would be different from now on. She was sorry, so it was my sin if I didn't forgive.

In the New Testament Jesus told his disciples to forgive someone not seven times nor seventy times but seventy times seven. But by the fourth grade I started counting.

I wouldn't understand for years the extent of the scar tissue, the exhaustion of my nervous system. A relentless urgency under my skin, the anticipation of violence.

There was another face of embodied fear. In the tension in my fists, the pounding of my heart, the shots of adrenaline at any perceived threat: fear made me angry. I wanted to fight the fuck out of something or somebody or anything or anybody. I wanted to hold somebody down and scream with my fists. I wanted to twist joints and break bones and kick spines and let this stifled anger live in someone else's body for a change. I was angry; I was so goddamned angry.

But anger was not something a Mormon girl should feel. Hell, of only five named women in the Book of Mormon, one speaks up against her husband and is promptly and divinely muted.

Anger coated my cells instead. It lived in my body's hormonal patterns, her quick-trigger flooding of adrenaline. In my brain, the stamp of fear in my amygdala. In my soft tissue, quiet, wrapped close around my bones, where I distrusted relationships as inherently conditional, fragile, and hostile. It gnawed my vertebrae.

But a Marine could be angry. Right? Could be calm in rage. The military was how I'd find ease in my body, deserve confidence in my own two legs.

I was wary of men, but I straight up dreaded women. Well. I glanced at Artigas. Some women were okay. As far as I could tell, the qualifying factor to be a woman I trusted was to be hard as steel. Gentleness was suspect to me, velvet thin over claws.

I chewed my lips. Monterey. I would forge myself skinny when we reached Monterey.

CHAPTER 4

THE PRESIDIO

Marines are the things that go bump in the night. Don't worry about the mountain lion that stalks the Presidio [of Monterey] . . . it's the hunched form of a Marine in the gloom that should terrify you. Of course it is all urban legends and myths, until two Marines stab a civilian jogger just to see what it's like, and stuff her body between the rocks, and then it doesn't seem so ridiculous anymore.

—*Ryan Leigh Dostie,* Formation

ONLY THE BEST WILL HAVE THE COURAGE AND DISCIPLINE TO BECOME WORLD CLASS LINGUISTS, screamed scarlet and gold letters in the stairwell. DO YOU HAVE WHAT IT TAKES?

We had arrived at the Defense Language Institute (DLI) in Monterey, California. Artigas and I stood in front of the master gunnery sergeant at crisp parade rest. His was real rank, acquired over years that Artigas and I, wee baby bootlings, couldn't imagine. He'd been a Marine longer than I'd been alive. His rank blackened his collar.

Master Guns eyed us.

"Either of you run for shit?" he asked abruptly, leaning back. "I'm damned tired of the Commander's Cup going to the Air Force."

Hurriedly we assured him, yes, Master Gunnery Sergeant, we ran for shit.

"That Commander's Cup . . . my females just lost, again. Get ahold of Tucson in fifth platoon. Have her take a time trial. Alright, go on."

He peered after us as we left. "Williams."

I accidentally elbowed Artigas as I leapt to parade rest. "Aye, Master Gunnery Sergeant."

"You gain some weight recently?"

Inside I screamed.

"Yes, Master Gunnery Sergeant."

"This is what happens when we tailor uniforms at boot camp. Your trouser legs are about an eighth inch short above your Corframs at the heel. Square it away."

"Aye, Master Gunnery Sergeant."

Uniform trousers no longer draped from jutting hangers of hip bones. Devouring MREs re-established a decided ass, which strained against trousers tailored to anorexic hips, that is, not having them. Thank God he couldn't see the disaster at my waistband. My guts were still a worm of compacted MREs.

Then again, while I weighed a certain number of pounds that seemed mammoth to me, it fell tidily between weight and height requirements. Well on the low end, in fact. Master Guns probably meant: *Take your trousers to a tailor. Have them let down the hem.*

I heard: *Starve yourself, you lazy, fat piece of shit.*

Artigas and I stepped into the hall. I was fairly sure checking in with Master Guns was our last task of the day, having been stamped, filed, and spun around by the S shops—staff shops like admin and logistics—who had checked our teeth, issued us bed linens, and made sure we weren't complete shitbirds before we stood in front of the senior-most enlisted.

I looked to Artigas. "Wanna run?"

"New joins!"

Artigas and I turned. We'd made it through the NCOs. We had a last introduction: our peers.

A Marine stormed toward us.

"Stand at parade rest; I'm corporal-select."

We stood at parade rest.

He had a face for recruiting posters, all dark brood. He crossed muscled arms. "So, new joins, huh? What are you going to be?"

"We haven't received our language assignments, Lance Corporal," Artigas said smartly.

"Not what I mean, devil dog. What kind of Marines you going to be?"

A pause.

"What . . . what?" I ventured. ". . . Good ones, Corporal-Select?"

He imitated me in high whiny falsetto. "'*What, what*?' Real professional, Williams. Hope you're not in my platoon. What kind of *females* are you going to be?"

I glanced at Artigas.

"There are three kinds of females in the Marines. You should know this. You can be a bitch, a dyke, or a whore. So what are you going to be?"

"Good Marines, Lance Corporal," Artigas answered in a low voice.

It sounded different when she said it.

The lance corporal narrowed his eyes. Artigas ground her jaw. I intervened. "Which do you suggest, Corporal-Select?"

He shot a furious glance at me, sure I was mouthing off, but advantage of my upbringing, I was extremely versed in absorbing blame, affecting remorse. I widened my eyes, dropped my chin, and—yup. He nodded curtly, appeased I'd deferred. "Whores are female shitbags always nursing some bullshit injury. At least bitches do their jobs. Sometimes. Sometimes they complain just because they like to complain. We're not supposed to have dykes but somehow they get in."

He waited.

"Aye, Lance Corporal," we mumbled.

"You," he pointed to me. "I heard you were smiling at some Marines when you came in."

That I had. Fellow privates held the red doors open and helped us throw our seabags across the threshold. We'd thanked them.

"You want to fuck those Marines, devil dog?"

"I do not, Corporal-Select."

"You sure? They sounded pretty pleased you're so friendly."

And yet. "I am sure, Corporal-Select."

"Do *you*?"

Artigas stiffened. "No, Lance Corporal."

"No? Huh. You don't want to fuck those Marines either, new join?"

"No, Lance Corporal."

"Yeah, I bet not."

Artigas looked ready to rearrange his face but only jerked her chin back.

"You'd better start acting like it. You're here to learn a language. Not fuck around. We'll see. I think I've got a pretty good idea what one of you is." He dismissed us.

Now, I so dearly hoped, we were done for the day. I'd put creamer in my coffee that morning, and this private needed to run NOW.

Artigas and I shot up the stairwell to our room, ripped off our Alphas, hung them neatly, and shoveled into running clothes. We transformed from taciturn uniforms to the stressed athletes underneath. We were, after all, Marines, even as spooked boots, and running was our idea of emotional processing.

We sprinted out of the barracks, red doors clanging behind us. The late September afternoon shone bright, and the magnificent trees growing in front of the barracks waved welcomingly in the fresh Pacific wind. We said nothing, lost in our private panic.

I heard the aspiring NCO tell me I was seeming real whorish for smiling. I blamed my body. If smiling expressed sexual interest I didn't have, it was my damn hips' fault. I figured I could refrain from public smiling until I was skinnier. Actually, that sounded pretty good to me. I didn't much feel like smiling. Maybe when I got to be an NCO I could laugh without accidentally seducing somebody. Maybe I'd be thin enough by then to deserve to laugh, really laugh, the kind of laugh that screwed up my face. I couldn't laugh like that now. It gave me a horrible double chin, and anyway I didn't like exposing my throat.

We bolted up the trail to the hilltop track. But Artigas kept running so I followed. She barreled past barracks into the woods, shooting across the pinecones. I was doubting that I'd be able to keep up with her much longer when she slammed into the chain link fence, where base shared a boundary with a forest called Veteran's Park.

Somewhat less neurotically, she understood he'd given her a warning. He'd not bared teeth, but there'd been a hint of canine. *Watch it*, he'd nipped. *Don't talk back.*

You're not even supposed to be here.

Certain details ignored, a waylaid civilian could mistake the Presidio for a college campus. Disregard defunct tanks used in exterior design, or red-faced sailors standing at attention and bellowing, "Permission to come on deck!" to enter their own barracks. Ignore soldiers screaming motivation as their frantic squads dive and pivot through battle drills, and massive Air Force PT formations in synchronized jumping jacks. Dismiss fire teams of Marines with highly motivated high-and-tights sprinting down the sidewalk in combat boots, calling cadences so filthy they affront the Air Force. Fail to observe Marine NCOs mulling by the smoke pit, spitting dip and placing bets on which Navy kids huffing around the track will throw up or fall out and telling lurid stories about stabbing people, and sure, the Presidio's school houses and barracks could be any other collegiate campus.

The barracks lined Rifle Range Road. Even without the eagle, globe, and anchor staked aggressively in the yellow lawn, the Marine barracks stood out. The Air Force barracks had a sandy volleyball court, the Army barracks a gazebo for smokers, the Navy, a fast-food kiosk. The Marines had pull-up bars. Rare was the moment a motivated squad weren't hauling themselves up on those bars, cranking out sit-ups between max sets.

In addition to Marines stationed at DLI to keep operations running, the detachment hosted a loose cadre of NCOs, who more or less kept us alive while learning a foreign language themselves. Because of Monterey's appeal as a reenlistment incentive, many Marine NCOs lat-moved into linguistics from other MOS. These NCOs were relieved to spend a year in a coastal California town, studying with electricity and indoor plumbing and absolutely no one shooting at them. Most of them had combat action ribbons, and this, to startled junior enlisted like me, was the red badge of credibility. We looked up to these NCOs with gravest respect. Marines who spoke offhandedly about Iraq and insurgency, firefights and extractions, white phosphorus and pistol-whipping insolent Iraqi teenagers—they were our heroes.

We too would go to war, Higher Ups promised. We just needed to knock out fluency in a foreign language real quick.

The Defense Language Institute was the Department of Defense's mightiest language school, and we learned what DoD said we should learn. The DoD concerned itself with the languages of enemies, or those whose enmity we feared. We learned Arabic. We learned Mandarin and Korean and Russian. We learned Pashto and Dari, Urdu and Farsi. We learned Spanish, Indonesian, and Tagalog.

Arabic burned with certain intensity. We learned it in the tracks of light armored vehicles, stories told with heads shaken of good Marines killed when we invaded Iraq without Arabic linguists. Higher Ups hurried to remedy this error, throwing baby linguists at the language and hoping for the best.

Everyone else was reminded we never knew where conflict might break out. We Marines, the tip of the military spear, must always be ready. We took this seriously. Marines in Russian learned the Cold War never ended. Won't get rid of their nukes, they repeated sagely. Can't trust 'em. Urdu Marines got hopeful every time the Pakistanis moved their nuclear weapons around. Farsi Marines perked up whenever the ayatollah of Iran threatened to wipe Israel off the map. The Korean platoon strutted with renewed relevance when North Korea completed its second nuclear test in 2009. Arabic Marines wore T-shirts with a nobly kneeling warrior, bold print proudly declaring themselves *kafir*—infidel. The truly overly motivated—the unfortunate slang was "motarded"—slapped bumper stickers on Mustangs and Chevys that said, "We speak [insert language here] so you don't have to," or "God bless America" in Arabic, Russian, Mandarin over aggressive lettering, "If you CAN'T read this, THANK A SOLDIER."

What I'm saying is, we Marines bristled for a fight. We didn't give much of a damn with whom.

We embraced our boot status in the reputedly nerdiest school in the military. We ran around base in our defiantly short green silky shorts, screaming, "Who are we? What are we for? WE ARE THE CUNNING, CUNNING LINGUISTS OF THE UNITED STATES MARINE CORPS." We ran around shouting infinitely variable cadences about cunning linguists and firmly believed we were playing a vital role in the War on Terror.

It was easy for me to understand how I fit into the military hierarchy. The S shops maintained a board with photographs of our chain of command. Chain of command looked familiar to me, like the fold-out charts in the Mormon magazines my parents read. Prophet on top, along with the First Presidency: three men of the highest priesthood. Then the Quorum of the Twelve Apostles. Beneath them, the Quorum of Seventy, who oversaw stake presidents. Stake presidents resided over geographic clusters of wards, each of whom had a bishop. The bishop, too, had advisors, and then members of the congregation were called to lead the young men, young women, and women. Even within our packs of teenage Mormons we practiced small-unit leadership: boys were deacons, then teachers, then elders, as they matured into greater responsibilities of priesthood. Girls had stupid names like beehives and maids. Each age group had its own president and advisors.

I felt comfortable in clear assignments of authority. Small unit leadership was an excellent way to map a large social organization, if its goals benefited from a not insignificant forfeit of individual decision-making, especially from the rank and file.

The Marine Corps was similar. There was me: the boot. Among the vast multitude of the insignificant. Above me, my fire team leader. Above him, my squad leader. Squads composed a platoon lead by platoon sergeants and, more loosely, staff NCOs. A group of platoons formed a company; companies formed battalions. Over these battalions the great Higher Ups stalked, officers far above my pay grade, and above them, my personal prophet, Commandant of the Marine Corps James T. Conway.

When I enlisted, our commander-in-chief was President Bush. Shortly afterward, his portrait was replaced with President Obama's, impressively doubling the number of Black men on the board.

There were no women on the board of leadership, just as there had been no women in the Church magazines.

But here we stood a chance, theoretically.

Artigas and I lived stacked on top of each other in the smallest barracks room on third deck. On Thursday the barracks NCO divvied up tasks for field day, a weekly scrub down of everything in sight. He ordered me to scrub the showers in the male head. I was a spanking-new private. I therefore sprinted to do precisely whatever the hell literally anyone told me to do.

I bent over in a shower stall, scouring away, when a boy stepped across the entrance.

"Devil dog," he grunted.

He wasn't wearing his blouse, so I didn't know his rank. He looked young, but most NCOs were. He could be a squad leader or even a platoon sergeant inspecting field day. For all I knew he was a war hero. I hunched in an awkward half-parade rest, my hands folded politely behind my back.

"Does it bother you to clean the showers?" he inquired.

I didn't love how he stood, blocking me in the narrow stall with his arms crossed. My shoulders crept up but I half-smiled, ready to secure my face and spring to parade rest if I figured out he outranked me.

"Of course not," I said humbly. Corporal? Sergeant?

"Why not? It's the *male* head."

Like a private gets choices, regardless of gender. "I was ordered to."

"It doesn't bother you at all?"

"Not really."

"Doesn't seem normal, females not minding cleaning male showers."

"It's really not a big deal."

"You know there's jizz in there. Like, you're surrounded by jizz right now."

. . . oh.

"That doesn't bother you?"

"It was an order."

"You don't mind living with males?"

"Sure don't." I spoke lightly. I minded shower walls against my back. I minded not being able to see an exit. I did *not* enjoy being cornered. I felt a familiar pulse in my neck.

"Yeah? You *like* it?"

Was this guy . . . possibly just really stupid?

"It doesn't make a difference." What's your fucking rank?

"So you're a woman who doesn't mind living with mostly men."

This kid could be as new as I was. I stood up straight and realized I was as tall as him. It embarrassed me, to be bigger than him.

The truth snapped off my tongue. "I have way too many brothers to give a shit."

The boy blinked. "How many brothers you got?"

"Four."

His eyebrows lifted. "You Catholic?"

"Firmly agnostic."

The kid slunk away.

I learned brothers gave me a half-second distraction. Having brothers, normalization of being the only girl, suggested I may've had a few scuffles. No one needed to know my brothers were priests.

On the day I was assigned my platoon, I stood at my barracks door, mystified. I wasn't sure what was on our door handle, but something told me it was not something I wanted there.

I peeled it off with the head paper I carried in my cargo pocket in the event of an errant period, and opened the door into my room, calling to Artigas, "Hey, is this what I think—"

I stiffened. Artigas wasn't alone. There was a man in my room.

A big man, in particular, with a relaxed face and slate-blue eyes. He turned away when I walked in. I knew him, or anyway felt like I did. He leaned against my desk, beer in hand, wearing a black Red Hot Chili Peppers T-shirt.

He had always been there. In my room, on my desk, in my being. Without a shadow of a doubt this man would not harm me.

For the first time in a couple of years I exhaled completely.

"*Ah-salaam ah leikam*," he said, half-raising his beer bottle. "Welcome to fifth platoon. I'm Harvey. I'm your fire team leader, so I am generally responsible for you. Let me know if you want help with Arabic. It's a ridiculous language. Oh God, do not stand at parade rest for me."

Artigas tilted her head. "Why are you walking around with a used condom, Williams?"

I blushed hot. I still held out the tissue. "Um, this was on our door handle."

"What?"

"Just now, when I opened the door. This was, um, over our door handle." I gazed at the floppy rubber I'd peeled off the door. It contained something white and of strange viscosity. "I kinda thought that's what it was," I added. Neither Mormon nor Marine sex ed covered contraceptives, but there had to be a limited number of options. "That's good to know, I guess. Um, why was it on our door? Does that mean something?"

Harvey laughed. "I wouldn't worry about it. Some asshat is just messing with you. Women new joins get a lot of attention."

"I'm not sure I like being messed with."

"People are idiots," Harvey said peacefully. "Junior Marines in particular." He stood and offered the trash can. He was tall, even bigger than Artigas. "But if anyone bothers you, let me know."

This was not something to be bothered about, then. I flung the condom into the trash.

The next morning I reported to my first formation with my new platoon. Fifth platoon mulled by the chain-link fence. In green woodland cammies, strangers blurred together and into the trees beyond the fence. I scoured for a friendly face.

That's when I saw her.

The woman stood out among them. She glinted like a silvery scalpel, a slightness to her under her camouflage, narrow but tempered. Her tightly pulled back hair accentuated the sharp angles of her face. She returned my gaze. Something in her unsmiling face made it clear she knew me, knew my type, and she wasn't going to let me get away with it that easily.

I dove behind Harvey.

"*Masa alkheer, sadeekee.*"

"Good afternoon, Lance Corporal."

Harvey groaned. "No, seriously, don't stand at parade rest to talk to me. This is Griffin." He indicated his massive friend. "And this is good afternoon: *masa alkheer.*"

"*Masawkahleer.*"

"Here come the NCOs," Griffin said, gazing across the parking lot.

Fifth had two NCOs: a furious-looking male corporal and a compact female sergeant. As they walked toward us Harvey narrated. "Marianne—Sergeant Walker—seems all light and bubbly, but she's solid. She's there if you need her. She's pretty focused on Arabic. She was a fire dog in Iraq—basically a firefighter," he explained, seeing the look on my face. "Tim—Corporal Jackson—is a great dude. He takes everything way too seriously, don't take it personally. He's just used to the infantry. If you ever see him drunk he'll tell you about three people he killed in Iraq, but don't ask him about it."

The two NCOs took mental inventory.

"No Tucson?" Corporal Jackson barked. He wore delicate silver glasses over a scholar's face. A currently furious scholar.

Griffin grunted. "She's got run team, Corporal."

"Roger," allowed Corporal Jackson. "Squad leaders, come talk to us." Griffin, a wry Doberman of a fellow, and the blond girl who'd stunned me with a glance joined them. I ripped my eyes from her, again. She, like, absorbed light. Her name was Lance Corporal Jane McCone.

I turned back to Harvey. It was weird, being near him. Like I stood under a gracious tree. Near him I felt I could talk like a normal human being. "So what's this Commander's Cup?"

He grinned and stretched his cammies sleeves over his long arms. "You'll see. Tucson'll probably try to rope you into it."

"Is it like . . . I mean . . . there's a team, or something?"

"Yes. The run team. Each branch—" Marines, Army, Air Force, Navy "—has a male and female team. They're always training for the Commander's Cup. Couple times a year there's an all hands at the track. There's some bullshit pomp and circumstance, then we all get to stand around and watch them run in little circles for two miles. Pain in the *teez.*"

"The Marines always win, right?"

"The males do."

"And the females?"

"They generally manage to beat the Navy."

"No!"

Harvey laughed at my dismay. "It's not great. Tucson's been going crazy. All her females keep going on chit." Chits were a military order from a doctor, limiting physical activity due to illness or injury. "Half the female Marines around here are broken. Let me know if she tries to recruit you. Unless you like running, then, I mean, go with Allah."

"I would like to join, actually. If I'm fast enough."

"For *run team*? You will be. You could probably run it backward and still be faster than some of the *hoots* around here."

Precious Arabic word: *hoot* meant whale.

At that moment the squad leaders returned to the platoon. Harvey nudged me to stand beside him in McCone's row. When we were in order, Sergeant Walker purveyed us cheerfully. "Let 'em have it," she said.

Corporal Jackson roared, "If you drive don't drink, if you drink wear a condom. Don't change the population one way or the other. It's payday Friday, so there will be a lot of drunk Marines doing stupid, stupid things. Don't let it be you or your squad. Alright, go get laid. *ALLAHU AKBAR*!"

"*AHHHHHHHLLAHU AKBAR*!" the Arabic platoon screamed back, and with that I guessed we were released.

Artigas also noticed Jane McCone. We both gaped, to be honest. McCone lived in the room next to us. Artigas pointed out approvingly she didn't fly out of the way of men. Only for senior enlisted did she politely step aside. She didn't flatten against the walls when any boy at all came charging down the hall, like Artigas and I did.

McCone moved like a dancer, upright, passing down the barracks in jeans and plain sweater. All high cheekbones, tall and graceful, and more than that.

McCone scared the hell out of me. She intimidated me beyond all reason. Her beauty, her serpentine poise, and something else.

There was something I noticed about this woman I could not explain. Though she was only a few months further into training than us, she was more of a Marine than her mere year in the Corps would suggest. She had been somewhere, had a shadow of a rifle over her shoulder.

She was also my squad leader.

"She's a squared away female," Artigas decided.

I dropped my head over my Arabic books. Ziploc bags of ice boot-banded to my shins seeped through my trousers and dampened my socks. I was trying, damnit. I was trying to be as thin as her.

My attention floated off Arabic toward my weight, my horrible, obvious weight. I bent to remove the ice bags on my shins. "I'm going for a run."

Artigas bowed over Arabic. "Again?"

She didn't look up as I traded trousers for silkies. Artigas rarely looked up from her desk. Sometimes she stress-smoked eye-watering cigarillos out our window, blowing smoke toward the formations below with a hint of fury. Artigas did most things with a hint of fury. She got dressed in the morning in a drumline of slamming drawers. She was gentle with me, though. When my nightmares shook the whole bunk bed, she woke me up with her foot to the underside of my mattress. "Williams, you're running in your sleep again," she'd call sleepily from the rack below.

I changed my clothes hunkered over, pulling my T-shirt over my hips before dropping my trousers. I hated exposing skin, even in the privacy behind my wall locker.

I tumbled down the stairs and ran into the brilliant Monterey evening.

I felt hyper aware of the sun on my thighs. It was a new sensation. My silky green shorts were Marine issue. They were also the most immodest item of clothing I'd ever worn. They were damned comfortable for running, though, and I'd be the only one on the track at this hour.

Evening runs were softer, base drained of Marines of high enough rank to really screw with me. Dusk falls over California's central coast so sweetly, even on military bases. I could plug in my music and run in meditative loops around the track and soak in the luxurious calm of being the fuck alone.

Below the track I passed junior Marines coming out of the PX. I tugged at the hem of my shorts and shyly ran between cars to put metal between us, embarrassed at the movement of my thighs.

As a Mormon girl, I was taught modesty, above all. Nothing more important than covering my body. By this, I'd be safe. I'd protect others too—protect young men from temptation, from luring a future missionary to stray from his path. Ah, the souls lost to Christ, youth leaders wept, young men unworthy to serve missions as they instead underwent painful repentance processes because they had sinned, they had wanted, had been waylaid by *you,* young women. Your bodies have power, bared shoulders, knees, power to CORRUPT! And so we shall learn to sew sleeves, girls, on all of our garments, lace onto the hems of our skirts to give us a few more pretty inches of coverage. For our job, our role, is to be modest.

It's a form of self-respect. If you don't respect your body, how could men?

Was this respect, then? The way I cowered when I undressed, even when I was alone? Horror at my body uncovered, the intense itch to be concealed at all times?

During all those years of modesty lectures I glanced longingly at my brothers, who also had Church youth groups. The boys ran around hollering and flinging hatchets and making fires and, later, prepared to receive the Keys to the Kingdom of Heaven.

I learned to lick a thread to fit through a sewing needle. My task, should I care to love God, was first and foremost cover my body. By this I'd be pure to marry, be sealed to one of the boys screaming down the halls, and in the next life he would be a god and I would be his helpmeet, his silent and unsung support. Along, of course, with the other wives God would give him, as polygamy remains doctrine for the highest completion of priesthood.

Kind of made me want to fling a hatchet.

As Mormon children we sang pretty songs about our bodies as temples. It wasn't a *bad* concept. An ancient and tender compulsion, the creation of a temple, to set aside a sacred grove, sanctify a space of beauty for spiritual contemplation. It would not be bad, to feel my body was a holy space.

Except doors to Mormon temples, towers of smooth white stone, were guarded.

You had to be Worthy to enter. To enter a Mormon temple required obedience, ascertained in an interview with a priest.

As a teenager I sat across a desk from a bishop. I dressed modestly, skirts covering the thighs I hated and burned with matches, to see if I was Worthy—only if he approved would he sign consent, grant me literal card-carrying proof of Temple Worth.

Did I obey the commandment to pay my tithing?

Did I obey the word of wisdom?

Did I obey the law of chastity; was I virgin?

I always said yes.

Perhaps a polygraph would have shown the burning shame the question evoked. I felt like I was lying. My neck burned and my stomach turned. I frequently left bishopric interviews and threw up.

I kept my face soft and allowed myself to blush and decorously reassured him, no, Bishop, I'd never had sex.

Was I lying? I couldn't remember. I had no words. Besides, whatever that had been, the paralyzing memory I tried to obliterate, the church hallway that haunted my dreams, the reason I was such an easily startled child, that wasn't . . . sex. Right?

And yet, when youth leaders told us modesty would keep us young women safe, I twisted my ankles around the legs of my chair, their cold metal leaving imprints on my legs, like I could weave myself into reality.

And yet, when youth leaders told us again our virginity was our most precious jewel, a pearl of great price, to be given away only when we were sealed in marriage for time and all eternity, all I felt was shame. Burning, overwhelming, breathtaking shame. I wore it like an itchy garment, and inside, I could not sit still.

My stepmother had no idea she'd inherited a traumatized child, one who wasn't entirely in her own body, and she didn't notice the traces it left. I was an easily startled child. I didn't like to be alone, reported hearing strange sounds and seeing dark shapes. Certain foods disgusted me beyond all reason; I refused textures that closed my throat. Melted cheese. Salad dressing. Things white and of strange viscosity.

When my stepmother married Dad a year after the accident, the one where my mother died, something already percolated under my skin, an electric burning wrapped around my spine. When she seized me and threw me onto a kitchen chair and wailed I was cruel, I made her feel so *unwelcome* in our family when I wouldn't eat the food she'd made—the textures I couldn't swallow—my entire body lit up like a firework on the Fourth of July. Sparkling with flecks of flame and the acrid smell of singed flesh on the inside.

I think it's why I remember her hands worse than my brothers do. I lived on edge, prowled my childhood like a cat, unsure I was safe on planet Earth. Each time she grabbed me, I heard it again: Others have the right to throw you around. In fact, it's your fault.

On the track, I slowed to a walk.

What was wrong with me? My iPod played crisp dopamine hits of Tchaikovsky. It was a clear, cool evening. But I wanted to stop. I was tired.

That was the thing, though, in training a body in obedience above all. I didn't feel fully sure my body was mine. Its inhabitation required permission; someone else decided its Worth. I looked outward to make decisions. Never inward.

The hell was I, to slow down, to stop because I was *tired*?
Up the Tchaikovsky. Damn the wall. Run on.

Back in the barracks I showered. I let myself into my room and rolled sweaty running clothes into my hamper. I wouldn't be eating tonight; I'd eaten a chocolate bar after class. I lay on my rack on my scratchy issued blanket, wooly and olive, and gripped the wings of my pelvis. I often fell asleep like that. Unbelievably soothing, the hard, solid grip of protruding bone. Reassurance in the white walls of stone.

I'd left home. I'd left the Mormon church.

But my body sure hadn't.

CHAPTER 5
LANGUAGE

The words we speak become the house we live in.

—*Hafez*

Ar-Rahman. The Merciful. *Ar-Rahim*. Giver of Mercy.

Artigas and I sat in the barracks hall. She wanted a beer, which wasn't allowed in our room because I was underage. We therefore slouched against our door frame with our legs out the door, where I was apparently less likely to become an alcoholic. Artigas sipped her Rolling Rock with Arabic flashcards fanned around her. I balanced ice packs on my shins.

As-Salaam. Peacemaker.

Artigas campaigned through a dog-eared Arabic workbook. I'd gotten as far as opening my journal, where I was meticulously copying the ninety-nine names of Allah for no practical reason whatsoever.

Al-Maani'. The Withholder. *Ad-Darr*. The Distresser, Balancer.

I could not be rallied to give a fuck for my quiz tomorrow. I was going to fail, and that was that. It was weirdly freeing to admit cramming would avail me little. I was weeks behind, distracted and sheepish and entirely overwhelmed in class.

Instead I traced Arabic calligraphy and absorbed new names of God.

All at once a Marine smashed through the red doors and dropped her shoes with a thud. "Shit," she grunted. "Sorry."

Tucson darted out of some desert where women rode horses and never felt compelled to slow down on foot. Five foot two of galvanized muscle, she routinely drank enough to fell a fire team and bounced up the next morning to outrun everybody, men included. People threw whore at Tucson but it didn't stick. It was like she didn't care. I saw her take off on a relay with a cigarette actively burning in her mouth and still churn the crud out of the gravel. I figured you'd have to catch her before you could pin whore on her.

She swayed in a short, curve-clinging green dress, barefoot. White platform sandals dangled by the strap in her hand.

"Fuckin' Franklin," she whisper-shouted. "Fuckin' . . . sobriety hill." The Presidio peered over Monterey from high atop the longest road uphill, with the nickname sobriety hill for its sobering effect on Marines staggering back to base. It called for a good buzz or not insignificant athleticism to summit on foot inebriated. Tucson had done alright.

"Dude. Corporal Kingsley was at the Crown," she said. "Goddamn!" She laughed and, attempting to lower her voice conspiratorially, sent hissed words echoing down the hall. "I'm not saying I would, but my gawd, he would be worth the NJP, you know?"

She let herself into her barracks room in an alcoholic bubble and slammed the door. We heard her shoes drop again, another "shit," then her rack jolt as she crashed.

Artigas shuffled her flashcards sternly. I bowed my head, grinning.

Al-Ghafoor. The Ever-Forgiving.

Tucson pummeled us the next morning, dark bags under her eyes and all. I couldn't stop laughing. She looked slightly gray but spirited the run team—three females in Russian and me—through warm-up sprints, led the charge out the gate into the sleeping civilian town. Silently we wound down along Asilomar Beach to Lovers Point, a finger into the bay ringed with jewels of cypress.

We ran onto Cannery Row. Tucson and I eased ahead of the Russians.

Hungover Tucson spoke with dignity. "Williams, I've been meaning to talk to you. I want you here. But if you don't eat dinner, or if you throw up, do not come to run team the next morning."

I said nothing.

She continued, "I know I'm not an NCO, but this is my billet and I order you. We have no damn female NCOs, so we kind of have to take this on ourselves."

"How did you know?" I held my breath, waiting for her answer. Did I look . . . thin?

"McCone talked to me. And I kinda knew. A girl on my college team was anorexic. She thought it made her faster. It did, for a while. But then she couldn't run, like, at all. She missed our state meet because she was in the hospital or something. I know you want to be here. But taking care of this is more important. I don't want you to get hurt because this—" she threw a hand back, indicating the trail. "This, comes and goes. You—functioning—that stays."

I marveled. I was going to ignore her, obviously, but it amazed me she took my eating disorder seriously when I wasn't thin.

"McCone talked to you?"

"She asked me to look out for you."

I bit my lip. McCone. Why was she trying so hard to frustrate my commitment to quietly, obediently disappear?

For every mile you run, you may eat one hundred calories.

Anorexia was like that. Like Grecian monsters, female. Clerical. Tidy and authoritative. Not like any woman I'd met, necessarily; one of both power and absolute reserve, but one I wanted to be. Assuring in her conviction. If I fucked up—if I ran only seven miles but inhaled a sheath of Oreos after a perfectly reasonable dinner of lettuce doused in low-sodium soy sauce—this wasn't a failure in her plan; it was a failure of me.

For every one hundred calories you eat, you need to run a mile.

So after puking the Oreos in my wall locker—back into the plastic container, so I could estimate how much I still had in my stomach and therefore how far I needed to run—I laced my tired running shoes and legged it to the track.

Numbers fenced my thoughts. Building a refuge with math was either hyperrational or absolutely insane, but for math, those weren't necessarily contradictions. Counting and multiplying and subtracting in running commentary. Math set order to my day, a structured system of success and failure. A direct cause-and-effect morality. Equating one hundred calories with one mile forged a mathematical warranty I ran off everything I put in. I estimated the baseline caloric necessity for the background noise—bodily function and platoon PT and, I didn't know, growing toenails or making blood or feeding thoughts or whatever a body not actively becoming fat did—would shed weight for me, in the minor details of just living, if running alone battled off input.

I could fit a run in first thing in the morning. There were spaces I could plug with short runs, fifteen to twenty minutes between class and formation if I booked it and formation was in PT gear anyway. And I could always run at night. The black. Building the bank. Putting the calories *into* my day, as well as compensating for ones eaten before. A mile. There's an apple for dinner tonight. Three more miles. There's the chow hall packet of peanut butter. I ran along the water and thought of whales, the mighty baleen straining in unfathomable loads of krill. We *boots* needed to move to eat.

The first time I ran sixteen miles I nearly cried at the indulgence of 1,600 calories. I'd been counting down the days, and calories, and double-checking for miles. Then one Sunday morning, getting up early and really and truly doing it: running my favorite sweep of trail, the long ballast of the Monterey coast, eight miles out and back, twice.

The blessing of low-fat granola from Trader Joe's, the entire box emptied into a Tupperware, incredibly stamped by my eating disorder's approval—such mercy!—together with a measuring cup of skim milk and half a bar of sugar-free dark chocolate I slivered with the pocket knife Harvey had wordlessly handed me after the condom-on-the-door-handle thing.

A meal—an entire meal, all at once—tasted like a Biblical promise remembered.

The next day I planned to rest. It was Monday, and there'd be formations and whatever PT the NCOs lobbed at us, class all day in between. That would keep me occupied and away from eating. I planned to subsist entirely on coffee.

I learned not a word of Arabic that day. I stared straight ahead and nearly hallucinated a protein bar in my mouth. The weight of it, the dizzying combination of sweet firm outer layer, the cloying heaviness inside.

I stayed at the track after platoon PT. I told Harvey I'd be in for Arabic tutoring in a minute. Then I ran a quick 2.5 miles, dropped down to the PX and bought a 250-calorie protein bar.

The primary language the Defense Language Institute taught Marines wasn't Arabic. Not for me anyway.

In the barracks my heroes were everywhere, lionized in two dimensions against the cinderblock. In one poster: a tired gunney, velvet blood coursing down his thigh, half collapsing, still gripping his side arm, arms thrown around the shoulders of fellow male Marines. Their uniforms were covered in blood and debris—the same uniform I wore, remember. I hooked my fingers under my ribs accusingly. The text read, WHAT ARE YOU DOING FOR <u>HIM</u>?

Is puking Oreos in your wall locker serving or honoring him in any way? No, it is not. Go run, you selfish sack of shit.

Another poster: a photograph of a Marine with shaken eyes, face blackened with dried blood, staring far away from under his Kevlar. Stern printed remonstration: WHAT HAVE YOU DONE FOR <u>HIM</u> TODAY? That poster, strangely, was for a doomed antismoking campaign.

Boot Marines became fluent in how we spoke of Him. We would often speak of Him. Everything the Marine Corps does is for the lance corporal on the front line with his rifle, we echoed. A mantra training our attention outward, out of our own asses and to our brothers overseas. Everything we did was for the infantryman, always infantry*man*, because the infantry was exclusively men. The pinnacle of actual Marines in the actual shit meant forever and always He. You, Marine, are learning a language to support Him. When you are tired or Arabic irregular verbs make no damn sense, you need motivation: you need to remember Him. You do not have it as bad as Him, here in cushy Monterey, California, and so you can run another mile or stay up an hour later.

Marines often spoke of Her too. A warning. She was a phantom, the female Marine accepted as the standard, an allegory. She was an overweight, nondeployed corporal who was promoted for sucking dick. She spent half her life on chit nursing some bullshit injury and had, apparently, notably loose labia. That she was sexually repugnant yet slept with everyone—which would mean everyone slept with her also, no?—confused me deeply.

Males had their standard to prove. Be like Him.

Females had our standard to prove. Don't be like Her.

If anyone asked me why I committed to running with religious fervor, I would've shouted I wanted to be like the men. Marines who fought at Guadalcanal and Iwo Jima and Fallujah. I wanted the brilliant devil-take-it of Mad Dog Mattis, a hero-worshiped general who exhorted us Marines to be polite, be professional, and have a plan to kill everyone we met. I wanted the war-weary wisdom of the Viet Nam lieutenant who wrote, "Courage is endurance for one moment longer."

I wanted to be like them.

I did not want to be like Her.

A strange thing happened, and increased in the months I scrambled to retain anything, actually anything, in Arabic from day to day. As I ate exclusively one hundred calories per mile I ran, my body did an unexpected thing.

She fought like hell.

Hunger chewed me as I ran. My stomach felt like it was shattering. I was pleased, normally, at the scrape of hunger, but when I held it long enough, a day or two or four, hunger morphed into something savage. Less dull knife. More delirious, rabid animal trying to scratch its way out.

In reply, I smashed my fist into my abdomen. Wake up, I growled. *Do* something. Digest last night's unhinged mauling of Kind bars. An entire box inhaled in rapid succession. Hard to vomit, Kind bars. Woody texture. Almonds gouged soft throat tissue. Too unprocessed to easily puke. I'd scratched at my throat, rabid myself, howling in frustration they wouldn't come back up. I only ran five miles this morning. That compensated for just two of the Kind bars. Probably less.

So shut up. I fed you yesterday.

I never once considered I wasn't eating enough. Never in my perpetual daydreams of starvation, fantasies of slinking about base with newly refined cheekbones and poise, did I understand *this* was starving. Snarfing food left unsupervised, a Hot Pocket Artigas left in the fridge, shoving it down cold and gagging it up in the woods, fighting my body for it when my stomach was a vise, my legs shaking until I sat down on the pine needles with my head between my knees, then careening to my car and driving to Trader Joe's for a box of granola bars, purging in the shower, plugging incomprehensible Arabic homework into my ears, itching in irritation then becoming so blackout furious at my own stupidity I flung my issued iPod at the cinderblock wall and then sheepishly knocking on Harvey's door to fix it, as it was now in seven pieces: This. This was hunger.

Harvey had figured out I was absolutely insane and was deeply bemused trying to talk me down. He suggested possibly a hundred times

I try eating three meals a day and seeing how that went for me. I tried to explain why this was, of course, immoral.

Insane, sinfully gluttonous, to think I always wanted more food because I was *hungry*. As my miles ratcheted up I was eating thirteen, fourteen, fifteen calories a day. That's what magazines said a woman trying to lose weight should eat. So the screaming desire to break my fist through the windows of a bakery and bury my face into a vat of dough—that was me being weird.

It couldn't be hunger because underneath my ribs I was secretly fat. Self-indulgent, orally fixated. A fat-ass in size two. A BCP Marine the day I let up on myself. I had to relentlessly stand guard against this clinically disordered compulsion to eat.

No, this wasn't hunger, longing for more. It was weakness. Ignore it.

Then the universe slid sideways, I was bingeing, and I despaired anew how profoundly all my haughty resolutions toward infinite and controlled order were complete and utter bullshit.

Bingeing—the slingshot effect of borderline constant hunger—propelled me across Monterey in frantic shaking trajectory. Even though I hadn't run off all the Kind bars, I gnawed through another box as I drove downtown. I parked and sped from one restaurant to another, jostled into civilians, apologized. At the Mexican place I jolted and pranced impatiently and ate three baskets of tortilla chips while my food was prepared to go—hurry hurry hurry. I ate standing on a vacant street and vomited in the next restaurant's bathrooms, tortilla chip sharp edges spiky in my throat. A hundred dollars flung from my debit card for thousands of calories inhaled up and down Alvarado, snarfing pounds of chocolate chip cookies from Trader Joe's, still chewing, ripping, eating in my car while I drove to the outdoor mall, then I vomited at the Del Monte Center bathrooms until the skin on my hands and mouth broke and chafed. I vomited until wrung out, promised myself I was done, for real this time, then stood and stumble-bolted for FroYo, feeling a black hole in my core. Purge and purge, the sweets still cold when I heaved them back up. Wandering Whole Foods, dizzy and dazed and pleased to be, the black currents of low blood pressure evidence I puked enough. I still felt, impressively, hungry, thinking, *Well, I'll try to be gentle*, staring at the broths. *Maybe something to settle my stomach*, picking up vegetable broth, putting it back, picking up low-sodium vegetable broth, putting it back, comparing labels, and finally heading to the checkout with a carton of organic fair-trade low-sodium vegetable water and congratulating myself, look at me, finally starting to really take care of myself, starting to learn something from all this, starting to understand, but then the berries looked so good, bursting with aliveness and promise of health, but also sweet sugar I didn't deserve until I starved myself for a few days at least. Well just a treat. Then I spied the vegan gluten-free carrot cake and fuck it, today sucked and besides, cake is easy to vomit, moister than bread, which formed owl pellets when shucked back up, but only if I get some milk too. Forty-two dollars on a forceful purge in the Starbucks bathroom.

I grocery store-bathroom-restaurant-bathroom hopped all the way to Seaside, dry firing until hands and throat were too swollen to vomit. Then I sat in my car, debris from chips and popcorn on my fingertips, plastic wrappers littering the passenger seat. I wailed wordlessly, my stomach so full and distended I looked like I was in my second trimester. Furious and erratic, unaware of the merry hell I was asking of my insides, I slugged back to the barracks, carrion-pecking cold french fries left in a to-go container on the floorboards, promising myself to throw it all away at the dumpster barracks and throw up again when my throat cleared.

Bulimia was a Grecian monster, too, one with two faces. One reserved. One howling.

I woke up the next morning cold with fear at the unknown mass of calories metastasizing in my belly, rolled out of bed and ran fifteen miles. Black coffee for breakfast. Gym for lunch. Organic fair-trade low-sodium vegetable water for dinner.

Then I was mystified when I woke up the next day with my stomach growling like a cornered animal. I couldn't be hungry. I was still fat.

And we were back to square one in the maddening Sisyphean game, bulimic Chutes and Ladders, calories paired with miles. I'd play for a day or five or ten, until hunger became less a feeling than a feral animal I tried to tame with an electric prod. My body fought back as if my conscious mind had no power. She hummed with a vibrant electricity, an insatiable urge to unhinge my jaw and swallow prey whole. It did not matter what I thought in mathematical terms of enough: my body had other damn plans.

Now I can see that power without hating it, I recognize these physical uprisings were an honest thing, an integrity in my body herself. She fought as a starving animal will do, to the pulse of something strong and real. Private Williams didn't know anything valuable existed between skin and bones, that body was anything more than bone and muscle and probably a few important organs.

I didn't understand my body was those things, but she was other things too. Relationship and fire and light. My body resisted hunger with instinct grounded in something I didn't yet understand: deep in my bones, I wanted to live.

Days balanced on a wobbly suspension bridge, jolting and jerking to create perfect tension between what I ran and what I ate. Every shred of ferocity I possessed I tapped to tear down extraneous weight. I had no attack in reserve for, like, my job. In Arabic I was timid, avoided eye contact, muttered answers when called.

I learned only the Arabic I heard the most, words my platoon used.

One: فقط انضباط. Fuck-it in-za-butt. It meant "only discipline." We shouted it often. We shouted it at field day and on company runs. Marines consistently found this funny. Example: "McCone needs more only discipline, you know what I mean?"

A teammate bought a cake, and the platoon roared. I learned another word leaning over the table, reminding myself under no conditions did I eat icing: "Fifth platoon, get some *shnukel*."

"There you go, Williams. That's a good one to know."

"What does it mean?"

Slang for vagina.

Other populars were أسماك كعكة and كعكة جزر. The first was a nonsensical expression—it meant "fish cakes"—but it was gleefully pronounced "ah smack my cock." I learned it when a Marine stood from where we sat in the hall and announced, "Well, I'm gonna have some fish cakes and rack out." I looked at him in blank confusion and politely told him I hoped he enjoyed his fish cakes, and Harvey laughed for about a week. The latter meant "carrot cake," but any whimsical association with confectionery was misplaced as it was pronounced, unfortunately, "cock jizzer."

When a grinning Marine stopped me in the hall, his hand to my arm, and asked if I wanted carrot cake, I was unaware what he meant, but I had an eating disorder and therefore told him no thank you, thank God.

Hoot was shorthand for a Navy woman. The Navy had the lowest physical standards, highest percent of overweight service members, and no chance of forgetting it, as Marines seemed to have taken some vow to continuously remind them. The female Navy barracks stood across from ours, and there was much speculation that what we saw through their windows was flirtatious.

"Those *hoots* leave their blinds up on purpose when they change over. They want us to see their rolls. You know how a Marine seduces a Navy female, right? You point and say, 'Come here.'"

We had other services' females all figured out too.

Air Force: "The *chair force* females are so much hotter than our females. Why can't our Wookiees look like theirs? See, all females try to join the chair force first, so they only have to take the hot ones."

The rare Wookiee within earshot mostly shook her head, annoyed by the jab we'd've tried to join the Air Force. Disdainfully, we said they got promoted by turning on one another.

Army: Female soldiers were more or less in the same boat as female Marines, with the advantage of numbers and hope of female NCOs. They had the fuck-all awfully mythologized Jessica Lynch legacy to deal with, though.

"Captured without firing a single shot," Marines delighted in reminding one another. "At least our females would pull the trigger. They might even hit something."

Mostly, though, we were whores.

I knew the word, obviously—the Bible fairly runs on them—but it had new connotations I'd not learned in Sunday school.

Girls were whores because they were junior Marines, and men smiled indulgently. "She's young and ain't used to the kind of attention she's getting here. In the civilian world, she wouldn't be getting any." Women were whores because they were senior Marines, and men's faces soured. "She picked up sergeant? Probably sucked dick." Girls were whores because they struggled. "She's on chit *again*. Seriously think she just joined to sleep around." Girls were whores when they did well. "She's only good in class because her squad leader exempts her from everything. He's going to get disappointed when he figures out she's a tease." Girls were whores because they were pretty. "I would fuck that female new join so hard. The blond in third platoon? Total whore." *Really*? "You saw the amount of makeup she was wearing in my Marine Corps uniform, right? And she was laughing with her platoon sergeant. She's been here a week and she's already looking to move up." Girls were whores because they weren't. "God, she has like, eight chins. She'd never get any attention in the real world, and fucking Gillis in third already proposed."

Girls were whores because of behavior that taught me I had grossly underestimated what whores did. In the chow hall a group of male Marines held the door open for a female. One of them snaked out a hand, touched her waist. She batted his hand away but laughed. Later I heard that because she laughed, you knew "she's going to end up knocked up and keeping the bastard to get out of nine months of PT."

It startled me. I, too, laughed when I was uncomfortable.

Boys called each other pussy and cunt and cocksucker. The constant use stretched the vulgarity of the words until they burst and ceased to shock anymore.

Whore retained power.

WM meant women Marines, but no one really used the retired acronym except to cleverly propose it meant walking mattress. The dozenth time I stopped wincing.

Corporal Kingsley smoked with us before formation. Corporal Kingsley, the unabashed war hero among us. Could be a staff sergeant, the lance corporal underground circulated, but took the fall for someone else. He unapologetically wore faded cammies soft from Iraq. His shaggy hair was a shade past regs. He kept his hands in his pockets and simply gave no visible fucks, like most of the 0311 Marines. He was the most admired NCO on base.

Corporal Kingsley pointed to a Camry in the parking lot with a paling bumper sticker. The car belonged to a PFC who ran errands for Master Guns. Her bumper sticker read: WM: WOMEN MARINES. THE FEWER, THE PROUDER.

"You know, WMs," said Corporal Kingsley, the combat veteran. "Walking mattresses."

One Marine grinned uneasily at me, trying to catch my eye. I stared off into the woods, trying to remember a forgotten line of a Dylan Thomas poem, as us mattresses are wont to do. I also said nothing.

Undeterred, Corporal Kingsley underlined *the fewer* with his cigarette and laughed. He said, "Thank God."

The PFC who owned the car had rotund hips, blond hair soft and squared away. She seemed like a hard worker, but it was clear Marines thought there was some other reason she might be hanging around. Because she was curvy, we knew what Corporal Kingsley meant. The dreaded female association with softness. Anything but that, in the hard Corps.

Far more common was the affectionate term Wookiee. Wookiee, a lasting nickname given to women in the Marines, originated in the imagined horror of hairy lady bodies after boot camp. Naturally we didn't have razors for the thirteen weeks of basic training, as we had slightly more pressing shit to do than shave. Our genital regions, according to the always stunningly well-informed lance corporal underground, returned to some primal, Kashyyyk form.

Personally, that one amused me. Who doesn't love Chewbacca?

Let the Wookiee win.

NCOs summed us up with exactly whatever the hell we were. "Williams, Vagina Type. Morris, Black Type. Evans with the Funny Head. Cole Who's Not Asian." Ponderously inventive, Marine-issued name calling. Sometimes they even used our first names.

We celebrated our lack of decorum, claimed it offered strategic advantage. Take your liberal safe-space trigger-warning BS and shove it, we aren't in the business of pandering to pansies. I was Williams Female Type when there was another Williams. Once we had Williams, Williams Female Type, and Williams Who's Black. Insist it was nothing diminutive, a military issue tag, a clarification. Except it forever asserted the standard was the white guy.

Alternatively, yes, I was Williams Vagina Type. I supposed they weren't wrong.

It gave me a gross feeling though. Like I was inside out.

Harvey was Old Man Harvey. Obscene to live in the barracks at twenty-five. McCone, who counseled me on my youth, was twenty-three. I was young—I'd enlisted the week of my eighteenth birthday. Most of us were in the surreal bracket the federal government trusted with top secret compartmentalized security clearances, but not with beer.

McCone didn't have a nickname I ever heard, except, in grudging admiration, cunt.

To openly brag about touching a woman without permission crossed the gossamer line into fucked up. At least under the commanders-in-chief whom I served, pussy grabbing wasn't locker room talk.

But there were strange silences.

Two Marines rejoined fifth platoon. Wherever they'd been had an inkblot over it. I heard the brig. I heard something like the brig, but less severe. I heard permissive temporary absence of duty (PTAD). I heard it was really none of my business.

Harvey told me Corporal Jackson called him and a few other men in the platoon, warned them to keep one of the returned Marines away from female Taylor. "Don't let him anywhere near her."

The returned Marines swaggered down the barracks hall in an odd triumph.

Taylor never said a word. She shut herself into her room. A phalanx of Marines boxed her in at formation.

Somehow, I didn't hear it.

But there are no female Marines.

Only Marines. Stumbling, I sought a way that denied my abhorrent femaleness: the path of most resistance. Marines, both peers and leadership, occasionally recanted. Females who were extremely physically strong, like professional athlete strong, and serious, showing no humor, no mirth, nothing but relentless drive and indifference, tended toward exemption from blanket female criticism. "She runs a six minute mile. She's hard." "She keeps it locked down." These stray lines formed cairns along the path to an invisible standard, a way to claw respect from the hands of Marines who casually said they didn't like female Marines.

Be so exceptional you earned it.

No one told me my particular female body was fat or ugly or distracting or evidence of the softening of the Marine Corp and indeed the moral decline of the American people, but commentary in person and online splattered female Marines, as a collective, like overripe fruit. Pussified, was a fun word I learned in a Marine Facebook group. As in, women in the Marines were evidence of the pussification of the Corps, as if perhaps our genitalia carried infectious frailty.

The odd thing about debating whether women should serve in combat was it utterly missed the fact women were, in fact, serving in combat. As boots sat there speaking out their asses about whining Wookiees, no shit women Marines were no shit serving in combat. The whole stupid conversation distracted from more important conversations, like questioning whether anyone should be fighting in the first place.

Women did real things in the Corps. But She was on no barracks posters. I heard no stories of Her doing her job well.

I heard a joke before the clinking of beer. Thank you for your cervix, ladies.

I didn't know what was true. I didn't know what was a joke and what I should . . . maybe say something about. I had no context for the vernacular. Despite my best efforts to get in trouble, I was still a bishop's daughter. When I saw *Jarhead* in the barracks, it was among the first R-rated movies I'd seen.

I kept my mouth shut and ran.

These were the good guys, I told myself sternly, when my stomach dropped. This must be how people outside of the church talked. Words twisted my stomach when he bragged she was easy after enough alcohol. Words made it okay for eyes to follow me when I walked away, because it was only a joke that my ass in a skirt made a Charlies inspection worthwhile. The comment and the teasing whistle made me horribly aware I did fill out my skirt, and I walked away determined to carve those damn curves away. I never did take my uniforms to be tailored from my anorexic shape.

I shouldn't be bothered, I told myself. Personal weakness, that living in the barracks left a taste in my gut that made me want to puke. Right?

I didn't know.

All I had was what those words made me feel. The clinks they made in my body. The surge of adrenaline, the pulse quickening in my soft neck, the unbearable urge to run.

How male Marines spoke of us females made me feel . . . watched.

CHAPTER 6
HUNGER

The logic goes like this: every thin person is healthier than every fat person, every fat person can become thin if they try hard enough. . . . As such, size becomes an indicator of character and willpower. . . .

. . . America is a meritocracy, we insist, defined by hard work and tenacity, the hallmarks of a true Protestant work ethic. Bodies become a symbol of that work ethic, the American exceptionalism that we have long believed defines Americanness itself.

—*Aubrey Gordon,* What We Don't Talk About When We Talk About Fat

Restless before an afternoon formation, I paced Harvey's room. My stomach growled so audibly Harvey tried to order me to eat Goldfish, which I wouldn't touch because they were processed and contained Lord knew what all.

Harvey had accepted with equanimity his new responsibility as eating coach for a teenaged girl, though it confounded him. "You're supposed to eat three meals a day," he offered, his mantra with me. He rattled the carton with one hand, beer in the other. "You can also eat snacks. I've had about a million of these damn things and guess what? I will also eat three meals today. You're going to run it off, Wills, you run like you're on crack."

"Normal people are supposed to eat three meals a day."

"The hell are you?"

"I'm fat."

His mouth was a straight stern line. "There is no way in hell you actually believe that."

"How in hell could I *not* believe that?" I wailed. My knees no longer showed the interesting movement of patella when I walked. "Maybe you can't tell because my cammies are baggy. But underneath them, I am fat."

"Your tiny-person cammies are baggy, and that hides that you're secretly fat? I've seen you in skivvies, Wills. You're fucking tiny. For God's sake eat some fucking Goldfish."

Validating, but my eating disorder struck a quick counter. "I probably just seem small to you, because you're a foot taller than me. But for my height, I'm close to overweight."

He groaned. "How much do you weigh?"

My face caught fire. I would rather slice my skin than admit it. "About a hundred twenty," I mumbled. Four. Point nine. I'm working on it.

Harvey leaned over his computer, pulled up Marine Corps Order 6110.3. "'In recognition that Marines are *warrior athletes*—'" he laughed aloud "'—program that will enhance Marine wellness . . . combat readiness and personal appearance . . .' yeah, 'cause those are the same thing. Great God, it keeps going. 'Weight redistribution program'? That's one way to say 'PT the hell out of them.' Ah, okay, here we go. Height and weight chart."

The Marines decreed for my height, my minimum weight could be one hundred ten, maximum one hundred forty-five. My thunder thighs and I fell between them with a wide margin on either side. Well, average isn't good enough. Marines don't applaud mediocrity.

"I can do better—" I began, but Harvey interjected.

"You would have to gain twenty-five pounds to be overweight."

My body's insurrection at MCT rocketed me up twenty pounds to my current size, so this wasn't reassuring. Anyway, fat wasn't a number. It was a quality. A state of being, available at any size.

"Wills, you've got to fucking eat like a normal person. I'm not saying you're normal. You are very far from normal. You run five hours a day."

"I average two," I corrected compulsively. "Some days I don't run at all."

"But most days, Wills, *most days*, you run like ten miles, right?"

That wasn't very much. Other people ran more.

"Let's do this. Let us calmly and objectively consider if you are eating remotely enough to sustain life. You had run team this morning."

"Just speedwork."

"Be that as it may. We had platoon PT this afternoon. Ammo cans were involved. Do you recall lifting heavy things above your head many, many times? Bear crawling while dragging Taylor, an entire human adult, holding on to your belt? Do you recall carrying Payne, who has to have thirty pounds on you, across your shoulders and running down a football field?"

What did that have to do with anything? I mean, that burned, what, two, three miles worth of running?

"And then you ran how far?"

"About ten miles." Glacially. "But just on the track. It's not like it was hills or anything."

"And you did this on the dinner of carrots and *mustard* you ate last night. What is that? Like five hundred calories?"

Defense flared. "I only ate sixteen ounces. That's one hundred fifty calories. Mustard doesn't have any."

Harvey blinked. "Okay, you're really not making this better. Look. Wills. Bailey. Bails. You are going to fucking destroy yourself. What you are doing is absolutely insane."

"I don't want people to think I'm faking something. Harvey, you're one of the people who's said all females break and go on chit."

"You are not doing that. The females who get onto BCP are the ones who join because they think it makes 'em badass and post Facebook pictures 'in the field' when they're really in the combat zones of North Carolina at MCT. Then they realize, oh no, it's actually hard work to be a Marine, *mufaja*! Then they mysteriously break and go on chit for four fucking years. It's *not* the females who work out as much as you do. You are *not* fat."

I wasn't actually sure who Harvey meant on this one. McCone was willowy and Taylor was big and Tucson was stocky and I was basically ginormous quads and elbows, but we'd all been hauling men bigger than us down the field.

The red-faced Marines in the Body Composition Program huffing by, driven by a cynical artillery corporal, made other Marines strangely livid. *God, they're running like ten minute miles. Civilian fat fucks. Fat-asses desecrating my Marine Corps uniform. This is the goddamn Marine Corps. Fuck, she had her baby like three months ago. Put down the fucking fork.*

"Fat is not something the Army abides," writes soldier Ryan Leigh Dostie in her memoir. "In this insular community, where there are no physical disabilities, no deformities, no elderly, no sick, nothing but youth and mandatory fitness, no one is more of a *shitbag soldier* than the one who is fat." That's only the Army. Given the Army slaps wrists where Marines lunge for the throat, we straight up bullied overweight Marines. Before weigh-ins, gym saunas slow boiled Marines frantically cranking out jumping jacks in sweats and garbage bags. Marines OD'd laxatives or went on liquid diets or ketogenic diets or all-protein diets or whateverthefuck diets, you know, for their health—self-effacing maneuvers that made my eating disorder seem not all that outlandish. Hydroxycut flew off the shelf at the PX. A platoon mate discouraged by their nauseating side effects passed a nearly full bottle of the metabolism-boosting pills to me. If a few are good, more must be better, ran my myopic logic. I swallowed red capsules, deliberately oblivious to pinching pain in my gut. I bit it during a platoon PT, heart barreling. I blamed Hydroxycut, knowing damn well I'd been throwing up every few hours for a week and was a bit unsteady on my feet.

"Oh yeah," said a sympathetic squadmate. "Some people have really bad reactions to that stuff."

"She's probably too little to take a full dose," another seconded, which I found deeply flattering as I lay on the earth trying to remember which way was up.

McCone confiscated the bottle and hissed the hell did I think I was doing.

"Motivated," cheered friends when I declined pizza in the barracks, indicating the apple in my hand. They didn't know that was all I was eating for dinner, but that was degree, not principle: Good Marines eat good food. Bad Marines eat fat kid food.

I wasn't alone in an especially military-female terror of fat. A study notes of servicemembers with a quote-unquote healthy BMI, 0 percent of men but 29 percent of women saw themselves as overweight (holla!); 81 percent of these female servicemembers were working toward weight loss. So statistically, in any given unit, a quarter of women who already conform to body standards are still actively trying to shrink. The study concludes: "Military members may be in a unique position to misperceive their weight status because of the expectations of military service-specific body composition standards and sex-specific ideals of body image."[1]

Sex-specific, indeed. I hated my ass and hips and thighs and stomach and breasts and somehow failed to notice I hated my body's expression of being female.

I stared at the chart. At 145 pounds, apparently, I'd be a fat, malingering, unmotivated Marine. Disorder scrambled Harvey's words to confirm I could eat because I ran, so if I stopped running, I shouldn't eat.

"*Now* will you eat the goddamn Goldfish?"

"What if they make me fat?"

"You would literally die before you could eat enough Goldfish to make you fat. They're some whole-grain bullshit."

"But they're inherently fattening, if there's a point at which eating them will make me fat."

"Fuck's sake. You haven't fucking eaten today."

"But I—"

"I do not care if you ate yesterday, or last weekend. You need to eat every day."

"No, I—"

"Yes, Williams, you do. You are trying to live on empty and it is a ridiculous way to live. It's a snack. You're not going to spontaneously expand fifty pounds."

"But what if I do?"

"That is an impossible thing. We are now talking about impossible things. It's called magical thinking. It is the basis of religion and also, I now know, eating disorders. We may as well say 'But what if the ceiling falls in and crushes us all as a punishment from God?'"

This was not at all reassuring. I'd read the Bible. Collapsing architecture was absolutely on the table.

"What if I put them in a bowl for you? Would that help?"

I paused. Oh God, I wanted Goldfish. I wanted anything.

"Like just," I started slowly, "If you cover the bottom. But you'll still come running with me before dinner, right?"

"Will you eat the goddamn Goldfish?"

"Just the bottom of the bowl."

Harvey muttered something I didn't understand as he poured Goldfish into a Styrofoam bowl. My heart was pounding. I couldn't. I had to. He wasn't making me. Jesus, Williams, put down the fucking fork. The smell of them. My mouth was watering.

"That's way too many," I cried.

"Just try—"

"If you don't put most of that back, I am not touching that bowl." The heaviness of it freaked me out even in his hands.

We negotiated a scant school of fish, enough reassuring white Styrofoam between their orange. I commenced eating them one by one, holding each fish between my tongue and the roof of mouth until it dissolved. They split in two when they dissolved, neatly, down the middle, and I squirreled one half in my cheek while holding the other on the tip of my tongue, savoring every flint of salt. I was unaware of closing my eyes.

Harvey spoke. "It is such an EO violation for me to be the one to tell you this, but someone needs to break the news to you." I opened my eyes and realized how close he was to me. "Williams, you're hot. You are stunningly beautiful. You make men stupid."

"That can't—"

"Trust me on this. You are make-men-stupid-hot. When *I* first saw you, I thought—I mean, I knew you were in my fire team, so I figured, okay, be professional—but my first thought was, *Wow. That is one incredibly beautiful woman.*"

"Didn't you meet me pissed off and in cammies?"

"Yup. And my first thought was still, *Holy shit.* Alright? No one is making fun of you. Has it occurred to you that some of the truly stupid shit these children say around you, in particular, is because they have lost blood supply to their brains?"

"By Marine Corps standards? Wookiee nine, so I'm a civilian two point three?"

"Nope. Unfortunately for you, you're genuinely gorgeous."

"Please stop." I wrapped my arms around my stomach protectively.

Harvey stared. "You honestly don't know what you look like."

"A beluga?"

"It's called an *hourglass*. You look like a woman *should* look." He broke off and addressed the ceiling. "*Ya Allah*! Is this really my job?" He stood. "C'mon, it's ten until fifteen early. We're eating dinner tonight."

"After a run."

"Fine. But I'm not doing more than six miles. And you are finishing that bowl."

I stood dramatically and seized the handful, crammed them in my mouth, planted my boots and stared at him as I chewed.

He raised an eyebrow. I blushed and dropped my cover on my head.

He held the door for me. "Look, Williams, I get it. I weighed 250 when I lived in Tulsa. I lost 50 pounds for boot camp."

"Wow! How?"

He laughed, a quick bark. "Went on a whiskey and Doritos diet. I'm not recommending it. You can eat whatever the hell you want, just eat less than what you use. My point is I get it, it's hard to be comfortable with your body. But you're in the damn Marine Corps. We kind of get a lot of exercise. You can fucking eat."

McCone knew something was awry. I think she could smell my fear. She stopped me in the halls to demand whether I'd eaten. I dropped my eyes, ashamed how often I did. She noticed me smashing back into the barracks sweaty and happy, running shoes in hand, but too often, morning and afternoon and evening. She snapped at me to knock it off.

<You're not going to do anybody any good if you break yourself,> she texted.

I was kind of flattered she thought I would break. I wasn't remotely hardcore enough for that. I snorted at Harvey's concern, at people who thought you needed to eat every day. No, the black veil that brushed over my gaze when I stood up was a *good* thing.

The women around me seemed so much stronger than I was. Berlinsky, sprinting uphill with me, objectively. Her quads were like torpedoes. At the top of the hill we turned around and jogged back down.

When I ran with the female run team, I talked to women in other language platoons. Berlinksy studied Mandarin. As we jogged back down the long hill she laughed off the sting of her NCO asking her stance on anal sex in front of her squad.

"If I laugh it off, it makes me DTF, you know? But if I act like I don't like talking about it, suddenly I'm a prude. I'm not, it's just like . . . time and place, dude."

Francis studied Tagalog. She was even colder and tighter than me. My hands turned white when we ran in the cold; hers turned blue. At her wrists translucent skin stretched over carpal bones. She burst out about a lance corporal who kept watching her, brushing against her whenever their platoon fell in or out of formation.

Oh, we talked about boys too. Boys who fixated or skulked. Boys who texted constantly under the guise of leadership or being helpful, withholding or angry if we didn't respond. Boys who went ballistic.

I knocked on Harvey's door. He opened it wearing a black T-shirt that said "I Support Single Moms" over the white silhouette of a stripper, hooking a pole with her stiletto. I winced, which he misunderstood.

"Don't worry, this is just bullshit," he assured me. "C'mon in."

Harvey was probably the best adult in our platoon and definitely the most computer literate, so the NCOs conscripted him to shepherd us through an annual online training. His massive flatscreen monitor displayed the first lesson. Harvey sipped a beer. "You can just click through them," he advised, pulling up a chair beside me.

He picked up his book, Christopher Hitchens' *God Is Not Great*, and resumed reading. Harvey was the first openly atheist person I'd ever met. It was as shocking as meeting a Democrat.

I sat at his atheist computer.

Personal protective equipment. Click.

Sexual assault hurts us all. Click.

Know blood alcohol content limits. Click click click.

Zero tolerance for hazing. Which option depicts hazing? Yes, hitting new kids with soap in socks is hazing. Don't do that. Click.

I froze. I swear I could always tell when McCone was coming. The bawdier of the barracks dick-measuring consultations shushed down the hall. My shoulders shot up to my ears.

McCone slunk across Harvey's doorframe. The angular blond coolly announced she'd come on a mission from Higher Ups.

"Williams. I don't care about your personal life. But I've heard some disturbing things. You need to keep your threesomes out of the barracks."

My honest first thought was I was so fat I couldn't believe one man would want to sleep with me, much less two.

I met her eyes on that one. "Do *you* think I'm having threesomes in the barracks?"

McCone's face softened, marginally.

"Personally I don't think you've even had time to fuck all the men who say you have."

"Thanks," I said weakly. Her face closed again.

"You're really young. You need to be careful. Males will say anything. Are you signed into this male room now?"

Harvey spoke up. "Um, Jane. Hi. I'm her fire team leader. And your friend, for the last eight months? Mari—Sergeant Walker told us to make sure our Marines get this shit done, remember? The door is fucking open. It takes two minutes."

McCone kept her eyes on me. "See, this is exactly what I'm talking about. He's in your chain of command, you trust him, you're working. *I* know it's okay, *you* know it's okay. But any passing Marine sees you in a male's room—that's how these rumors start, Williams. When you're young and . . ." Something closed in her eyes. "When you're female, you need to hold yourself in such a way that, not only does no one have any reason to doubt your integrity, you can't give them anything to *fabricate* doubt. Do you understand what I'm telling you?"

Not at all. This diatribe felt so irrelevant to me, who was so whale-like in form surely I attracted only barnacles. "Yes, Lance Corporal."

"It's professionalism."

"Aye, Lance Corporal."

"It's for your own fucking safety."

"Aye, Lance Corporal."

McCone gave me a final hard look and left.

Harvey stood and pointedly closed the door. "She has no right going off on you like that," he fumed. "She acts like she's such hot shit when she's sucking an NCO's dick."

Her fiancé was a corporal in Mandarin. "Weren't they together before he was promoted?" I braved tentatively. Prior relationships were the exception to the don't-date-NCOs-oh-my-God rule.

"Yes, fine," Harvey relented. "Sorry, Williams, I don't mean to yell. I don't like that she picks on you. I was here when she showed up. She only started getting her shit together a few months ago. Stopped drinking, lost weight, started running, doesn't do anything but PT, study Arabic, and police you, evidently."

"Was she heavy before? Like, as heavy as me?"

"Williams, you are tiny. But no, she's always been skinny."

Drat. "Want to run down to the water with me?"

He groaned as he set down his beer. "I guess that would be good leadership."

The severity of McCone's leadership style made sense to me. How men treated females was one thing. How we treated each other could be even worse.

A new private had recently joined fifth platoon. She sighed and wandered off sometimes. Delicate blond tendrils escaped her bun and wafted after her. Her first name fascinated Harvey: Star Blue. Hippie parents, we marveled.

"You don't meet a lot of Marines raised by lefties," Harvey wondered. "Is this how liberal kids rebel? Cut their hair, say no to drugs, and join the military?"

Star Blue was in Griffin's squad, and it was very funny to watch. The enormous man stared at the delicate girl, baffled.

Shortly after Star Blue joined the platoon, Harvey called me to his room to—as far as I could tell—despair of teaching me Arabic. For once

I'd bothered to sign in, leaving my ID with the Marine on duty to keep track of females in male rooms. Sex in the barracks was both verboten and presumed. Duty passed by the open door every so often to announce, "Still not fucking like rabbits? Cool, carry on." We females were told this was for our safety.

Harvey and I were both marveling at how disturbingly far I'd made it into Arabic on charades alone. Harvey opened to the first page of the first lesson from a workbook I should have mastered a month ago. He clucked, "*Y'allah.*"

Fortunately Griffin barreled in to put me out of my misery. He flung a notebook over my Arabic. I jumped. "I can't handle this," the huge Marine moaned, sinking onto Harvey's rack.

Harvey picked up the notebook. "What is this?"

Griffin's eyes bulged. "I *told* her to write an essay! I can't even *read* this."

Star Blue was late to formation often, and Griffin was losing his mind. He couldn't motivate her in the usual manner—0400 death runs, digging a foxhole on the beach during an incoming tide, etc.—because she was pregnant. He therefore ordered her to write an essay about accountability.

Harvey and I peered at the notebook.

She had written him pages and pages of poetry. There were fairies and dew and meadows glistening in sunshine. I had no idea what she was talking about. Harvey and I spoke together."What in the actual fuck?"

"I can't do this," Griffin moaned. "I've got to move her to McCone's squad or I'm going to . . ." he shook his head.

How dearly I hoped he would move Star Blue to my squad. I would love to see what McCone would do to her. Strangle her probably. I would. That was *our* credibility she was pissing on. The men had Iwo Jima. We had Star Blue.

"She's malingering too. She got off chit for an apparently asymptomatic twisted ankle, then got knocked up three days later."

Harvey reached into his minifridge for a beer. "There's always a few. Females who think they can hang and realize, oh shit, I have to actually work. Then go on chit forever. Like Davis Broke Type."

Davis Broke Type limped. Platoon mates carried her schoolbag as she shuffled to class on crutches. When we PT'd as a platoon, she stood silent vigil one leg tucked beneath her, while we yelled and lunged across the field. Marines muttered that when she didn't think anyone was watching, she walked just fine.

Griffin nodded and downed the offered beer.

"Fucking females," he said tiredly.

I pushed back from Harvey's desk and excused myself. I needed to run. I had no idea if Star Blue or Davis Broke Type was malingering, but they were, whether I liked it or not, my team, we, the fucking females. One of us had to keep it together.

So yeah. How McCone policed me made sense. But I was missing something.

There was something I didn't know about the young woman who knocked on Harvey's door on a mission from Higher Up. Well, I didn't know a damn thing about her. But this particular thing I didn't know would, when I learned it, set me on a course that changed my life forever.

I believed it, by the way. I believed what we said about females who complained about male attention being kind of intense. She's immature. If she can't hack it, she shouldn't be here. She's making a big deal out of nothing. He didn't mean it *personally*. I believed if one of us was actually assaulted, it would be a whole big thing. I believed if one of us was, God forbid, raped, we would take that shit seriously. We'd apply the full force of the ferocity we threatened in our existence as Marines. We'd strip any rapist his right to wear the eagle, globe, and anchor, if, indeed, we let him out alive.

McCone knew better.

While I was still at boot camp peacefully meditating on my concave pelvis, Marines in McCone's platoon—our platoon—had gang-raped her one night in the barracks. All I heard of it was McCone kept to herself, focused on Arabic with laser intensity.

Only years later did she reach out. I shared a story I was writing, this story I kept writing because of her. She called me up and told me exactly why she kept to herself, why she stopped drinking. Eventually, she texted, she'd had to have surgery.

<But at least my asshole doesn't look like cauliflower anymore.>

I didn't know that then. I didn't know real things were happening to the women around me that we weren't talking about. I recognized a tension around McCone, a tight-lipped solemnity when she came up in gossip. The three oldest men in the platoon, Harvey and his friends in the Old Man Club (who held wisdom gleaned from such ages as twenty-five and twenty-six) shut up jokes about McCone's body with a mere glare.

I didn't understand that was the extent of the justice McCone was going to get on this one.

High-minded, oblivious Private Williams didn't listen to girls, so I didn't hear McCone's warning. I heard her say it didn't matter who I was, only how I was seen. I didn't hear what I now believe she was trying to say.

Wake up, woman. If you don't hold your own, you are going to lose it.

PART II

TAKING

CHAPTER 7

VETERANS DAY

Shame is a slow creeping. The most powerful things are quietest, if you think about it. Like water.

. . . That is shame. A warring within, a revolt against oneself. It can bury you standing if you let it.

—*Sarah M. Broom,* The Yellow House

The Marines outside my door discussed the mechanics of a gangbang, a term previously unknown to me. I was receiving an alarmingly detailed definition.

"But you'd have to avoid the balls, or it would be gay . . ."

". . . hanging titties kinda flap . . ."

I stared at incomprehensible Arabic, forehead in hand.

Certain words repeated in my head. Words from a Mormon story. A cold jailhouse in frontier Missouri, the prophet Joseph Smith hunched in chains and taunted by the jailers. Then the prophet stood. The prophet was a big man, more than two hundred pounds, and witnesses claimed he radiated light and filled the jail with a leonine roar. Damn good fighting words for a preacher. As a child I traced the words on the page again and again, his declaration: "Silence! . . . In the name of Christ I rebuke you, and I command you to be still; I will not live another minute and hear such language. Cease such talk, or you or I die this instant."[2]

That was pretty much what I wanted to say. Or, in the vernacular: Shut. The fuck. Up. I felt heat in my hands, the readiness to back words up with fists. You are ten feet from where I live and sleep and read and change my clothes and puke into plastic bags. I do not need to hear you ponder how much better a woman can take dick when she's into it compared to when she's not. Fuck right off.

But to stand one's ground? To lead? Rebuking was a task ordained to men.

When Dad was a bishop, he went into hospitals to place healing hands on sick friends. He baptized me and my brothers. He ordained my brothers to the priesthood. Sometimes when Carol was really out-of-her-mind upset, tempestuous enough that even Dad knew about it, he would stand behind her, put his hands on her head, and quietly use the voice of God to ask her soul to peace, be still. All holy covenants were enacted by men. We believed the creation of Earth itself was an act of priesthood. Men performed miracles: spoke in tongues, cast out devils. Priesthood revelation illuminated scripture, rendering Dad the moral authority of my family. Men called Sealers presided over temple weddings, claiming otherworldly authority to seal marriage not until death do us part, but for Time and All Eternity.

To be a righteous Mormon man was to embody the power of God on Earth.

Girls . . . could have babies.

That was. Pretty much it, yeah. And the hell power was motherhood? I hadn't had a mother, and look, I was doing just fucking great.

Of all the scars I carried as I sat twitching at my desk over my Arabic, perhaps the most disorienting was this: I did not believe I had the same right as men to dissent. The aftershock of a male clergy, an absolute lack of female spiritual leadership: I'd learned to trust men more than women, including myself, including the discomfort of my own body.

Wifehood was sacred, Dad insisted. He posited Christ was married. Marriage and fatherhood were sacred covenants necessary for the fulfillment of the higher priesthoods (so wifehood was sacred for the doors we opened for our husbands' expansion of priesthood), and since Jesus was the perfect example of all things, it stood to divine reason he married and fathered children. And of course he had a heavenly mother. How else could the only begotten son of God be, you know, begot?

This was a rare private conversation, had at home, stories we told before bed. Never did I hear the mention of a mother in church.

"Why don't we talk about her?" I'd wondered.

"To protect her," Dad had said. "God's heart hurts every day at the iniquity of his children. It would break his heart to see her name called in vain."

To protect a woman was to silence her.

Men had heroes to look to, the mighty prophet-warriors of the Book of Mormon, the panoply of male leadership. If I looked for divine female leadership, what I got was . . . silence.

I loved my dad. Whatever he said was true. God Himself wore my dad's glasses.

I didn't remember my mother's face.

Why was I here? I stared at Arabic and tried to focus. Why did I want to be a Marine?

That drumbeat resonating through some deep aching part of me. I'd wanted to be a priest. I didn't know why. I just did. As far back as I could remember, the idea of being a priest filled my entire body with a sense of calm. To have the intention of life be walking with God, befriending whomever I could, studying the sacred, uplifting those who despaired? To live life as the embodiment of my faith? A life of peace and meaning? Of course I wanted that.

That I felt called to ordination didn't mean a damn thing to the Mormons, unless I wanted to press the point and get myself excommunicated. I couldn't join the clergy of the Saints, though I went ahead and excommunicated myself anyway.

But God help me, I was American. I could join the armored priesthood.

Like a man of the cloth, a man in uniform is told he is a little different. Set apart. Tasked with something. Temperate and honorable, though fierce when called. His struggles will be the grand old ones, the stories of good and evil. He will fight terrors the layperson cannot know—not for glory, but because someone needs to fight them. He may need to make difficult decisions and unknown sacrifices, ones that civilians can never understand, sanctified by his calling.

And so I sat, forehead in hand, staring at Arabic.

No wonder the female Marines around me were stressed out of their minds trying to be non-female, given what passed for female around here. She was getting gangbanged out in the hallway, flapping hanging titties and all, and she loved it, the dirty slut.

This must serve some purpose. Did being a Marine—our ultimate purpose, after all, to kill more proficiently than our enemy—necessitate insensitivity to human bodies? Did we need to speak bodies into nothing worth caring about?

Was the fact I didn't like it simply indication that I was still a pussy not tough enough to hack it?

Was this practice?

If so, for what?

It wasn't entirely true that I couldn't stand up for myself. Harvey called me challenging at least twice a day. What quieted me was doubt I had any right to be queasy. They were just joking. This was another one of those things I wasn't supposed to be bothered by. Right?

Next to me, her ears buried in headphones, Artigas crammed every spare space of her Arabic workbook with inked notes.

My Arabic workbook was weirdly blank in the exercise spaces. But the margins were thick with ink. Numbers, certainly, page after page of caloric accounting. But I also traced Arabic letters along the corners, carefully copied words I was slowly beginning to know.

Al-Mumin. The Guardian of Faith. *Al-Muhaimin*. The Protector. *An-Noor*. The Light.

I didn't know why. I just did.

The names filled me with something. The whiff of a memory, a time when right and wrong had been immutable walls, great divisions explained through Book of Mormon stories of war and military operations. A time when there had been great and clear order to the cosmos.

I had a new order. I shoved back from my lackluster homework, walked to the head, and threw up.

It's just teasing. They're just words.

So I told myself. So I acclimated.

After all, it's not like anyone's putting hands on me.

A few days before Veterans Day a Marine put hands on me. I was walking down the hall with my arms folded across my stomach, watching my boots. When the big hand seized me I watched the skin twist around my forearm. Startled, I looked up to see a Marine from another Arabic platoon. Peters stood a foot taller than me so I got the feeling of looking up at the ceiling as I smiled and said, "Um, excuse me, please—"

Peters leaned on me so heavily I staggered. Realizing he was drunk I wavered. Though every fiber of my being fired *Rip away and leg it*, I hesitated. My Mormon ass worried, *Oh dear. He's really drunk. Should I get him to a doctor or something?*

The Marine swung me into his room. Astonished, I pled my suddenly pounding heart to calm down. Be polite. Peters asked if I wanted a beer and pressed a can into my hands without waiting for an answer. The condensation on the aluminum worried me, as if the moisture had calories that could seep through my skin. I set the beer down on his desk. My refusal wasn't a Mormon thing. I didn't drink beer because I was bulimic and fundamentally terrified of carbs.

My eating disorder found her usual way to make herself relevant. *This is because you are fat*, she hissed, gripping my thighs. *Do you see squared-away McCone swung into places she doesn't want to be? No, you do not. YOU, however, look like a shitbag, because you are fat.*

Peters slurred, words I missed. I couldn't hear him over where he stood, blocking the door. Blood rose to my head, pounding. I wanted to headbutt him and charge the door, ramming speed. I felt my thighs turn on, almost quiver with the urge to run. I felt so charged I felt fairly sure I could throw myself against a brick wall and crash through it.

Still I strained at my mouth to be polite. I ignored what I felt. I didn't doubt the man in the room would've defended my sudden unwanted imprisonment as no such thing. Merely a friendly beer.

But I didn't want it.

I ventured, "Actually, I'd better go, thank you. I was about to rack out."

He scoffed. "It's only 2100. C'mon. I could use company."

"I have to wake up early."

"Your platoon has no PT in the morning," he slurred. "C'mon, have a beer. Formation's not until zero seven."

"I know. But I have PT."

"What, with the run team?"

"Yes."

"Isn't Tucson on leave?"

"She is."

"So who's running it?"

"I am."

The big man wasn't buying it. "Well, so, if you're in charge of it, you don't have to have run team in the morning. It's not like anyone'll show up." He reached over and opened the beer I'd set down. "Here, let me get that for you."

"Thank you," I said, then wondered why. "Look, I wake up early to go running in the mornings because I want to. I'm going to leave now."

He took a step forward, blocking me. He still smiled. "It's only 2100," he repeated. "C'mon. You're not the sort of girl who goes to bed this early."

What fresh hell. "I am, actually. I'd like to leave now, please."

"No, c'mon. Stay." And Peters pressed me, still smiling, still friendly, to sit on his bed. "Wait. Just one second. Just hang on."

Peters ordered me to stay, then sat by me, away from the doorway. I had a clear shot.

I didn't move.

I trusted men more than I trusted women, including myself. I needed his permission to leave, felt it like an iron clamp to his bed. I wrapped my arms around myself, trying to make myself smaller.

If I could reach across the years to tap that girl on the shoulder, I would love to stand in her place. I wouldn't even speak. I'd just growl. It would be low and deep in my throat, and I would stare down that young man. How much younger he would seem to me now. But to growl requires power within my throat, a relationship to my own guts. Back then my throat was slick with acid.

What got me out was how awkward I felt, suffocatingly awkward. I was aware of my feet dangling off the side of his bed, the emptiness beneath my soles. I hated it. How much better I'd feel if my feet were on the ground.

My soles magnetized to the floor. "Thank you, but I think I'd like to leave now," I said cheerfully, charging the door. "Good evening."

His hand circled my wrist. "No. Wait."

But my body was hauling ass and I guessed I was going with her. I swung my arm free. I continued swinging my arms wildly as I shot down the hallway. Lance corporals flung oatmeal patties at a pyramid of empty beer cans. I booked it past Artigas, who was in the supply closet hauling herself up on the pull-up bar. Stepped over Harvey and Griffin, seated at the end of the hall heatedly discussing Middle Eastern politics over a bottle of dwindling whiskey.

I'd known these Marines were in the hall, but I hadn't considered calling out. I'd heard what we said about females in male's rooms. It would be my fault for being there.

I shoved open the red door to the fire escape. The heavy door slammed behind me. The Presidio stood still, Rifle Range Road empty and dark, the schoolhouses silent. Down the hill a crescent of electric light outlined Monterey's curve around the bay, fading into the Santa Cruz Mountains. I glanced down and considered. Green shirt, cammie trousers, and combat boots. Boots and utes were authorized PT gear. I clambered down the fire escape, combat boots clanging on the metal stairs. I tore into the dark through the trees, running to my sanctuary, the empty track on top of the hill. When I got there I ran.

Wasn't I supposed to be wired like this? When challenged I threw my body at something. Wasn't that the Marine way? Weren't we all getting ready to *go*?

On Veterans Day the Presidio held a ceremony called last call. All four services shouldered together in dress uniforms on Soldier's Field, an elegant knoll above the ocean. The commanding officer called names. Last name, twice. Then into the silence, first names. Names of servicemen who had been through the Presidio, stood where we stood, and died half a world away. We didn't know them. We didn't have to. They were on our team. We heard the flags shifting in the coastal breeze as the voices of ghosts, saying, *Be better. Stand up straighter. Try harder.* In my case, *Be thinner.* We accepted those who couldn't answer in final roll call would agree wholeheartedly with the purposefulness of the long wars.

That silence swallowed a lot of protest. This other roll call was why I never said anything when we spoke shit about women. There was a real war going on. It made caring about our routine insult seem very small.

FALL OUT. We split into platoons. Corporal Kingsley lit a cigarette, cupping the lighter and quick flicker of fire. He glanced at Corporal Jackson. Veterans Day loosened stories that begged to be told, crimson stories that lived in the backs of throats. Choking regret, that boot-ass first lieutenant who should have listened to his goddamn NCOs. "We didn't know" and "He was a good kid." A cat yanking brain matter from a corpse. Swerving from plastic littering California highways, conditioned to assume IEDs.

Yeah. Who really cared about a word like bitch? I assumed only a Mormon, and I wasn't one of those anymore.

I wasn't sure what I believed. But there was a hearty philosophy available to me, great spinning cogs in my head that rendered my theology of nothing-you-feel-matters rational:

Remember why you are here. Your nation is at war. Don't forget your existence in some small-cog way supports this. Never forget you are here for your team—not for a sliver of a second. No matter how useless an order, you are being trained to support the lance corporal on the front lines with his rifle. You will leap to follow said useless order in his name, to practice embedding instant obedience to all orders into your bones. No matter how maddening the boys around you, this isn't about you, and hey, you're learning to withstand personal discomfort, to try to fit in when you don't, when you stare at a rape joke and try out how a smile feels on your face, like maybe that's the secret, to just let it go through you.

You can always do better. Anything less than perfection is to forget the dead and the suffering, and anything less than striving for perfection at all times in all things in all places insults the heritage of every Marine since Tun Tavern, and so fuck you. Try harder. Haze yourself. Get it right.

Semper Fidelis. Always faithful.

If it weren't so sad, it would be kind of hilarious how much I insisted I wasn't Mormon. It was a stamp in my brain, the driving need for redemption, Puritan work ethic speckled over a deep sense of not-enoughness.

Veterans Day called us to fall in for our dose of motivation, like we filed through gloved nurses for flu shots. Good for a year.

I wasn't saying shit. I didn't have it as bad as him.

CHAPTER 8

THE DESPERATE LOVE INSTITUTE

I can tell you when the body feels out of place it will cling to anything that looks like life. Cities. Homes. People. Lovers.

—*Porochista Khakpour,* Sick

Lance Corporal James Trom was an excellent Marine and would go far in the Corps. Incidentally, he had scathing things to say about all female Marines who weren't me.

I was drawn to Trom because he was, in his own way, a deeply religious man. Irish Catholic, sure, I could work with that. More alcohol in his faith, more sarcastic humor when contemplating the grand design, but his imbued guilt levels were right up there with my Mormon sensibilities. He was as driven to self-flagellation as me. As desperate, perhaps, to be remade.

For about a month I nearly levitated with pleasure. Here he was: a man who was adoring and attentive to me, but forceful and driven, even brutal in the standards to which he held himself and others. James Trom attacked Afghan Pashto like it insulted him personally.

I didn't yet understand that how a man saw his own life—whether it was peaceful or a struggle, a game or a threat—was how he'd treat you one day.

I ate with Trom whenever possible because he would nod approvingly and call my salad motivated.

The chow hall played Fox News. Fox reported on what we cared about: disrespect against veterans, kids these days aren't raised polite anymore, and what is that socialist president thinking, investing in frivolities like solar power and healthcare while terrorists rampantly attack Our Troops in Iraq?

My morning run pulsed against my shins like a bruise. I sat with Trom and men from his platoon, two boiled eggs and half a grapefruit on my plate.

A patchy-faced sailor sashayed past to deposit her tray. Strands of hair fell out of her messy bun. Trousers unfolded over her boots. Her belt squeezed tight around her promising middle.

A cue, any girl walking by.

"Gotta love 'em a little thick."

"She's a little heavy, man. Kinda looks like a shitbag."

"That just makes it easier. You know how a Marine seduces a Navy girl, right? Just point and say . . ."

I focused on the news. Stern faces bemoaned the proposal to repeal Don't Ask Don't Tell. A lacquered blond asserted it would demoralize The Troops, The Gays coming out and making their coworkers uncomfortable.

I wondered what she knew about being a troop. From where I was sitting, I figured if sister enlisted looking like that, Marines would place bets on whether she bleached her asshole too and who'd be the first to find out, and I would get to hear about it.

"I think it's okay." A Marine nodded toward the debate. "Pulling back DADT. It's not like we don't have fags anyway."

Trom scoffed. "They know what they're enlisting into. I don't think they should be allowed in infantry. Not in all-male units. We have rules for a reason."

"It's alright by me, so long as they don't hit on me," said the first Marine who'd appraised the Navy girl. Oorah.

He raised his eyebrows at me, the sole woman in the huddle. "Williams? You down with The Gays joining? 'Course, it's not as bad for a female when another female hits on them. Then it's just hot."

Helpfully, the boys had lesbians all figured out. There was another Definitely Not Gay female in Artigas's platoon, but since she was small and had a soft face she wasn't spared, even when she cropped her hair. She didn't shut up the peanut gallery the way thundering Artigas could. The barracks philosophers asked her (1) if she was lesbian because she hated men; (2) wouldn't she really prefer a nice guy; and, most commonly, smirking, (3) can I watch? Somehow feminine female queers were for men's entertainment. No one really took lesbians seriously. If you weren't butch you were a porn star.

Though DADT prohibited queer expression, I hadn't made any particular secret of my attraction to women at first. I bargained it to be one of the guys. Yeah, dating women. "Irrational, man," I'd nod, agreeing, like I was something other than *those* women.

Then McCone combed my Facebook and ripped into me to take down a high school photo of me kissing another girl if I didn't want to be dishonorably discharged, equivalent to a felony in many states. Panicked, I got awfully rude at a civilian girl I'd been flirting with, snapped at her I was a United States Marine and couldn't be sexting a girl. It didn't feel great. I checked my queer after that.

I surgically removed an egg yolk with a spoon. I wanted to say I appreciated days I made it through breakfast without being reminded women's bodies were free game for speculation. I wanted to say his fear of being hit on was dazzlingly ironic. I wanted to say The Gays were most definitely already here, and Uncomfortable Troops themselves. At the very least I wanted to throw my grapefruit at his head.

I was raised to be polite. I stood and said, "I'm going to get more coffee. Does anyone want anything while I'm standing?"

Often Trom and I ate from to-go boxes after spending our lunch break at the gym. One midday work out, he spotted me at the bench press and told me about his Pashto teacher.

"He was a doctor before the Taliban threw him out. He told us about this Afghan woman who kept coming in beat to hell," Trom said earnestly. "Finally he asked her why she kept coming in beat up, and it was because her husband was beating her."

"God."

"It gets worse. He was beating her because she wasn't getting pregnant."

"How idiotic. It could be his fault." I had no idea if that was true, but it sounded plausible.

"It was," Trom said grimly. "He was fucking her like a boy. So, no shit."

"Wait, what?"

"Man love Thursdays. You haven't heard of the Afghan dancing boys?"

I shook under the weight of the bar. "No."

"The Afghans take little boys and dress them up like women and fuck them, because it's haram to sleep with women. I guess they think pedophilia is better. And then they grow up thinking that's okay, and fuck over the next generation. You should look at Pashto, Williams. Fucked up, backward language for a fucked up, backward people." He helped me set the bar back. "This might sound fucked up, but it's motivating as hell. I'm going to learn this language because I'm contractually obligated to, but knowing all the fucked-up repression that happens over there makes me want to end some woman-beating fuckers."

How often I heard this refrain. How eager Marines were to defend women.

I sat up. Blood rush. "I suck at Arabic."

"Christ, Williams, again?"

"Sorry."

"You're the smartest woman I've been with. Learning Arabic shouldn't be hard for you."

"And yet."

"Why do you think you're not getting it? You're probably doing fine."

"Because I'm stupid, I would hazard a guess."

"You are not. Just commit to why you're learning it. Marines die because of shitty linguists."

"Then it's lack of self-discipline." I considered my reflection in the mirrored wall. A little gaunt in my face at least, but no hiding the curve at my waist, or my obvious existence. "Same reason I'm overweight."

"Don't start. Can't we have one goddamn day without you talking about how fat you are?"

"I am?" I cried, alarmed.

"No," he snapped. "You *know* what I meant."

I didn't.

"Look, you're stressed over nothing. Stick with it, you'll be fine. Learning a language isn't *that* hard. Marines are doing a lot harder shit than learning Arabic, that's all I'm saying."

We were going to war, damnit. Now was not the time to fuck around. Linguists were on front lines, and our mistakes could contribute to Marines coming home in flag-draped boxes. From slamming awake on a coarse government-issued green blanket to passing out, ice packs boot-banded to my shins, I didn't forget I was a Marine.

We weren't supposed to.

Fifth platoon continued to scream *ALLAHU AKBAR* until we pissed off a passing infantryman. Corporal Jackson was also infantry, but his scholar's face burned red as he announced, "We're not going to do the *Allahu akbar* thing anymore. An infantry brother just pointed out—a really good point—*Allahu akbar*, that's the last thing a lot of Marines ever hear. So. We don't need to go around shouting it. Remember that in class today."

Motivation, Marine Corps style. Yes, actually, what we were doing might matter.

Trom got it. We faced homework like a skirmish. We spoke as if life or limb was on immediate line. Every mistake warranted scolding. *You should know this by now. What's wrong with you? Compare irregular verbs to what He is doing. Marines die because of shitty linguists like you.*

When we slept together I executed strange maneuvers to stay under sheet cover. I bolted to get dressed immediately after, I guess before Trom noticed I did, in fact, have a body. At first Trom found my eagerness fantastic, but he quickly understood I felt little pleasure. I sought something through sex, a confirmation of desirability I never felt.

We screamed often. We were devoted students quick to pick up nuanced ways of getting under each other's skin. We admired each other. We wanted to see the other do well. We simply didn't know how to convey it without shouting. It was how we knew to talk to family.

We said I love you a lot, and broke up most weekdays.

Our fights came early and they came often. At first they centered on my eating disorder. He exhorted me to clean up my act so our future children would be healthy.

I argued the curly fries I'd just puked weren't going to help either said imaginary pregnancy or my chances of getting pregnant in the first place, a comment he didn't find nearly as witty as I did and was I seriously questioning my commitment to him already because I didn't *need* to be attractive to anyone else; he found me pretty so why was I *so* obsessed with my eating disorder. I'd twitch in frustration: because *curly fries.*

During one such spectacularly idiotic argument I walked out of the barracks, head swirling, craving clear night air. I liked walking around the base at night. I liked it then. The hills were still and quiet.

My phone buzzed. A photo of his bare chest: he'd carved my initials over his heart. If I walked away, if I didn't stay with him tonight, he'd kill himself for sure.

I cannot begin to explain how utterly the Book of Mormon had not prepared me for this situation.

Harvey rolled his eyes and said my boyfriend was certainly a motivator. He couldn't forgive Trom for yelling at me. Harvey dismissed my defense that, well, I yelled at him too.

Even Artgias looked up from her books. "He's squared away," she conceded. Artigas approved of Marines who worked out as hard as she did. "But you get he jerks you around, right?"

"What! He's so kind to me." He tolerated me.

"You gotta get out more, Will."

McCone watched too. She ordered my lackluster Arabic and me to evening study hall. I ran in late, sputtering apologies. Parting ways with Trom was always a bit of a to-do regardless of how short a time it would be until I saw him again.

McCone was unimpressed. She said I wasn't mature enough to date anyone, which prompted a passionate flurry of victimized journaling—during study hall—about how I was mature enough to join the United States Marine Corps where men my age honorably laid down their lives for our nation every day, so, yeah, she was not wrong.

Base emptied at Christmas. We called it Exodus.

I met Trom in Colorado, his home state. We went up to the spacious white mountains. We crossed a frozen lake, admiring crystalline fractures under our feet. Cold wind blew powder off the peaks. He asked me again, was I sure I only wanted a plain silver band for my ring? Not even a small diamond?

I hiked in ballet slippers, and the snow brushed my bare ankles. I brought my combat boots, the ones I wore every day, but in a heavy voice Trom reminded me real Marines are wearing those in combat right now. The ballet slippers were all else I had in the car. My feet froze but presently went numb, which was convenient because I could focus on losing my mind.

In uncertain words I tried to explain that even if religion was the opiate of the masses, etc., still, it meant something to my family. It made me sad, is all, that marrying outside the Church would be a big, ugly deal. No, it's not you, Trom. It's that you're not Mormon.

Trom offered, "Well, I'll convert to Mormonism. I don't mind marrying you in their temple. So long as I can sneak a beer every once in a while."

I wailed. A white barb of hilarity flew out of me. I couldn't stop laughing. My guts spilled everywhere. In the white mountains I laughed and found myself saying everything I'd hoped, if I never spoke about it, would stop being real.

"If you convert to Mormonism, you can't just not sneak a beer, you can never go anywhere they serve beer, or you're going to be tempted and become a raging alcoholic.

"Not only can you never have a beer, James, you'll have to hurry to turn off the TV when there's a beer commercial, and you have to grieve when your young daughter asks you not to, because she doesn't know what beer is but she likes the Clydesdales. You will need to mourn and scold her for liking the Clydesdales and warn her this is the 'Devil making sin look fun' and therefore she is 'being tempted by a trick of Satan.' Her older brother will try to cheer her up by telling her maybe the Clydesdales are slaves of the evil beer people and therefore not, themselves, evil Satan-following, beer-drinking Clydesdales."

"Oh, Christ, babe . . ."

"I never lost that sense, like I was missing some moral compass. Like when I didn't cover my eyes in the Getty and my brothers did. Because apparently marble statues of Athena and Aphrodite are pornographic."

"There's no way your family was that intense."

"Um, my brother ran across the hall with his hands over his eyes, and Dad told him he was proud of him for 'feeling the stirrings of the Holy Ghost,' which told him to feel uncomfortable in the presence of such immodest art. The curators had to ask them to stop running in the museum. Safely in the Rembrandts, Dad explained *that* was the sort of immorality that was responsible for the decline of the entire Greek civilization. A woman's body: the downfall of Greece. Meanwhile I was standing there wondering what was wrong with me because what I saw when I saw goddesses didn't make me want to cover my eyes and bolt, at all.

"The thing was, those statues, they looked like *me*. That's what *my* body looked like. I saw someone with a body like mine standing up straight, unafraid, maybe even fucking hallowed, and we acted as if they were evil, and it made the holy priesthood holders run so they didn't get 'feelings they shouldn't feel outside of marriage,' and damn the entire civilization. So that made me feel kind of crazy."

"They were just trying to protect you."

"We also ripped human anatomy out of the encyclopedia. Terrifically threatening, the nervous system."

"That's . . . weird."

"The medical illustrations were the only immodest things we had in our house. The only things that suggested human beings could exist without clothing. My little brother confessed he felt titillated. We felt about sex the way I felt about food when I was anorexic. Terrified, mostly, that it could rocket out of control at any moment. Surely we can't believe the body itself should regulate such inherently bodily things."

"You're losing me, babe. What does this have to do with me becoming a Mormon?"

"If you convert to Mormonism and we get married in the temple, you'll get to know my true name, the name God calls me, but obviously I don't get to know yours, because, I mean, come on, why would we be equals, *you* have the priesthood. And you, instead of hearing 'what man is, God once was, and what God is, man can become' as the most saving graceful poetry imaginable, you will teach this in the literal masculine sense of man, claiming it is talking about the perfection of the priesthood. So *you* can aspire to Godhood, and *I* can aspire to being kind and patient with the woman you marry after I die, because you'll be married to both of us after Judgment Day, when *you're* a god and *I'm* a fucking sister wife, HURRAY!"

"I don't want two wives. Wait, is that still a thing? I just want you."

"But you'll remarry after I die anyway because you want your infant son to have a mother, and in Mormonland, temple marriages are for time and all eternity, so the whole damn church raises your kids believing don't worry about mourning their dead mom or anything, because we're all sealed and we all get to live together in the next life in our happy little *polygamous* family, so, whatever. Sorrow would have docked us points in God's 'test of our righteousness.' That's how my mother's death was explained to me. A trial. A test of my obedience to God."

Trom had moved from amused to confused to horrified. "Well fuck, if you don't want to marry me . . ."

"But you're missing the best part! This little rebel, our daughter, will grow up and somehow not become a raging alcoholic even though she drinks sometimes, my God, the statistical anomaly, *but she will seek extremism in everything she does*. This will *astound* you, that you've raised an extremist. Abstinence is extremism and extremism is easier than moderation. Though, as a bulimic I might tell you, moderation seems like a real good thing to fucking learn.

"You convert to Mormonism, and she will glue herself to the most intense human she can find *in the fucking Marines*, because this is the takeaway: You can never lose God by pursuing perfection. God is perfection. There is no too far. There is no good enough, you are never good enough. And if you sit down and rest, you're not moving toward God, so you're falling away. It's a good thing to lose yourself, to be like Him.

"So, no, you can't convert to Mormonism and still sneak a beer, because God requires devotion. Devotion requires obsession. We say, 'The natural man is an enemy to God.' You have to safeguard against your natural being at all times and in all things and in all places. First you'll slip a beer in, then you'll stop coming to church as much, then you'll commit adultery. There is no acceptable amount of sin. The way to God—the ONLY way to God—is straight and narrow and prescribed by men who speak for Him. You don't understand. You don't understand. No matter how much you try, it's not enough. *You,* inherently, your *natural state,* is *not enough.* All you can do, is just . . . your best."

"You think I'm intense?" Trom asked frankly.

"My feet are *blue.*"

"That was your choice."

"OH MY *GOD,*" I screamed, my voice echoing. In a steadying movement he grabbed me and pressed my face against his chest.

"Jesus. You're going to start an avalanche." He released me and I stared, feeling his palm on the back of my skull, the press of his jacket against my nose. I hated, hated, *hated* more than I could articulate, more than made any sense, a hand over my mouth. I felt rocketed back, a time before memory.

He sounded tired. "I guess it's true. Female Marines *are* fucking insane. Talk about your standard-issue daddy issues."

I could not swear at him deeply enough. I conjured the most profane sacrilege I could muster. "It's God. I fucking hate God."

I was. Um. Somewhat unready to marry him.

Headlights punctured the snowy road as we drove down the mountains. I told him yes, of course, I was excited to marry him. I told myself I'd lose twenty-seven pounds so I'd be beneath a hundred with enough room to eat a slice of wedding cake.

He suggested the local diocese. I flatly refused. Monterey's city hall, and you're wearing your blues. That night I composed a running plan that concluded in running an eighteen-minute three-mile, the perfect fitness score for men. I would be my husband's equal by the only standards I cared about, the body, tamed complicity of flesh and competency of sinew. In the morning I ran in the Denver slush, daydreaming of wedding cake, forbidden sugar and carbs. My stomach growled. I imagined myself a bride. I'd wear my blues too. Maybe a soft French braid bun to juxtapose newly sharpened cheekbones.

Somehow Trom and I survived leave. But an icy edge crept between us, a cold shoulder. I'd said too much. I'd admitted it: I was lost and confused and hungry, and no, I wasn't sure marrying him would make me happy. I'd shown the rage I denied. I was obeisant not from girl-next-door sweetness, but from a harsh reading of a faith that had crumbled something in me. I felt terribly disobedient and deeply sorry. But the words insisted on being said, and I couldn't undo them.

CHAPTER 9

LION

The problem is . . . you're too busy holding on to your unworthiness.

—*Ram Dass*

In January I flopped on my back in my barracks room, combat boots up the cinderblock wall, and softly swore. Eventually, I figured, I'd rally, go downstairs, see about dinner. I had a whole five hundred calories left. But the idea of walking down two flights of stairs made my shins scream in protest.

Aching shins were such a common malady among female Marines I didn't dare admit it. Another female broke and went on some bullshit chit.

I kneaded my shin.

What if "cut it out" wasn't reprimand but instruction?

A pair of nail clippers easily snipped through the skin. I pressed fingers into the incision as far as I could. Ha! I felt something tear, something soft and webby.

I held the conviction bodies should be hard. I wanted all soft stuff eaten away, leaving only cavernous hollows, but caverns of rock. So when the filmy webbing tore, it felt good. If it could so easily tear, it should.

As to the stomach-turning sensations of digging into my own flesh I gave no shit. My old stress fractures were in the Marines now and needed to get their shit together. As I saw it, the entirety of naval tradition rested on their ability to bear my weight.

I'd read about Russian runners who jumped from ladders barefoot, intentionally desensitizing their shins. If the Russkies could do it, a Marine could. I slammed through runs all week, pounding hard onto my right leg. Wanna ache? Yeah? Little high-school-cross-country-bullshit-stress-fractures? You weren't even fast.

McCone noticed when I trotted in from an afternoon run, clotted Band-Aids dropping off my shin. "What the hell now, Williams."

"It's nothing. I fell . . . ?"

Each night I camped out on my rack and excavated the hole in my shin. The small wound was a porthole into my body. Its aliveness fascinated me, the ways tissue tore, infinite textures and varying densities of fluids over my fingertips. Some thin sheets of webbing tore with a grainy sensation. Others required sharp jabs or dull hacking. I studied focused and fascinated, a naturalist in a very small ecosystem, my Arabic ignored.

One night I felt lightheaded release. A *rip*, a minute relief in pressure. I extracted something, an irregularly shaped shard. I held it to the light. A yellowish rock, some kind of hardened tissue. The way my stomach swooped when I saw it, at last noticing it was a dead thing—what had been a living thing—glinting with the possibility it was time to stop digging. Blood flowed warm down my calf. Ha. The fattened calf: one of the old sacrifices. I was bleeding quite a lot. The darker kind, velvety where it pooled. I took a skivvy shirt and tied it around my shin before the blood seeped into my issued blanket.

Barracks rumor had it a female in third platoon failed a room inspection because of *blood* (the private telling me the story gagged) on her sheets. My face hadn't registered the appropriate shock, so the boy insisted, "You know. Like, *period blood*."

I startled. "How did they know it was period blood?"

"It was on her bed."

Afraid forever that someone, somewhere, might think poorly of me, I leapt down from my bunk and stomped around the barracks room, skivvy shirt knotted around shin. I embraced the reverberations charging up my leg. Yes. I'd done something. Pinpoint black pressure pressed behind my eyeballs. In a glimmer of rare lucidity I wondered why I couldn't just take up smoking like a normal stressed out underage Marine.

I told Harvey because I always told Harvey. I said it grinning, punch drunk, daring him to laugh. I didn't expect him to respond as he did.

"Williams," he said slowly, placing his beer down on my half-assed Arabic. "What in the hell do you mean, you *pulled something* out of your leg?"

Artigas burst into laughter.

"It's not a big deal. Like this . . . brittle clump, thing, but I mean, it's out now, so, whatever."

"The fuck was it?"

"Huh. I don't really know. Old scar tissue? I've had stress fractures before, maybe like a shard of—what's the sheath that covers bone? Probably just scabbing. Hey, don't look at me that way. My shin feels way better. You know, I bet I blasted the area with a mega-shot of dopamine or—what's the pain one? The reason you feel high when you cut—when you hurt yourself. It would've been cool to see it under a microscope. It had cool little maroon clots in it."

"Hold up," Harvey said. "You just . . . threw it away?"

"Well, yeah."

"Why?"

"What was I going to do with something I pulled out of my leg?"

"You take it to medical," Harvey finally roared. "You take it to medical and you say, '*Holy shit, holy shit, this just came out of my goddamn leg.*'"

Artigas couldn't stop laughing.

"That honestly did not occur to me."

"Trousers off, Williams."

I unclipped my boot band and rolled up my trouser leg, fingered off the drenched bandage, embarrassed how anticlimactic it was. I tried to see the knothole as he would. Small, if a bit. Well. Purple.

"Sweet fucking God, that's deep." Harvey sounded amazed. "Surely that's not your fucking *bone*?"

"The white stuff? Nah, I don't think so. It's soft."

"Williams." Harvey gently put his hands along my calf. He looked up, his long face not unkind. "Did you do this to yourself?"

"It hurt. There was something in there. I had to get it out."

Were we looking at the same wound? It was *tiny.* At least, it wasn't actively bleeding. I'd had wounds like this. White soft gunk would colonize it, sometimes yellow or green. I'd debride it—well, I'd keep poking at it—clearing out the crap and stuffing it with Neosporin. The skin that grew over it would be unbelievably soft for a while, an obvious dent underneath. This was an old, old way of self-soothing. Mortification of the flesh was not my original idea. It would heal.

"Really, it's nothing. I drained my knee in MCT and it made me feel better. It's like that."

"You've done this *before*?"

I elected the path of self-righteousness. "You know what, it's my body." I could torture her as I pleased.

"We're letting Sergeant Walker know."

"No!" I yipped. "It's nothing." Even I recognized compulsion toward uninformed self-surgery wasn't the sort of thing that won people major sanity points.

Harvey was already texting. "Have you eaten anything today, Williams?"

"Ah."

"You threw up?"

What I could.

"And you *ran* on that?"

"Couple miles."

"Williams."

"Like six."

"Wills."

"Seven point eight."

Artigas shoved away from her Arabic. "Really? *Really*?" She still shuddered with laughter. "Williams, you have got to cool down. Calm the hell down and be yourself. You don't need to break yourself to prove you're hard. What are you even doing? I thought once you started eating you were bucking up a bit. What the hell is this? Just be yourself, Wills, you're not that bad."

"You won't go on chit either," I dodged. She treated plantar fasciitis by rolling cold tennis balls under her feet as she studied. We had a tube of them in our fridge.

"Well yeah, but I know how to manage it. I've had this since college. I'm not the one running around gnawing my bones out of my legs."

I sat on her and buried my face into her shoulder, her familiar scent of freshly laundered cammies and Old Spice. "I love you."

"You're an idiot, Williams." She wrapped freckled arms around me and squeezed. "A goddamn idiot."

Harvey sighed. "Come on, Williams, I'll buy you a burrito."

"I don't eat burritos."

"That wasn't actually a suggestion. That was an order. We're going to Chipotle."

A burrito was far too terrifying, so I leapt to outrage. "Are you ordering me to dinner with you?"

"No. I couldn't do that. It would be unethical. However, I am ordering my fire team to an emergency mandatory team building exercise.

Lunsford is on special lib and Anders is on duty. Looks like that leaves you and me. Come on. I will buy you a goddamn burrito."

"Get out of here." Artigas shoved me off and turned back to Arabic.

I couldn't sit still in the restaurant, unnerved by people between me and doors, sure everyone was watching me, judging me for eating, despite my obvious weight issue. Harvey compromised. We took our food down to the ocean and sat in the sand.

Though I'd never admit it, I was ecstatic. Harvey had threatened to babysit me all night to keep me from throwing up, which meant I got to eat a normal-ass human meal like a normal-ass human. It felt like a holiday or something. I placed a lime tortilla chip in my mouth and closed my eyes. The air smelled like salt. I was pretty sure eating was some kind of sacrament. One I hoped one day to be decent enough—as evidenced by, skinny enough—to deserve. I texted Trom I was *so* sorry not to see him tonight, but Harvey was my *fire team leader*, and my *platoon sergeant* wanted to make sure I ate, then set aside that particular death spiral for the night. He would be livid I was with Harvey, whom he hated for the reason obvious to everyone but me that while I might be in some tumultuous heart-baring romantic enterprise with Trom, Harvey, I simply loved.

Harvey spoke up. "I'm sorry I raised my voice. I am confused as why *b'isma Allah* you think you need to torture yourself."

The waves crashed against the sand again and again.

"I feel stuck," I admitted quietly. "My brain isn't working right."

"It might help if you ate enough."

I snarled. "Why does it keep coming back to this with you? I eat *so* much. I *binge*, Harvey." I brandished a tortilla chip. "All the fucking time. 'Not eating enough' is *not* the problem here."

"You don't have to be super skinny to do serious damage to your body, Wills. You throw up all the fucking time. I threw up once last weekend. Griffin and I got loaded and played *Call of Duty* until zero six, and then when the sun came up we were feeling all moto and said fuck it and went running." He laughed. "God, I threw up more pizza than I even knew I ate. I felt like a bag of smashed ass all day. And like hell half the next day. You're literally that violent on yourself all the time. I don't understand how you function, much less run as much as you do. You need to eat normally or you're going to fucking die."

My heart sank. "You don't think I'm super skinny?"

The order came swiftly: stop running. Sergeant Walker and McCone forbade me to run until the puncture in my leg closed. I did lunges from one side of my barracks room to the other until I heard Artigas' key at the door.

When Sergeant Walker decided the strange hole was healed enough for PT, I turned and sprinted after my platoon, jubilant. I felt strong, a fact I attributed to whatever more or less beneficial god accepted blood sacrifice.

Yes. Yes. This one thing, I can do. I may not be fast, I may not be strong, but I have this going for me: I don't give a shit about my body. I will run through anything.

McCone knew damn well I'd hurt myself. She prohibited running unless I ran with the platoon or run team. I didn't rate to contribute to the injuries of Marines the world over, even if the Marine in question was only me.

Conveniently enough, however, Tucson was in the home stretch of Arabic and cramming for the formidable final language exam. Right as McCone told me to sit my ass down, Tucson declared me her fire team leader. When still-awake Tucson would text me at zero dark thirty to cancel practice unless I wanted to lead it, I'd text the two or three other women on our ever-amorphous team practice was optional.

Then I'd roll off my rack and run to the track.

If no one showed after I trotted around the track until zero six or so, I'd turn and run to the ocean, head north, and haul ass as far as I could.

I felt fairly honest claiming *leading* practices fell within the dubious capacity of my sort-of billet. Admittedly, my fire team was highly theoretical. If it was only me, well, *vamanos.*

The primary desire to skirt McCone's order was, of course, battling fat. Rabid to run, desperate to scorch calories and fry fat and melt lipids. I'd rip out my ovaries if it made me weigh less.

But I had other reasons, harder to put into words. I loved it. Running quieted the whole world into a pulsing forward rhythm. With the music in my headphones and the dawn lightening the clouds above the Pacific and the seagulls crying and my blood pumping, I felt brave and tough and focused. Like Him. I felt powerful, independent, goddamn virtuous. I felt less like a girl, or at least what I understood being girly to be.

I was never going to mandate practice. In obvious indication of my ineptitude as a leader of Marines, I had no desire to command or order anyone to do anything. But if anyone *wanted* to run . . . Not every female ran alone, I knew. Though other girls were eager to go off base, see the town, explore the trails through the woods, for reasons I didn't understand some wouldn't go alone. Some girls wouldn't leave base and run until even the lights of Monterey faded behind and the iconic towers of Moss Landing loomed ahead, returning to the barracks long after dark, sand coating bare legs.

But some girls said it was cool I did.

I wasn't so sure about girls as a general concept, but girls I knew as people, I generally quite liked. I was painfully shy and spent my free time alone—running or feasting in private—so had no friends. In some lonely part of me, where I privately suspected some of the shit we said about girls maybe didn't apply to *all* of them, the girls around me had planted a tiny, tiny seed: if anyone did show up to the dark track, I wanted her to find me there.

So. As long as I sent out a group text offering an optional run team practice before I ran. Any day. Any time. However many times in a day. It was *basically* run team, right?

McCone figured it out by early February. She kicked my door open so hard I thought it would sail off its hinges. Insubordination. Flagrant disobedience to a direct order. It did not help—it really, truly did not—that I had taken a razor to my forearm that day. I thought she might actually NJP me for this one. Hadn't we been over this? She ordered me into her room and slammed the door, crossed her arms and paced.

She exploded: "Marines are out there having their legs blown off, and you're *cutting yourself*?"

Good point.

McCone's fury flew like Chinese throwing stars. "You're going insane with this running thing. You're so self-absorbed in your own little problems, you don't see that other Marines rely on you to act like a fucking adult. We *need* you, Williams. You are smart enough to learn a language. Do you even realize where you are? Everyone smart enough to be a linguist could've done something else with their lives. We chose to be here. The work we do matters. It's my job to open your eyes, *A Clockwork Orange* style if I have to.

"Stop smiling at everyone. You're giving people the wrong message, and you know it.

"I see how hard you're trying, but you are missing the point. You can't fucking cut yourself or starve yourself or fucking throw up every fucking thing you eat. That's not honor, Williams. It's not fucking sacrifice. It's making your time in the Marine Corps about you, and it isn't. None of this is about you.

"It's like this thing with the run team."

My stomach clenched.

"If you'd just asked," McCone said. "If you'd come to me and said, 'Look, this is what I'm doing, and why.' I get it, Williams. You're actually trying to be a leader, in your own childish way. But you have to do things on your own terms. That's not how the Marine Corps works. Good initiative, shitty, shitty judgment."

Had she been a man, I would've bit my tongue and aye, Lance Corporal'd. But the Latter-day Saints had instilled me with a deflated sense of respect for women. I admired McCone, but didn't fear contradicting supernatural order by disagreeing with her.

I met her eye. "I ran when I shouldn't have. But I ran because I thought it was right. Lance Corporal, I don't know what the hell is wrong with me. I wish I knew. I'd do anything to fix it. But I don't know what's wrong."

She curtly ordered me out of her room.

I settled at my desk to write the essay McCone had ordered ("What the Seven Basic Principles Mean to Me"). Harvey knocked and made himself comfortable on my desk.

Sipping his hot toddy, he spoke mildly. "Here's what you need to know about McCone. She doesn't like to talk about this. She's not going to bring it up. But . . . with the whole 'Marines getting their legs blown off' thing, she's talking about a formation she remembers. McCone's brother is an infantry Marine. He got blown up in Iraq. Before she enlisted she was like, working at a record store in San Diego. Then she went and met him when he came back."

"Older brother?"

"I don't know. He got pretty fucked up. He's with Wounded Warriors down in Balboa. I think she feels she took his place. Or now it's her turn. So that's like, what's on her mind."

We quieted. Balboa, the Naval medical center in Southern California where Marines rehabilitated severe injuries, evoked a respectful silence. Harvey lifted his mug and sipped pensively.

Maybe that was why McCone was so grim. If my brother was wounded in action, I'd be wound pretty tight too. How had McCone clamped it? I couldn't imagine her puking in the shower. I couldn't imagine her shuddering to sleep in a fetal ball. I couldn't even imagine her laughing. She slammed PT and Arabic, the self-contained force all female Marines should be, as Corporal Jackson praised her.

How badly I wanted to be like her. Cauterized.

Later that evening I sat at my desk, forearm tender, trying to read *Crime and Punishment.*

It bothered me that I'd hurt myself in the old way. I'd cut myself from fourteen to sixteen but spontaneously stopped after my suicide attempt. When I woke up with a cottony mouth I felt a glimmer of something like gratitude. I'd stopped cutting, stopped throwing up. I even stopped trying to lose weight, for a while, until Parris Island. I kind of thought I'd done it: gone through the dark times, come out the other end, saddled up and moved on. I was better now, wasn't I? Sure I threw up again, but I was, well, maybe not in control of it, in truth.

Still. The cutting made my heart hurt. My own skin was telling me what I was refusing to admit, that I was maybe not doing great.

The razor lines on my forearm jolted like live wires as my sleeve brushed against them. I refused to bandage, preferring the pleasure I'd feel later when I took off my shirt, the way the fabric would pull each cut's seeping edges apart.

I don't know why I thought *Crime and Punishment* was going to help. Certainly it was something I obsessively sought to understand. The nature of original sin and all the ones I kept right on making afterward.

I felt myself tense, compressed out of Imperial Russia. Though my door was closed, I knew McCone stood outside.

Sometimes I thought of McCone as a mountain lion. I knew they lived in Monterey, in the forested hills I ran. I passed signs warning me of recent activity. I never saw one but once in a while saw a mottled bone pile of gristle and fur. Sometimes I felt a stiff prickle on the back of my neck. I knew to act big and bold in the woods when I felt the odd, tunnel-vision-inducing feeling of being watched. I'd hold my head up and swing my arms more vigorously. McCone was not a lion, but sometimes it felt like she, too, was trying to scare me into standing up straight.

An index card slid under the door.

I didn't stand immediately. I put Dostoyevsky down.

I admired her. I was terrified of her. Every time she was near me I felt so stressed I couldn't breathe. She was trying to keep me from hurting myself, but I ached for her to go away, disappear, cease to be. It would be easiest to hate her, but her sheer force of presence amazed me. She was a force of nature, vital and indomitable. She made me exquisitely unhappy.

No wonder we didn't get along. I felt toward McCone what I felt toward my own body.

I bent to gather the index card. What new order? Mandatory Arabic tutoring? Another essay prompt? I flipped it over.

Neatly handwritten was a list of phone numbers for every mental health resource available to active-duty military. She wrote a note at the bottom. *Let me know if you need any help.*

None of the numbers really helped, but I kept the note with her handwriting pinned in my wall locker for months.

CHAPTER 10

NOW WE ARE HERE

I no longer believe that we can keep silent. We never really do, mind you. In one way or another we articulate what has happened to us through the kind of people we become.
—*Azar Nafisi,* Things I've Been Silent About

Night in the barracks. Next to you, Trom attacks Pashto like it poses an existential threat. You sit by him in the hallway, rereading Azar Nafisi's *Reading Lolita in Tehran.*

The red doors slam. The senior Marine on duty storms through. You leap to your feet.

"What are you doing, Marines?"

"Studying, Staff Sergeant."

"Reading a book, Staff Sergeant."

Duty eyes you. He's seeking, finding something to police. "The fuck are you reading for, Marine? Is it in your target language?"

Crud. "No, Staff Sergeant."

"You fluent in your language yet, PFC?"

"No, Staff Sergeant."

"No, huh? So maybe you should be studying like this fucking motivator." He leans his palm onto your door. "This your room, Marine?"

"Yes, Staff Sergeant."

"Let me in."

You do, because nothing Uncle Sam gives you is yours. Your roommate Artigas spins handwritten flashcards, habitual frozen tennis ball underfoot. When she sees a staff sergeant she leaps to parade rest. Her heavy wooden chair slams the bunk, and the tennis ball shoots into the baseboard.

"Studying, Marine?"

"Aye, Staff Sergeant."

Duty looks for a target. Your room is disappointingly immaculate. He picks up your trousers, draped over your rack. The muscles in your face contract, a tight smile squeezing your face. You've learned this normally helps with men. A smile means *please, no harm*.

Not this time. "Think this is funny, Marine?"

"No, Staff Sergeant."

"Why the shit aren't these folded away, PFC? Marines have died in this uniform." He drops your trousers to the floor.

He turns to leave. "Square your shit away, Marine."

"I will, Staff Sergeant."

You wait. You wait, because you feel the surging heat of eruption, and you will never, ever erupt in front of a Marine who outranks you.

"You can hear that, right?" you ask Artigas. You feel as if you might be floating. "Do you hear that? You can hear that?" You are now unsure whether you are straight up hearing things. Perhaps it is official. You are crazy pants. You are hearing the virtual gunfire that accompanies living in a Marine barracks.

"What do you mean, the video games?"

Thank God. "Yes. You can clearly hear that, right?"

"Yes. Williams, what're you—"

"You can hear Myers and Kole next to us playing video games, right? And down the hall too?"

"Well yeah, they've got their doors open. What does—"

Trom gets it. "He probably thought reading doesn't have the same combat applications. They're blowing off steam. You're just reading for fun."

Combat applications. You close your eyes. A streak of righteous indignation, reading impermissible where video games indulged, but something else *bothers* you. Why did he decide to police you? No one but Harvey knows how completely you are fucking up. No one knows your shin and forearm are seeping through their bandages under long sleeves. No one knows you puke so often your fingers feel your epiglottis, the soft flap at the root of your tongue, beginning to fade like a jagged moon. A hall of boys drinking beer and playing video games and a girl reading a book; why did he pick on you? Clearly it's your weight. You've run three hours today and you haven't eaten, but you gorged on Clif bars yesterday, and this is what this is about: your enduring lack of discipline. You want to do something violent, like run or vomit or scream. You are fucking *trying*, god*damn* it. You seize your keys and storm down the hallway. Trom hurries after you, alarmed or annoyed.

"Mountains," you sputter inarticulately. "I need fucking mountains."

Off base. Out Taylor Gate, the dark curve of the 68 snaking through the woods. You intend to take the 101 south into the Carmel Highlands, to a quiet beach where you can see the ridgelines of the Santa Lucia Range. In the dark the hillsides look like home, like West Virginia.

"I don't see why you're so upset," Trom finally says. "Did he say anything that wasn't true?"

"Nope."

"And, I mean, you could have folded your trousers neatly."

"Indeed. I could have. That were on my rack. In my room."

"It's not your room. It's government property."

There's nothing to correct so you don't. Your silence bothers him. His aggressively broad shoulders expand.

"What the fuck is wrong with you?" he yells. "Are we going AWOL right now? Because I'd really like to know now, so I can get the fuck out."

You've fucked up. You meant to drive south. Instead you're going north, peeling farther into the cement and artificial light of urban Seaside. You scream at your own incompetence. You can't breathe at your own marvelous stupidity. You can't even get on a highway going the right goddamn direction. It avalanches, your failures, your grades and your goddamn thighs and your warping sense of self, into this dreamlike hell-realm where you can't run away. Sprint or crawl, your scarred skin follows you.

You cut across two lanes, dive off the highway at the Sand City exit. You now get to self-soothe in the Home Depot parking lot. Wonderful.

A homeless gentleman passes by headed toward the overpass. You clench the steering wheel. *Get it together, Williams. You really don't have it so bad.*

"Why the *fuck* are you so stressed out?"

"I don't know."

"He didn't say anything that wasn't true."

"I know. I'm a fucking shitbag."

"Oh, calm down. You know you're squared away."

"No, I'm not, apparently. I wasn't even thinking about dishonoring the entire United States Marine Corps when I took my pants off."

"They're called trousers."

"Damnit. God, James."

"Well, they are." Trom glares. "You seriously need to learn how to take criticism. He wasn't even criticizing you, necessarily, he was just pointing something out. Sweet Mary, how did you survive boot camp?"

"I didn't eat, that's how. It was its own absolution."

"What the fuck are you talking about?"

"J, can you just say, like, something encouraging right now?"

"You could do a lot better than you're doing."

"Thank you, love. Truly. That's helpful. I'll think of that when I'm slitting my wrists tonight."

He gets good and mad then. "Why do you always get so fucking stressed out? This is the Marine Corps. This is what it's like. You don't need to take it all so fucking personally."

You squeeze your eyes. He's right, he's right, they're all right, which means *you* are wrong. None of this is about you. You are tremendously, horribly wrong to feel upset, unnerved and scared out of your mind two-thirds of every day. Cars rumble on the highway.

Would she be hospitable or hostile when you walked in the door? Would she seize you and slam you against a wall and wail on you about your whore eyeliner? Or would she mull over a Church magazine, pointedly ignoring you entirely?

Your stepmother was more physical with you than some parents, not as physical as others. She never beat you, not with concentrated effort. Her violence was explosive and stochastic, when anger spun out of her in directions neither of you anticipated. It was between shocks, when everything was quiet, when you'd find yourself going very still. You'd find yourself sitting at the top of the stairs, straining to listen as she spoke on the phone, spying on her through the railing. You strained to gauge her rage like barometric pressure.

You read to disappear, to inhabit places far away. Your father approved of reading about pioneers, early Mormon history inextricably linked with westward expansion, and you read a lot of it. Though in shaded Appalachia, part of you lived there—big Western deserts, open skies—a little bit all of the time. On the school bus home you'd start to get that ache, that dread, and you'd sink your gaze into books about girls who moved unafraid under mountain skylines.

You dream of Utah. You're brave in mythologized frontiers. You're trustworthy. You're sure on your feet. You're calm and reliable and fair. You're definitely a cowboy but you're a rare sort: a diplomat, a peacemaker. You don't start fights, but if you have to end them you're swift and judicious.

You're not a man, exactly, in your fantasies, but you're a version of yourself not defined by being a girl. You move freely in your own body and no one labels you, no man claims the right to tell you whether your appearance pleases him or not. Your clothes cover your skin from the sun and cold and wind and have no actual messaging beyond that. Your body is yours. You live in it fluidly.

You're not a hero in your childhood daydreams. You're still alone, on the edges. The other cowboys think you're weird because you don't drink and you get along with the Indians. But it's a damn good kind of weird. It's a weird that breathes. It's the weird of someone who carries herself with so much self-respect she just doesn't care what people think. A wild freedom, self-worth.

That will be your adulthood, you promise yourself, hiding in your closet, hoping your stepmother doesn't know you're home. One day, you will stride off alone under clear blue skies, at ease in the wide wild world.

Then the explosions.

You bounced off most surfaces in your house or slammed against them. Walls shook and you cracked when you landed on tile and you flew into bookshelves hard enough to send *National Geographic*s cascading. Each surface bruised differently. You dreamed sometimes of the deeper impacts, landing dazed, the wind knocked out of you, like your diaphragm could bruise, until your vision bricked back into place. She stood over you. "Get up. Don't be so *dramatic*."

And if you were *dramatic*—if, for example, you held a newly tender wrist to your chest or got a bag of ice for the lump on your head—this would make it much, much worse.

Glass after glass of water she'd brought to your face if you cried, and you gulped, trying to get it down, to swallow, but it'd go up your nose and down your windpipe, she was shaking, and furious, "How *dare* you cry? Yes, I guess because I'm just *wicked*, your *wicked stepmother*," and you tried to assure her, *No, no, you're not but please*—but you couldn't speak because you were choking, you couldn't breathe but there was no leaving, no fighting, no recourse but to learn to swallow and know, know like a prayer, that soon enough this would end, as she chanted over you, "This is what my mom did for me. You can't cry if you're drinking water."

You learned. Just take it.

Why hasn't it ended?

Now you freeze before you answer a knock at the barracks door, correct yourself, brace yourself. You smile too easily and often, agree with anyone who yells at you, reassure them their anger is valid and important. Your heart pounds around anyone who has authority: police, NCOs, librarians. You are guilty, you know this, you got it, you absorbed all those corrosive sermons; at some point, you got it. You. You are what's wrong. You are the problem.

If you don't want to be hazed, get it fucking right.

Want mercy? Earn it.

So what if the rules change? So what if the rules are draconian and surreal, shifting and morphing as you try to understand them? Figure it out.

You do not differentiate between discipline and torture. You will rip shards of hard tissue from your legs and puke until you splatter the barracks toilet in blood, and this will seem like an appropriate treatment of a body, because you were drilled to understand what you felt didn't matter, in fact wasn't even real.

You should be past this. You're an adult. You're a goddamn Marine.

So why does your body live like you're anticipating an explosion? Why does your heart squeeze, why are your hands in fists, Marine, why are you braced for an emergency landing?

You escaped. You got out. You tore out West. So where is the sureness you thought you would find in your feet?

Stop dwelling. Pick up your pack and move on. Buck up. There's a war on. There is not a creature on Earth who benefits from you moping like a—like a—you think of the worst thing you can call yourself—like a *girl*.

I was nineteen. I sat in the Home Depot parking lot gripping a steering wheel.

Trom sighed. "Why are you always so dramatic?"

"I'm sorry. I'm so sorry. I'm just having a bad night."

"Yeah, well, you need to plan your bad nights better. I have a quiz tomorrow."

I drove back to base. The silence strained between us. I chose this moment to revisit the conversation of the hypothetical child we assumed we would one day have.

"James, if you ever hurt our child, I wouldn't bother divorcing you. You'd never see either of us again."

It was the only way I knew how to express what felt like a gaping chest wound, a limited way to say I'd thought about it and formed the groundbreaking conclusion that bullying kids was pretty fucked up, honestly.

And then we were off. His horrified response that I'd think that of him slamming into whatever wires were misfiring in my needy little noggin.

I picked a fight with Trom craving release. The chemical high of punishment. My body tensed. It wouldn't release until brutal penance. Until body slammed wall.

I hoped he would finally just hit me. He didn't. My nose tingled in anticipation anyway, waiting for blood.

All through spring Trom and I teetered on the edge of a precipitous decision. We heard the other's hesitation. We pulled back at the right moment. We breathed a sigh of relief. Then we turned and shouted in each other's faces.

We didn't break up so much as we detonated. My grades, always nosing just below passable, collapsed.

CHAPTER II

CAPTAIN

It takes time to plug into the land. "When you plug into it, it is strong, beautiful. But in many ways we're still not there, not strong enough to be there." That's why we run.

—*Noé Álvarez,* Spirit Run

It validated my disordered calculus that it was my body that kept me at the Defense Language Institute.

Higher Ups called me into an academic review board. A tribunal of senior enlisted Marines surveyed me critically across the conference table. I sat ironed into Charlies. Master Guns spread my transcripts out in front of him, but looked at me as he spoke.

"Williams. I was surprised to see this come to me. I see you working out every day at lunch. And I see you running all over the damn place with that run team. Seems like every time I drive out that gate I see you running up that hill."

"Aye, Master Guns."

"And I see something angry in your eyes right now."

"Aye, Master Guns."

"Can you tell me why?"

"I can do better, Master Guns."

He nodded. "Any lance corporal with the self-discipline and motivation to PT as much as you do is a lance corporal I want to be one of my Marines. Good to go?"

My jaw twitched, but *thank you* wasn't allowed. "Aye, Master Guns," I nearly shouted.

I would long suspect one of the staff sergeants surveying me disagreed. He always looked skeptical that I was there after the review, like I must have cheated. I was used to it.

With kicking me out ruled out, the council could roll me to the beginning of Arabic or put me in a different language, one classified less difficult. They opted for another language.

Persian Farsi, the language spoken in Iran.

I walked to the on-base library, blinking. An odd thing: next to my unused Arabic dictionary sat the only three books I'd carried when I bolted west. My own best weapons: my favorite books, what words I'd chosen to keep on hand at the wary cusp of adulthood. Two were written by dead Englishmen. But the third—the one I'd reread recently—was written by an Iranian American woman. *Reading Lolita in Tehran* was about Iranian women who gathered to read banned books after the Islamic Revolution. I'd read the book again and again, amazed by their defiance.

The soldiers who glanced at me as I walked past them in the library would have seen a stern-faced girl in too-big cammies headed to the Farsi section with her head bowed. But inside, I leapt in ecstasy.

Farsi felt like the luckiest break in the world, and I only owed it to running all over the damn place.

Without any apparent study Harvey sat the final language test and graduated with the highest possible scores. He was still hungover when Higher Ups issued his orders to 1st Radio Battalion in Lejeune.

"Done." Harvey couldn't stop smiling. Arabic textbooks slid into the dumpster, thudded to its depths. "Done. I can actually move on with my life. I can go somewhere I'm not surrounded by children."

We sat in the sand at the beach. Harvey conjured a fire and cheerfully burned his notebooks. He passed a flask. I made a face. He laughed and said one day I'd learn to appreciate American whiskey.

On an overcast Sunday I drove Harvey to the airport. At the curb, Red Hot Chili Peppers filled my Volkswagen. I twitched under the siren call of the grocery bag of Reese's peanut butter cups shoved under my seat.

Harvey took my hand slowly, like he was amazed by it. "I'll stop drinking if you'll stop puking."

I'd be puking Reese's in about fifteen minutes. I shook my head. "I wish. But it won't help. I can't just . . . stop. I try every damn day."

"I'll try it anyway. I'm going to miss you, Bails. I don't think you see what you are. You're so much smarter and a whole damn lot more stubborn than you realize. I know I haven't always said the right thing. But everything I've said or done, I was trying to help. I love you, you hopeless lady."

He brought my hand to his face. He kissed each scarred knuckle.

Then he stepped into the Monterey airport, seabags over his shoulders.

McCone graduated shortly after Harvey. We didn't say goodbye, but I shyly knocked on her door and wished her good luck.

From the day I left Arabic I would never again have a woman in my chain of command. Sergeant Walker and Lance Corporals McCone and Tucson were all the female leadership I was ever going to get.

Tucson was leaving too. She barreled through Arabic and graduated in a whirl of minor sexual scandal muted by excellent scores. During her frenzied packing and clearing, she heaved possessions into cardboard boxes and ordered me over her shoulder to write an essay on Why I Want to Be the Female Run Team Captain. I wrote an impassioned treatise, though no one else wanted the job. She bequeathed me the female run team and a threadbare book of motivational quotes, and bade me good luck. Then she was gone.

Monterey did not lack for running trails.

That glorious summer I had a few months between Arabic and Farsi wherein my chief task, as I saw it, was to run. I told myself I was building a solid foundation for assuming the run team captaincy, because I needed a stern rationale for the joy I experienced, running in fresh air along the gleaming coastline.

I ran looping miles through the woods behind base. The trails interlaced and wove. I enjoyed them at random, following such things as mushrooms and the auspice of sunlight through the waving pines. Once I even stopped to inhale fistfuls of wild blackberries—for one startled moment no stoic warrior-athlete but a shaking, hungry mammal in the woods. I nearly collapsed with gratitude.

As I disliked speedwork because I hated competition. But also, as I began to hit ninety mile weeks as a matter of course, I, on such an occasion as a radiant sunset or an open trail at dusk, enjoyed sprinting as fast as I possibly could. I liked to see how long I could run—really run. Like my life depended on it. How far could I go *fast*?

Could I run up this hill? *As fast as I could?* If someone *needed me* to get to them up this hill, *would I make it before they bled out?*

I crept farther and farther from the Presidio. On base my shoulders lived basically in my ears. But off base, nosing the edges of the boundary, I ran east of Eden and great waves of stress rolled off my body, down through my soles. Hillsides that fell away into the Carmel Valley; magnificent, sprawling oaks; and the glimmering, endless ocean, all alive and vibrant under the California sunshine. I learned to love running in the hills at dusk, when I was most likely to see fellow quiet-footed crepuscular creatures. There was a world outside the gate, and it pulsed with an aliveness that coursed in my own veins.

Through running I was in my own way participating. When I ran and the coastal wind roved over my sweaty skin I felt deeply okay. Yes, I was an exercise addict. I was also—blindly, wordlessly—seeking God. Whatever lives we lead, there is a door to grace. I didn't need to throw my body against it like a battering ram, as I did; I was still so many miles from knowing that softness would do better. Still I believed there was something on the other side, and I craved it. Even though I wasn't eating, I felt unbelievably glad when I ran, like I could recharge on sunlight and miles, like my body was strong and resilient, like I, too, could keep going. What was one more run, at the end of a ninety mile week? Why not ninety-eight? What was another few miles; why not one hundred?

One overcast evening in high summer I forced myself to time a mile. I flew across the hundred-meter line on the empty track, ripped my wrist to eye level before I'd slowed my momentum. 5:47. A miscount, surely. Wait. I had four splits. I staggered to a stop. I heard a joyful voice I realized must be mine whooping, startling the hilltop's resident grazing deer.

I'd never run faster than a six-minute mile. Hell, I'd never run faster than a *seven*-minute mile.

Adrenaline spurred me all the way to Master Guns.

I wasn't at all sure I could do this—step into an NCO billet, capably lead a largely theoretical team. I felt like a walking bruise. I was constantly sore, hamstrings strung so tight touching my toes was a distant dream. I barely remembered my shins. Yet another toenail was precariously close to detaching.

But fuck it, I was standing. And I could run a 5:47 mile. I stood at parade rest outside Master Guns' door and stared at the wood. Maybe I stood as much of a chance to take on this billet as anybody.

Master Guns ushered me in. "Williams," he said good-naturedly. "You start Farsi when?"

"I'm still waiting on my start dates, Master Gunnery Sergeant, but I heard July."

"I'll ask around. Bet we have the roster and it's sitting on a lance corporal's desk somewhere."

"Thank you, Master Guns." I dove straight to the point. "I need a female all hands."

"Females not showing up to practice?"

"Not enough. I need more runners."

Master Guns nodded. "Takes time to train for distance, good to go. When do you want it?"

"Monday morning, zero-six."

"Alright." He flipped a page of his yellow notebook. "I'll pass this down to the platoon commanders. Female all hands—you want NCOs, too, Williams?"

I nearly passed out with power. "Yes, I need them too. Anyone who can run."

I stopped every female I saw on base even three minutes my junior and asked her if she could run. I fully recognized no one *wanted* to. We did, in fact, have a language to learn. But nonetheless we had been given this thing to do, seven female Marines, to run a race and win, and Master Guns had given me the freedom I'd been bold enough to request: run team outranked platoon functions.

I'd seen Tucson nearly lose her mind trying to organize one single time when women from all the platoons could run together. A Marine's fire team leader, squad leader, platoon sergeant, or so on—any level—could make anything mandatory. Formation, inspection, ass chewing. These compulsory, ordered blocks of time were out of a junior member's hands, and there was not a damn thing a lance corporal like Tucson, or now me, could overrule.

But Master Guns? If Master Guns said run team was more important than getting bawled out by an irate platoon sergeant because he was having a bad day, a fellow female could *choose* to come with me instead. It was the rarest thing in our lives, choice.

So join the run team, I could say. I will run with you any day, any time. Like for real, if you don't feel like going to PT that's "do all the pull-ups and then let's hit each other with things," text me, and I will go running with you and that will BE run team.

I talked shit. I threw down a challenge for any female Marine on base to outrun me. I ran two miles in under fourteen minutes, faster than the Air Force's winning time of 14:06. If anyone could outrun me, I needed them.

Team runs can be slower than running alone—it's a skill to pace in a group. Still, there *had* to be stronger and faster women than me. I was pretty sure they *all* were. I just had to find the other girls who'd hear, "Hey, want to do a thankless thing no one will remotely care that you did, but we've been tasked to do?" and go, "Yeah, that sounds like why I'm here," and we could do this. Shit, if I could do it, anybody could. If I could rally seven women who would run with me and my insane bulimic ass, as I cribbed Olympian marathoners' training schedules (We could do it. We were Marines, were we not?)—

We would win. By, like, a *lot*.

I hoped making it a challenge would shake out some of the reclusive female Marines, the quiet badasses like Artigas who did their own things as removed from the Defense Language Institute's neuroses as possible.

I was right. Within a week I had a team. Burkhart, from Colorado, who ran ultramarathons; Panno, a corporal from admin, our only NCO; skinny Francis, still cold but calmer now she was a lance corporal; and super-strong Berlinsky. Not enough to form the seven-woman team required at the Commander's Cup.

But now the run team was five women who could win.

I received my orders to Farsi. I squeezed Artigas and left for my new barracks over the hill. I carried my seabags in like conjoined turtles, one on my back and one on my chest. Between pillars of green canvas I couldn't see for shit but I could balance the stack of library books against my chest. I had commenced reading straight across the Farsi shelf at the library.

I conceded defeat to Arabic. I sucked almost entirely. To the very last sound it made no sense. I learned *hoot* and *shnukel* and *mufaja*, only discipline, stray lines of profanity, and a few new names for God.

CHAPTER 12

MARROW

. . . hope, for soft marrow lives in hard bone.

—*Hafez*

Farsi opened midway through summer. Soft hope met me padding across the cool courtyard. I felt durable, reinforced. I'd been running a hundred miles a week. Studying Arabic, however miserably, gave me a head start. I walked on tungsten legs and truth etched into my thighs from leading the run team: if you want to keep up, stay ahead.

Iranian teachers welcomed us into the schoolhouse, beaming. Come in, please, *befarmaeed. Khosh amahdi.* They ushered us into Farsi, the language of empires and tea with *shirini.* A language for poetry and revolution.

Our class filed in. Airmen, soldiers, and sailors, nervous or relaxed. I nodded curtly to my junior classmates. Like an ass, I sat in the back with the Army NCOs: I was the only Marine. Army NCOs were different from Marine NCOs. They spoke less sharply. Our entire orientation passed without anybody asserting if I didn't learn this language right, I was going to get someone killed.

Most Army NCOs sprawled as they sat. But one soldier stood against the back wall. He wasn't being rude. He was watching people file in.

Noticing where they settled. Aware of doors and windows. I noticed him noticing because I did the same thing. I felt his eyes on me and glanced back.

The soldier looked so relaxed he seemed to be dreaming, his tanned face at the charming beginning of creased. He leaned against the wall smiling easily, long legs in front of him, wrapped in a blanket of invisible mirth. I wanted to know what made him laugh.

My name caught me as I tottered to formation on sore legs. I turned. The laughing soldier strolled across the courtyard. I shot to parade rest. "Aye, Staff Sergeant."

"Hey, at ease. I hear you're running a marathon up in San Francisco this weekend," said Staff Sergeant Gerecht.

"Aye, Staff Sergeant."

"How ya feeling about it?"

"Wildly excited, Staff Sergeant."

"Good luck."

"Thank you, Staff Sergeant."

"I need to get back into running. Do you know any good runs around here?"

"I really do. There's amazing running around here. Just south, in Big Sur, you can run up this ridge and see the mountains break down into the sea, and there's cowboy cologne—it's a sage—so the whole time you're running you smell this amazing—" I caught myself like a knife hand to the chest. Shut up, boot. "Er. I know a few, Staff Sergeant."

He smiled easily. Damned if I knew what else to do, I said, "Good morning, Staff Sergeant," and went on, blushing furiously.

Endurance running tasted like iron and pulsed like blood in my heels. Long runs cruised to eighteen, nineteen, twenty miles. A marathon was the obvious next step.

All summer I'd passively trained for the San Francisco marathon. Impressively I managed to both over- and under-train. I ran twice a day, distance and hills and sand and trails and sprints and in combat boots. I lifted weights at lunch and slept like I'd died.

Still I didn't eat. I ran on coffee and good intentions.

The night before the marathon I stayed in a strangely lit shared hotel room in San Francisco. I ate a second peanut butter and jelly sandwich, which was stupid, because I couldn't sleep for freaking out about it. I lay on the sloping floor gripping my pelvic bones as if I could seize them tightly enough to keep them from sinking into all the saturated fat in that peanut butter.

You're going to run it off; just run faster tomorrow, I pleaded with myself. *Now go to sleep, damnit.*

The outer line of my hip ached dully at the starting line.

Eh, just tight from kipping on the floor. Let's go.

The reverberation sank deeper into my groin in the first few miles. Where the path turned uphill, my groin began to pang. Still warming up. Keep rolling.

Then, running through bright rose gardens in Golden Gate Park, the pangs came at a higher frequency, shudders of sensation closer together. I ignored them. I wondered what it would be like to live in San Francisco.

The reverberations sharpened to a stab. Knock it off, I hissed, swinging my fist back to punch my thigh at each step. This is nothing. Shut up.

What I said during the last few steps I had on planet Earth before how I walked changed forever was: This shouldn't even be hard for another ten miles or so. Stop bitching, you weak, fat-ass fucking—

Then the rose garden sharpened into the taste of white, a neon splitting yank. An electric charge so shocking it took blinded, startled seconds to place in my groin.

I reared back into a half skip. A pulse of the crowd passed around me, water around a sudden stone. The hell was that? I shortened my stride. The grander fireworks ceded. Okay . . . that was . . . shocking, but not lasting. The calf, for example, which for a moment had seized under a great wave of pressure down my leg, stopped trembling. Well, whatever happened it—oh.

Oh.

From deep in my hip socket, my right hip had finished early. The entire right side, from waist to midway down thigh, felt immobile. Apparently I would not be lifting my right foot higher than a few inches.

Words came to mind from *300*, an immensely popular movie among those of us who considered Marines the ideological progeny of the Spartans. A warrior loses his eye and carelessly declares, "The gods gave me a spare."

My left leg was fine. So this wasn't . . . too . . . bad. Onward.

CHAPTER 13

ONWARD

If my body can endure a marathon, then my soul . . . can blunder on too. . . . Endurance can help turn elusive sorrows into something tangible, like aching muscles and blisters.
—*Catriona Menzies-Pike,* The Long Run

The morning after the marathon I snapped awake in the barracks.

Damn it. Run team.

I laid back and squeezed my eyes.

I'd given the team a few days off around my marathon. "It's important to give yourself cycles to rest," I'd seriously said with a straight face, knowing full damn well *I* would not be taking a "rest day" after something as unimpressive as a marathon.

When my feet hit the deck I nearly fell over.

This was not the body I'd had yesterday.

Wake up.

I leaned against my rack and tentatively weighted each foot. They basically worked. I took a step. Fine. I took another. Off-balance, yes, but standing.

I felt tender, aware of jangled, torn-up roots across my pelvis. I didn't do tender. I rolled down my sweatpants to step out of them, running shorts underneath. Without thought I weighted my right side.

I crashed into my desk and fell to the floor.

I took a second on my side. Pressing myself up took new effort, angles and joints lax and clanking. Until now I'd relied on my body, especially my legs, my solid hips, some infinite capacity to bear and keep bearing. It was ridiculous that it was hard to stand. I scolded myself for being so lazy, so weak, it seemed gargantuan, Herculean, fuck, *interesting*, standing the fuck up. *Jesus, Williams, it was just a fucking marathon. You're training for an ultra. You're* fine.

Still the sensation incurred awe. All that was, all that had ever been, was the linoleum underneath me, the whitewashed cinderblock walls, and my body, suspended in an ocean of this sensation, immutable in its insistence. I felt pride, like answering a riddle correctly, accurately identifying something in a numbed body I only halfway inhabited.

Pain. This one was pain. This was no ache or strain, no muscular cramp or a light flesh wound carved with a dull edge. This was one was holy shit, searing, down to the bone *pain*.

A bit of a fiasco, hauling myself to standing, but once up I felt silly. *For heaven's sake. You can stand. So you can walk. So you can run.* I spun the circle on my iPod. Going to need Eminem for this.

What was wrong, really? I argued, launching myself off my desk and lurching toward the doorframe. Other than the feeling itself, which I did not for one moment consider valid information in and of itself. Pain was weakness, subjective and immaterial, and so neither rational nor as important as logic. What was *actually* different?

I walked off balance. A sharp, deep stab in my right hip peaked and subsided in waves. And I felt simply *off.* Sometimes after a run I walked through the tides, shoes in hand, feet sinking into the soft sand. The cold tide rolling out pulled at my ankles, and my sense of being fully upright tilted. That's how I felt. Like the ground under me was shifting.

I paused against the doorframe.

Fear felt like a heavy hand on my neck.

I hadn't eaten a meal after the marathon, ashamed of my shitty, limped-in time. I ignored finish line offerings, clusters of bananas, artisanal blueberry muffins on the bright wharf. I ate snacks, but less than I'd hoped for in the weeks I'd trained, fantasizing about what I'd eat when I could consume an entire 2,600 calories in a day. For recovery or whatever I'd planned on allowing myself a titanic 3,000. Instead I subtracted for the second peanut butter sandwich the night before the run and more for the embarrassing fact that I'd walked, had all but picked my way across San Francisco after the blinding moment of impact. I'd snacked on the drive back south, then shut myself in my barracks room and sat on the floor.

I thought the marathon would make me feel clean. I just felt dementedly hungry.

And so, that goddamn bagel. I thought I could justify one bagel—a forbidden fruit, too many dreaded carbs for civilian use, but if there ever was a day I could—eat one—

I'd stalked to the chow hall, snatched sad, boring Sara Lee bagels in a to-go container. I smuggled them into the barracks close to my body. I hated walking through the barracks with food, a clear advertisement that despite my weight, I ate.

Alone on my rack I'd curled around the first bagel. Its was a gruesome death. I skewered it first with my teeth, skinning the outer flesh off in strips, then ripped its underbelly apart in sacrament-sized morsels. I nursed each wafer in my mouth until it softened to film, letting tissue-thin sheaths dissolve on my tongue. Then I ate another, and another, in the same way. Nearly four hundred calories, lying on my back and staring at the ceiling, mesmerized by the transition of bread to film.

If I hadn't eaten slowly I'd've unhinged my jaws and swallowed the bagels whole.

Surely last night's bagels were still in my stomach. I couldn't *not* run.

For one moment I dropped my head against my door frame.

To stop running—to rest—didn't occur to me. I wasn't about to be another fat broken female on some bullshit chit. A real injury would give me no choice. Bodily injury took you out or it didn't.

I had to run because leading the run team was my stupid, idiotic, Uncle Sam–appointed piece of shit place of fucking duty *that I'd asked for*, and I had to run so I didn't get fat from the high fructose corn syrup in the Sara Lee bagel. I had to run because I actually had a team, women who impressed me, people I wanted to run with. I had to run because moving into Farsi meant I shared a platoon with Pashto, which meant I shared a platoon with Trom. Our on-again, off-again bond had outworn its elastic. Whoever had the silver engagement ring in our game of hot potato kept it. Still, I savagely wanted him to think well of me, and he'd told me his friends—my new platoon mates—at least agreed I wasn't a shitbag because I ran so hard. I had to run because the laughing soldier had asked if I wanted to go running sometime and I had said yes and not in this life was I going to tell a combat veteran, oh *sorry*, no can *do,* I *hurt* myself in fucking California.

Most mornings I savored walking down the barracks hallway when the rest of my platoon was still asleep, the potent aloneness unique to 0445. It felt different, that morning. Dread seeped into every joint. The red door opened a way I didn't want to go.

Hey. It isn't the end of the world.

The heavy red door slammed behind me. The cold air zapped my lungs the way it always did, the clarion call to begin again, and my injury and I went for our first run.

For the next week I hobbled down Cannery Row like a bowlegged drunk and experimented. I reengineered my stride. If I kicked with my left leg, I could swing my right around. It didn't feel comfortable or right. But I figured I was moving generally forward, in this as in all things, so onward.

Harder than overriding mechanics, harder than negotiating pain—*sensation*, I reminded myself, only sensation—was stomaching a prickling feeling. Deep in my belly, some animal instinct told me I should be sitting down.

In later years when I am studying an articulated pelvic bowl in my hands, my anatomy teacher will share Wolff's law. Bones break. Bones heal. They can heal differently, in a shape not quite the shape they were before. Wolff's law states bones grow as they're used. Bones heal to the environment they're in. On a deep level, the very bodily infrastructure we build to support ourselves is constructed by how we move through the world.

For better or for worse, this one was going to heal Marine Corps.

I knew something was wrong. It would be impossible to feel what I felt and not *know* that something was very, very the fuck wrong. But I genuinely believed that what I felt was unimportant. This, too, was something I should not be bothered by. I had carefully learned to swallow the right to claim my pain was valid. It created an odd homeostasis in my body, discomfort completely repressed by the sincerity of my delusion: I was a junior enlisted female boot in Monterey, California. The hell did what I feel matter, compared to the pain of a combatant at war?

And so I ordered my body to shut up and deal with it, whatever it was, and pain intricately framed the months I settled into Farsi. Pain rewired my thoughts, though I didn't know it at first, the months I sat down and stood up slowly and carefully.

Do we get rest? asked my body.

No.

Do we get healing hands, of any kind?

No.

Do we get food?

Ha. No.

What do we get?

YOU'RE A MARINE, MOTHERFUCKER.

"Congrats, you got a 300 PFT!" Trom beamed. "I didn't even get a 300. So you're the guide now, huh?"

"Yeah, they're on a PT kick."

The day we ran a practice physical fitness test, only two Marines in our platoon hit the perfect score. Our platoon sergeant wasn't wildly happy about it. The other Marine, already a squad leader, grinned to say well done when he saw me doing my damnedest not to limp to class, gripping the furled platoon flag.

"Did you run eighteen minutes?" Trom insisted.

"What?"

"The male standard for the run. I mean, I know you ran a 300, but you're a distance runner. Did you make it by the male standard?"

I bowed my head. "No. Twenty-oh-eight."

"Oh wow! Only a minute slower than me. I mean, don't worry about it. Good job!"

CHAPTER 14

DAMN THE TORPEDOES

Most fruits, if left alone on a tree, eventually do ripen, especially if they're not being yelled at.

—*Firoozeh Dumas,* Funny in Farsi

Gently I prodded the laughing soldier with my foot. "We need to talk about this."

He squeezed me and addressed the ceiling. "Nooooooo."

Our Farsi laid strewn across the floor. We'd met at his apartment purportedly to study, then proceeded to spend a lot more time making out than I suspected the ayatollahs would approve.

"You have more to lose than I do if we get caught," I said.

"What do you mean?"

"This is your career."

"It's your career too."

"But you've actually done shit. If we get caught, I'm just another whore who slept with an NCO. Your fifteen thousand ribbons are going to be a lot more notable on a newly demoted private."

Gerecht leaned out from underneath me to pick up sheets of Farsi verbs, a tenth attempt to refocus. "I would love to see this POG-ass command try to knock me down that far.

"And people who say shit about females just because they're females are fuckin' idiots," he added reasonably. "Wait until these boots get in country. They won't give a fuck who's doing the job; they'll only care they're doing it right. If anyone talks who doesn't have the combat infantryman rifle, fucking ignore them. If they weren't infantry, they don't know shit. As for . . . this, as far as I'm concerned, Marines don't have the careerist distinction, right?"

"ONE TEAM, ONE FIGHT, OORAH."

He grinned. "I like you. I like it when you're around. You make me laugh. And what the fuck ever, you're not in my chain of command. You're not even in my branch. Besides, I've seen you with your run team. If you were Army they'd make you an NCO for that shit. Marines are crazy professional. You're a shit-ton more squared away than female Army NCOs."

What could I say? He vibrated optimism and ease, and, freezing, I was drawn to him like he was fire. "Damn the torpedoes, full speed ahead."

He threw Farsi overhead and reached for me. "Damn the torpedoes!"

"من هستم تو هستی," sang Gerecht as he marched around the living room.

Miserably I marched behind. "من هستم تو هستی."

We'd untangled to study for our first test. Gerecht did well in class, laughing from one quiz to the next while I all but ate my workbook in panic. We were assigning conjugation to movement, marching Farsi into my brain.

"Whatever your block is, you damn sure know how to move, so make that Farsi," he suggested.

Frustration seized me by the throat like it could throttle me.

"Look, this is hard," he acknowledged. "It's okay. It's hard for me too. Just because it's hard doesn't mean you're doing something wrong."

I threw my head up. "من هستم تو هستی . . . . *ooo.*"

"*Hast*," he gently supplied.

"I am never going to learn—"

"Sweetheart, *you are allowed to not know*. We're three weeks into class. You're not expected to somehow *know* Farsi already."

"ما هستیم. شما هستید," I shouted at the ceiling and marched myself into the arm of the couch. "Genius."

"That's right, though," he shouted. I leapt back behind him. "Again!"

"من هستم. شما هستید. او هست. آن ها هستند."

It was the simplest use of language: to name I am. You are. New words to connect subject and action. New ways to understand that pivotal relationship.

We reached the end of the hall. Gerecht froze, then formally bellowed. "About. FACE."

We pivoted and marched back.

"ما هستیم آنها هستند." A cadence began to sound.

"Yes!" Gerecht shouted triumphantly. "Again! *Houhand*!"

I marched in Gerecht's footsteps around the living room. "من خواهم. او خواهد. آنها خواهند. شما خواهید."

Gerecht threw his arms up. "یک بار دیگر. One more time WITH CONFIDENCE!"

"من خواهم. او خواهد. آنها خواهند. شما خواهید."

"Brilliant!" Gerecht screamed and marched me right into his bedroom.

During the test I pumped my boots under my desk. من هستم. شما هستید.

We both scored at the top of the class.

In October I stood in Gerecht's kitchen measuring one tablespoon of peanut butter for a sandwich. Gerecht whipped the jar out of my hands and dropped to one knee. He offered up the Skippy, beaming. "Will you make me a happy man and move in with me?"

I would.

Gerecht and I ignored each other in class. In the hallways I sprang to parade rest and screamed good afternoon, Staff Sergeant with laudable professional vigor each time I saw him. It made me smile, seeing the quick turn of his mouth as he tried not to laugh.

"At ease, Williams," he whispered into my hair at night.

I wasn't quite sure who to ask, on this one. Living with Gerecht gave me a fighting chance. When I walked into our apartment my whole body softened. I could change my clothes without hiding in my wall locker, fearful someone was watching through the windows. I could laugh as loud as I liked and dance around in my socks. Gerecht had his own issues and could zone out in front of video games for hours; I'd go for a run and read, curl up beside him with library books and the strawberry smoothies that composed 90 percent of my diet. The view from our little deck was a coastal redwood.

Quiet. We had quiet. When I slept by him, I dreamed.

On the other hand, worries both religious and martial agonized me. I was Living with a Man Outside the Sacred Bonds of Eternal Marriage, so that prompted the occasional outburst of recovering-Mormon cognitive dissonance. Gerecht shepherded me to a Lutheran church. "It's like Catholic without all the guilt," he assured me. "Er . . . for what it's worth, *I* think God or whatever loves you. You're not a bad person, Will; you're just in a lot of pain. Not everything is your fault."

Professionally, I took the honor of being a Marine so seriously it micromanaged every aspect of my existence. Dating a Marine NCO would've been out of the question, but a soldier? My Farsi squad leader, Sergeant Wolf, knew perfectly well I was ghosting off base to live with an Army NCO, so I'm sure the rest of the platoon NCOs knew, but nobody cared because I wasn't a screw up. I had to give them no reason to care. My uniform was immaculate; my military bearing—the face I showed at work—neutral and empty. I woke up earlier and ran harder, grimly understanding between four and six miles my hip sort of stopped hurting because it sort of went numb and then I could really hit a stride.

There was no clear-cut rule about interservice relationships, but fraternization was a severe offense. It demoralized The Troops.

I wasn't sure if living with him was a sin or divine intervention. All I knew was from the time I moved out of the barracks and in with Gerecht, I stopped stressing about failing out of Farsi and started stressing about getting straight As.

The pain gnawed into my sleep, and I dreamed what I ignored when awake. My right leg caught in a metal trap or buried in rubble or immobilized under a writhing coil of black snakes. Once a lion looked up at me, his golden muzzle speckled with blood, then resumed stripping off my skin, almost delicately. I could move any time, but then the lion would starve. Whatever the trap, the dreams were all the same: I couldn't run away and so was eaten, chewed apart by gaping, insatiable jaws.

I woke Gerecht wailing this *meant something.*

He startled awake. "What?"

"In literature. My fucking leg. It's an incredibly bad omen. I keep dreaming I'm trapped. Hurting your leg is symbolic of losing your ability to fight or fly. When a character hurts their leg, it means *something bad* is about to happen."

He rolled to me. "Maybe fucking up your hip was the something bad. It already happened. You're in pain, Will. It makes sense you feel it when you sleep. I really wish you'd go to medical."

"I'll go when you go for your ears." Gerecht's ears sometimes rang so badly he'd come home and shove his palms over them, a souvenir of firefights from his infantry days.

"It's not the same, Will."

"Yeah, you've earned it."

"It's not the same. You deserve help too, Will. You fucked yourself up in a leadership role, encouraging females to run."

I flung the blanket over my head. "Your ears hurt from shit exploding in combat."

"What is it you can't run away from?"

"What?"

"In your dreams. What was it you couldn't run away from?"

". . . Zombies."

But he didn't laugh. We were watching our way through every zombie movie ever made. He began to go over our apartment zombie-attack defense plan. He lulled me back to sleep describing wiring explosives under the stairs.

After a really good day in Farsi, when my professors beamed at my novice attempts to speak, I had the strange thought, you know, I bet my parents would like to hear from me every once in a while.

I called Dad. He always answered on the first ring. He asked me to wait one second while he gathered up the cat, my parting gift when I left home, who had a name until my dad started calling her Outside Cat. I could hear him settling into his chair with the purring semi-feral.

I tried to tell him about this aching chasm between me and what was, actually, an okay life.

"The remedy to spiritual depression is to learn something," Dad advised. He told me when he was worried, he studied things. "Global warming fascinated me for a while." Currently he was on the American Revolution.

"Find something good, something that gives you joy, something that fills you with wonder and a sense of beauty."

"Running."

"Preferably something that doesn't destroy your legs. Find a way of serving other people. Paul tells us, 'When you lose yourself, you find yourself.' You have to lose yourself in something beautiful and virtuous and good."

"I thought that was the Marine Corps." I said it less certainly.

"Keep seeking."

My father encouraged me to seek the light with singleness of purpose. It was the way of saints. Or, more my speed, moths.

The progressive Green Movement swept Iran. It was an exciting time to study Farsi. Furious crowds burst onto the streets of Tehran, protesting a dubious election. Theocratic mullahs denounced and criminalized protesters. "In the name of God, the most mighty, the most merciful," they began, and explained how He endorsed the use of blunt clubs.

Thousands of miles away, a class of DLI students enthusiastically cheered those who marched against the government. I was in the most relaxed classroom, with students who were at the top of the class. Mostly Air Force NCOs, Gerecht, a few senior sailors, one junior airman, and me. We were unabashed Mousavi supporters. We loved to insult Ahmadinejad, the diminutive president with nuclear ambitions backed by the supreme leader, in pidgin Farsi. We rooted for Mousavi, the moderate progressive who seemed to care for, like, the nation's people. We voiced thunderous opinions on sanctions and human rights, our subjunctives falling off all over the place.

In the quiet of the apartment, I sat down and paid attention to my homework. Every day I listened to BBC Farsi. زنان was the word that caught my ear. Women. Then حقوق زنان. Women's rights.

Women were . . . participating in the protests?

No. رهبر. Women were leading the protests.

I listened.

Handwriting changed in Farsi. Arabic found me languorously strewn, tracing stray names of God in lavish calligraphy. In Farsi I kept a journal. I sat bowed over my lap and wrote as if chiseling into stone. Letters tightened, flourishes turned blocky with childlike concentration. *Gerecht prepared dinner. I ate vegetables. I am still a Marine today.* The Persian translation for Marine was *tufang dareier*. Rifle carrier.

I puzzled out Farsi sentences while I ran. *Here is the ocean; here are . . . ocean dogs.* (I made mental note to look up "seal.") *I have a pain in my leg. The sky is beautiful above the ocean. There is a whale! The whale is big and I am small.* I caught myself. That was an odd thought. *The whale is big and I am big. You sound like an idiot*, I thought, surprisingly kindly. *The whale is beautiful. I am a rifle carrier.* از دویدن خوشم میاد.

Run team arrived at the hilltop track sleepy, wrapped in sweaters. Serious-faced Duryea and funny Berlinsky, skinny Francis. Colorado Burkhart was on duty; that was legit. Panno, as one of like three female NCOs on base, got tapped to monitor random piss tests that morning. She'd already texted that she'll run with me this afternoon; all good there. And here was Cassidy, an overweight Marine sent to me for punitive running. Welcome to the party.

My eating disorder and I greeted the team with pretend ease. I'd already run for an hour.

"Marnin'. Easy warm up. Mile at your own pace. A good gauge is if you can breathe easily, carry on a conversation."

Next barefoot drills on the grass. We tossed shoes and socks behind us, small feet startlingly pale from days in combat boots. We ran drills on balance and alignment and center of gravity. Odd that I taught this. I read the books and studied *Runner's World* like doctrine. But when I ran, I did whatever the hell I had to do to keep moving.

Run harder. One day you'll be stronger, and it won't be so hard.

The team lined up. I echoed my old friend Tucson: "If you're gonna outrun me, you'd better time yourself." Across the white line, the clicks of four watches, eager tap of plastic.

"Ladders. One hundred meters, two hundred meters, four hundred meters. Reverse. Two hundred meters, four hundred meters, six hundred meters. Reverse. Four hundred meters, six hundred meters, eight hundred meters. Reverse. That last four hundred will feel just gorgeous. Easy two-mile jog after, short and sweet. I want these all at race pace.

Berlinsky, Francis, keep working toward that seven-minute pace. Think twenty-six, twenty-seven seconds each hundred meters. Duryea, you can keep up with me; we're rocking twenty-five, *enshallah.* Cassidy,"—she looked alarmed—"Run however the hell you can. Don't be afraid. Whatever you've got is great. No matter what, the team is only as strong as you, so don't break yourself."

She smiled nervously. We both hoped she wouldn't have to run in the Commander's Cup.

I ran. I ran as hard as I could. I ran and sometimes Duryea eased past me, and I swallowed my martyr sense of *but I'm in paaaaaaain*, as if that entitled me to something. *Shut up and keep running. Pain is weakness leaving the body. It's not yours to wonder why it lingers.*

At the end of practice, four and half miles of speedwork, the women gathered on the field, sweaty and eager as the sun rose, the crack of endorphins. My chest burst seeing them. Something about the first sun on the hilltop, filtered through the mist and Monterey pines, awake and alive and going for it while the base still slept, made standing sore and inflexible on the grass feel kind of grand.

In class my eating disorder curled in my lap, harsh and spiny, and I forgot to hate myself for whole hours at a time. Farsi unfurled in beautiful arches. The language transported me, riddles and symmetries falling into place.

Our professors welcomed us as guests, which by Persian tradition meant they treated us like royalty. They spoke as if we were visiting dignitaries who honored them greatly by choosing to learn their language. They politely but pointedly ignored a sailor's protestations we'd all been ordered to Farsi. Irrelevant. You're our guests now. Our professors practiced the Persian custom of *tarof*—courtesy in speech built into the very language.

I loved Persian Farsi.

Like Archimedes' lever it moved my world, hearing someone say I was doing a good job. I began to have moments, especially when my hip wasn't too bad, where I felt actually . . . okay. Like maybe I was doing enough even if I wasn't actively dragging injured Marines out of firefights. My shoulders dropped a micrometer. My eating disorder struck out a scaly hand to recount calories in the margins of my notebooks and I found myself writing a new word over and over: نترسی. I liked the swoop of it, the elegant way it flowed from a pen. Over months it filled my notes.

I'd spent so much time in Arabic writing names of God in the margins, I wondered, sometimes, if maybe I was finally hearing a response. The word was in the informal imperative, the way you'd speak to a friend.

نترسی. Don't be afraid.

CHAPTER 15

RUN

داوم على كسر قلبك حتى تفتحه

You have to keep breaking your heart until it opens.

—*Rumi*

Midway through Farsi the stars aligned, almost. With the addition of a serious-faced Marine in Russian, the run team scored six female Marines who could individually run two miles in under fourteen minutes, and we spent months running together. We could win the Commander's Cup, we six. But I had to run seven, and we had to run it together. The magical seventh revolved for months.

How I envied Higher Ups who ordered the Commander's Cup. I'm sure they saw it as a fun little morale-booster for The Troops. I imagine they slept soundly in their beds blithely unaware of one sleepless lance corporal anxiously pacing the barracks the night before, trying, again, to make one and one and one and one make seven. I'd text all the female squad leaders in my phone. I'd offer to PT their squads from here until Christmas if they would please send someone to run this effing two miles. I'd knock on females' doors from other platoons, anyone I'd heard didn't actively hate running. "It's fun," I said. No one particularly believed me, what with the ice packs taped to my shins, but I limped door to door proselytizing anyway.

Keeping the six we had was a perilous thing. A day before one race a Marine stomped Francis' ankle. She told me it was a PT accident. I swallowed the harsh voice that snapped, *Well, can you deal*, and borrowed the saner voice that came out my mouth: "Please don't run if you're in pain." I tapped Blake, a good-natured squad leader in Pashto, and gave her a borrowed pair of running shoes and about fifteen seconds to prepare.

I still wonder about one of the mystical sevenths. The next Cup, an Arabic squad leader sent me a sacrificial new join, a platinum blond with a promising seven-minute one-mile. Fox was so new to DLI the first time we ran together was the Cup. She ran great for two laps, then started wincing. I dropped back to run alongside her. She told me she couldn't breathe.

"What hurts?" I asked, prepared to present the Williams school of pain management, basically some variation of *Try not to think about it.*

"No," she said, gasping now, hyperventilating. Cheers of amassed forces around the track quieted as Fox began to cry. She sputtered hysterically, barely walking. She kept pulling at the hem of her shorts as if she could persuade them down a few more inches.

I did not have a strategy for this. I was watching my own greatest fear, breaking down, the grief in my body bursting out of control. Fox just had to do it right here in front of God and everybody.

I seriously considered seizing her wrist and leg and rolling her onto my shoulders—the rules said we had to finish together; it said nothing of "on a teammate's own volition"—but even I realized that was a touch dramatic.

The Army surged past. We barely crawled past the Navy.

After the race I gathered the team. I was livid. I murderously called a 0400 death run the next morning. We were sprinting hills until we died. Fox volunteered for duty, so we ran our penance without her. She went on permachit and left the Marines before graduating DLI, among a small but steady trickle of junior enlisted women. *Good riddance*, I figured.

Still I thought about that girl for years, our short, forced interaction. Only thousands of miles later, while running in a beautiful forest, will a new idea turn that memory over in my mind. Who in the absolute hell was I to react in anger? What if that wasn't faking it? What if she wasn't freaking out because of a lack of self-discipline or strength or military bearing or some stupid thing? What if she'd no shit been having a flashback or something? She kept pulling at her shorts, like she wished she could hide behind the tiny fabric. Intense self-consciousness being so bodily in front of a crowd, on display before the entire Presidio: I could think of reasons this could stress a body out. If she'd had sexual trauma, maybe, or, oh, I don't know, *an eating disorder.*

The next race I ran a pregnant PFC twelve minutes off quarters. I ran into her at medical while picking up free Ibuprofen, which I ate as non-bulimics might eat Tic Tacs. Sasha volunteered on the spot. "Honestly I wouldn't've even come to medical normally. It's just a fever. But I'm pregnant, and I never get sick, so I thought I should ask."

She was supposed to convalesce in the barracks until 1600, but we figured the race wouldn't get started for at least a quarter hour after that. The female Marine run team always kind of relied on guts, so I thanked her effusively.

On lap three Sasha passed the hell out with a fever of a hundred and two. After we disqualified we sat in the shade under the bleachers. "Well," she said, eyes glassy. "That went well." We were both giggling helplessly when two rare female NCOs came by to ask us what the hell.

My backside thoroughly muddied from sits-ups during platoon PT: a platoon mate quipped, "Damn Williams, looks like you're up for promotion."

A variation of that old stupid joke.What's the difference between a female staff sergeant and a zebra? The zebra doesn't have to lie down for its stripes.

Now that I had a team, routine teasing about females didn't make me apologetic. It made me apoplectic as all rabid hell. I looked at my team and didn't see a damn thing that needed to apologize for itself.

But what was I going to do? Tell a man, a *veteran*, to fuck off? I said aye, sergeant and no, sergeant and slammed in the front door and threw my running shoes at the wall.

This didn't surprise Gerecht.

"The Army has like three chicks on suicide watch right now," he agreed. "Though I don't get why anyone listens to the bullshit boots say. Saying dumbass sexist shit to show off in front of their equally dumbass boot buddies. You can't *listen* to that shit. I don't know why girls take it seriously."

"You don't know why we don't like being told we deserve to be raped?"

"But it's not real."

Then what was this hand across my mouth, this pressure clenching my jaw?

"What you need to understand, babe, is most of the time when males say stupid shit, they're not thinking about the actual females around them."

I opened my mouth and closed it again. Why yes. That was indeed the problem.

McCone and I hadn't said goodbye when she left for Goodfellow Air Force Base, but I swore to lead as she had: be so damn good your existence challenges the standing assumption it's funny to call females weaker. I strained for that. I ran to chase down good enough. While I growled and swore to sabotage the Marines' war on female-ism, *Bridge Over River Kwai* that shit and dance in ridiculous banana leaves over it, I had no idea how. So I committed myself to the laborious process of losing my mind.

I went nuts.

Press back up to one hundred miles a week. Crisp and clean, dicey hip be damned. One hundred and ten, crisper and cleaner. Twelve hundred calories a day, enveloped, ironed, and precious. Keep going.

Here's a neat little tip from a misinformed corporal during a vapid nutrition briefing so nearly entirely wrong it felt like being sandpapered: if you want to lose weight, pick your goal weight and add a zero to it, and that's how many calories you should eat each day. Intriguing. That allotted me 970 calories a day.

If you want to mess up your head even faster, run sixteen miles and still only eat your goal-weight-plus-zero calories. Then you, too, can wake up in the middle of the night with hunger kneading your stomach from the inside with a knobby fist.

I gnawed my knuckles in my sleep. I woke up with blood on my pillow, noting with mild interest I was resorting to self-cannibalism. I turned the pillow over.

I routinely slept with ice packs on bare shins. Frostbite blended in with other scars, mottled like blue bark.

"Damn Williams, you must be the first Marine to get frostbite in Monterey," an NCO laughed at formation. I laughed along. Hilarious.

If no pain, no gain, then I was rocking. Every time someone implied it was characteristic of females to be fat and broken, I furiously clocked another mile, right hip clicking along. When rumor circulated a female was malingering for going on chit, I flew out the door, shoelaces double knotted, shouting at my injury to go on, *hit me.* And when she was asking for it or she's lying, she wanted it, I protested by running long hauls along the gray coast. A strange self-hating protestation not so different from a strange self-hating apology.

I rarely cried. Sometimes, though, in the gray cocoon of oceanic fog, miles alone up the coast, hunger and need cracked into something else. Then I slowed on the sand, dropped my hands to my thighs, and took a few shuddering breaths.

Bulimia lingered like a rattlesnake in the apartment, camouflage its best defense. Fistfuls of protein-bar wrappers wadded into an empty mac-and-cheese box shoved into the garbage. It nested in the shower drain, me insisting I knew nothing about a clog, as if I didn't have bites on my knuckles. Disembodiment slithered into bed when Gerecht and I slept together. I retreated to my head as if I didn't exist underneath my chin, could repeal my existence back into my brain. It struck out and sank its fangs into runner's legs when I showered after a run and felt the heaviness of my quads as shame. I'd rush past Gerecht, muttering about mandatory study hall while kicking on my shoes and stumbling out the door to unhinge my jaw, inhale my bodyweight in iced brownies, and throw up at the Cannery. I always thought I could escape the serpent tailing me through this weird incantation, telling myself, always, *this time, last time.*

The rattlesnake shot out of the pantry unpredictably. Gerecht wrapped me in a bear hug no matter how I rattled. He was unperturbed, really. He didn't understand why I wanted to starve myself, but he'd seen this before.

"My ex-wife was bulimic," he said. "She kind of got over it. She found a diet that works for her, I guess."

This suggested a successful diet I hadn't tried yet, a way to live as a satiated skeleton. "Your first girlfriend post-divorce is not doing so much better at keeping her head out of the toilet."

He shrugged. "Least you give a shit."

I did give a shit. I'd accepted misery as a Marine. If you want to be a Marine, be okay with your life always sucking a little bit. That was part of the fun. Oorah.

But this.

The redwood outside our window. If we left the window open we heard sailboats shuffling at the wharf, rolling in the smooth promising pulse of the Pacific. Running shoes lived by the door, exciting to me every time I saw them, beckoning me down to the water. Library books stacked on a chair, Iranian fiction about censorship and poetry. A preposterously good person playing video games on the couch, who was somehow my partner in all this. Despite myself I'd bushwhacked to a good place. A small part of me understood I was going to miss it if I kept hacking myself skinny enough to deserve it.

So I ran and ate and purged and went to class, and didn't go to lunch, because clearly I couldn't be trusted around food. At the gym I vigorously pushed out skull-crushers, trying to tame the impermissible waggle at my upper arms literally no one but me saw. Back to class but feeling motivation slide away as a goddamn sugary ginger scone from the café imprinted itself on my brain. The shape of it. The texture. The satisfying crumble. I answered questions in class and dreamed about that goddamn sugary ginger scone. Then after class I walked with a sense of purpose to the café and ate that goddamn sugary ginger scone, then shifted my feet side to side during formation, praying it would end because I needed to puke. But sometimes, after formation, the urgency had passed. I went home without running, asked Gerecht if he'd like to do pizza tonight; after all, it was Friday. He'd light up, me acting like a normal person, and we'd watch zombie movies and eat entire pizzas, and I'd make something indulgent, chocolate chip cookies or White Russians, and say, I'm just really hungry today, repeating myself, pleading for him not to notice how much I was eating. I'm just really hungry, and the great irony is I was.

"Williams, why are you taking it so seriously? Run team's just for fun."

So fun. I smiled and said what I always did: "It's my billet."

"Honestly, Williams, it's all a joke. Don't *worry* about it."

Fuck's sake. Tell that to my team. Tell that to girls who ran like hell, who ran every early morning mile and sprinted split I counted in my sleep. They ran knowing full well in the only evidence anyone would ever see, the accursed Commander's Cup, we won't have enough people, I'll shove in an overwhelmed new kid, we'll have no evidence to show we tried at all, and our friends will try to cheer us up by telling us it's not our fault females are fat and broken. In this way, we ran to the soundtrack of denigration of the very thing we were.

My team shrugged and ran the miles anyway.

I sure as shit wasn't laughing. Crazed and cracked open, I felt I could not quarter. No matter how stupid my stand, it was my stupid duty to stand it.

Of course, nobody but me actually cared.

I stressed out of my mind over something literally no one cared about. I was accountable to no one but Master Guns. Not a single Marine on base could name who ran on the female team, though, in their defense, rarely could I name seven either. The only metric of success was the Cup, which no one seemed to care we routinely lost. I got Facebook messages from men I barely knew. "Good job with ur team, u motivate me." "Looking good Williams, ur an example to other females."

But were people looking at my team? We could win. We could be good. If we sprinted across the finish line first, definitive winners, maybe the invisible pressure grinding my jaw would lower. Maybe we could train more intelligently, with things like phases and cycles, instead of constantly, constantly charging. Maybe if we won, the injuries it took to get us there would be legitimate. Maybe if we won with a powerful thunderous charge, we could earn a touch—the tiniest breath—of *being fucking Marines*. Boot Marines, yes, young Marines, undeniably, but Marine enough that the next time someone told me female Marines expected to get everything easier just for having tits, I wouldn't get court martialed for punching them right in the goddamn face.

That tiny captaincy was my place of duty, and it possessed me because I was insane enough to believe not only *that* I held it but *how* I held it mattered. Mine felt like the smallest, stupidest billet in the mighty Marine Corps. But it was mine.

Slowly, being a Marine was teaching me to show up, bite down hard, and hold the hell on. Nothing about being a Marine was teaching me rest or recovery. I had no idea recovery was a crucial part of athleticism. I kept on running on my sputtering-near-empty tank.

By the time Farsi reached the future imperative, something in my groin was just full fucked. On dress uniform days I planned ahead to take as few steps as possible—high heels were a special kind of hell.

Often my hip buckled. I limped, and it pissed me off. Get it together, Marine. What the fuck are you *limping* for? Have you been shot? Have you *deployed*? Have you done *fuck all* for your country? No? Then *what the everlovingfuck* do you think you have a right to *limp* for? I invoked the Bataan Death March where World War II POWs were shot if they fell out, or a story told by Elie Wiesel about Jews evacuated from Buna-Monowitz concentration camp, forced to run through the snow and dark for miles and miles, malnourished and freezing. See? People can run. There is a level of endurance so much further than this. You're not suffering as badly as they did. So you can keep going.

This was the standard of endurance to which I held myself: death marches and concentration camps.

The arrogance astounds me, now.

Some days, from some unknown calculus, it didn't hurt to move around. Enthusiastic, I raced out the door, amazed anew by the ocean crashing against the coast. See? I'd gloat. Invincible.

But then I'd be fetal on the shower floor again, fluently swearing. Maybe other Marines have higher pain tolerance. Maybe everyone hurts like this all the time and oh my god, I am such a malingering twat piece of shit. *Christ, Williams, can you keep it together?*

If I have to.

Well, then it doesn't hurt too *badly.*

I'd taken it for granted, standing up from the toilet without bracing myself against the stall walls. I was suddenly old. I was twenty.

One morning the run team came to practice precisely on time. I finished my warmup run and waved good morning. They did something odd. The women sat down together on the track.

Francis spoke for them. They'd seen me falter. They'd heard me swear. They had decided as a team they would not run with me until I took my stubborn ass to medical.

I had assumed my injury was invisible. A private thing, deep in my groin, in mysterious anatomy I understood as a black censored block. My team's mutiny stirred something quiet. It felt so strange to be seen without feeling I'd been watched.

I took my stubborn ass to medical.

"Overuse injury. Common in females," the doctor added carelessly. "Have a chit and some Ibuprofen. Any chance you're pregnant?"

Females really aren't made to run long distances, scolded the second opinion. "Especially with a female figure like yours." (Perched on the crinkly paper, I immediately sucked in.) "The angle from your hip to your knee is more dramatic than a man's. Ease off the running, or yeah, you're going to feel a little discomfort."

"Labral tear," predicted the third opinion, when he jolted my knee toward my chest and I nearly passed out. "The labrum is between the head of your femur and the acetabulum, the pelvic socket, like a gasket. When it wears down or blows, the bone knocks on bone. I know it's hard to see when you're young, but you need to consider down the road. You need surgery."

"Sounds like a psoas thing to me," said the physical therapist I saw a total of once. "Except I don't think you'd able to run on that; it would be excruciating." He was a man so I didn't say what I thought, which was, *And why do you think I'm here, motherfucker?*

"I might guess a stress fracture," frowned the final, civilian doctor I saw out in town, a sports specialist. He spoke with me a few minutes longer than the military docs. "Though a stress fracture at the hip makes me wonder if something else is going on. If you're not getting your period it's possible you've reached the female athlete triad and you may be losing bone density. Are you careful about what you eat?"

"I . . . try to be."

"What you definitely do need is rest."

Well, that wasn't happening. My eating disorder had a few choice words on "rest." Rest was for real endurance athletes, and currently my gross fat body refused to endure. You're limping, for God's sake. That is not the body of an endurance athlete. Clearly I was too fat for my eating disorder to be relevant. Surely I hadn't worked so hard as to fracture my pelvis, that great solid thing I craved to bring to the surface like a sunken vessel, or torn major stabilizing musculature or some other real, holy shit injury. No one would run a hundred miles a week if they were in that much pain. Anyway, the fuck was pain? Pain was an idea. Pain was for Marines who actually suffered, not my bullshit little cush-ass enlistment in Monterey Bay. My disorder protested loudly.

For my world to make sense, what I felt had to not matter. If I let what I felt be *real*, if I actually let myself *feel* what I felt, I would scream. I would scream. That was pretty much what I felt like doing, all day, all night, all the time. I might not stop. I feared if I sat down, I wouldn't get back up.

I Googled the various diagnoses. Somehow seeing *ongoing pain* or *will not heal on its own* or *mechanical irritant* or *osteoarthritis* didn't reach me. The relationship between malnutrition, the cortisol and adrenaline constantly pumping to keep me on my feet, decreased bone density, and increased risk of fracture felt irrelevant to me. My deluded bony ass held as fact I was too fat to be unwell in any way. I clung instead to one article that claimed being overweight could be a contributing cause of labral tears.

That was it, my eating disorder decided. I'm so heavy it strains my hips to run. Fuck me, I'm not taking time off for being fat. I pocketed my chit and kept running.

I ran no risk of learning grace, but I did learn one sane thing in my fevered quest to captain that team.

As an eighteen-year-old private, when the first NCO scolded we females weren't just here to date, I thought, panicked, *Oh my god, I'm so sorry, no, I'm not, I'm sorry, whatever made you think that's what I want, no, I'm sorry, I'll square that away.*

When I was a twenty-year-old lance corporal and heard the nth NCO scold we females weren't just here to date, I thought, tranquilly, *We fucking know that. Do you?*

One Commander's Cup, we received reinforcement. Somehow my battle cry echoed down the road to the Marine officers studying at the Naval Postgraduate School. A captain with red curls promptly showed up fifteen minutes before the race to run with us. She wound her way through the crowd with a strange quality. When she shook my hand, I felt my feet planting through the track and my head lift. What witchcraft was this?

The strange quality followed her through our warm-up mile. I stared at her, fascinated. It dawned: she seemed calm. A relaxed woman in the Marine Corps. It was the strangest thing.

It was a strange day for me. I'd had another nightmare-laden night, a vision of the bones of my leg pulverized into a wall. I felt unnerved, touching my own thigh, not sure I wouldn't feel the sharp edges of bone jutting out. The calm woman's simple existence felt like a bandage. I felt some of the hot frittering tension in the injury cool.

The other girls stared similarly slack-jawed. Leadership, among us? A Higher Up come down from on high to help us?

Her presence lit us with rocket fuel. We hammered in with the Air Force. Officiants called it a tie.

God, it felt like a win.

CHAPTER 16

COLD

Symptoms like "depressed spirits" and "agitations" were commonly seen as pain's causes, not its consequences. And medicine's ongoing fascination with the pathological power of women's impressionable nerves and delirious emotions meant that their pain was considered almost always more a matter of psychical feeling than physical fact.

—*Eleanor Cleghorn,* Unwell Women: Misdiagnosis and Myth in a Man-Made World

Medical knew when Marines offered a MCMAP course, the Marine Corps' take on martial arts. The morning waiting room, usually stubbornly devoid of woodland cammies, flooded with grinning lance corporals trying not to laugh because ribs were cracked, bloody toilet paper shoved up our noses. We flashed pocket flashlights in one another's eyes to check for concussions, which we bragged weren't a good enough reason to miss class. Not for us Marines.

I disliked MCMAP. I disliked Gerecht's alarm, which played the part of the "1812 Overture" where the cannons go off, a guarantee I started my morning with heart palpitations. I disliked the heavy plastic smell of the gym, echoing shouts of "KILL!" and being slammed repeatedly to the mats. I signed up anyway because, you know, Marine Corps.

MCMAP supposedly drew from Brazilian jiujitsu and krav maga, but I never felt fluidity in it. Instead we executed the same moves repeatedly until we wired in reaction. The goal, like a great deal of military training, was to eliminate thinking.

"When you're grabbed," intoned the instructor, "instinct is to seize up. But that makes it easier for him. You're doing some of the work for him. Remember getting your drunk buddy out of the car, how hard that is? Yeah. Do that. Go limp. Dead weight. Make him work for it. Williams. You look like a virgin in a strip club. *Relax*."

I couldn't remember how.

I did enjoy the bullring. One Marine stood in the center, and the rest of us circled around him. We had no division by gender—there was one other woman in the course—or weight class. As our instructor shouted, there was no choosing your opponent on the battlefield, as if perhaps we lived before the invention of close air support. Once we started to play, any one of us—or more—attacked the Marine in the center from any angle, any hold.

I fucking loved it. I fucking loved that moment standing alone in the ring, bracing for someone to tackle me. How I lived made sense here. Constantly acting like you are in danger *keeps you safe*. Fearing for your physical safety *is good for you*. Living braced for imminent disaster *is realistic*. The cold crunch of collision, the poorly named Jaws of Life. It could happen any time.

The truth is a healthy human body can withstand so much corrosion.

That might be one of the reasons eating disorders weren't seen as all that dire—they take such a long time to actually *kill* you.

First they make you cold. I'd been borderline cold forever—not as cold as I'd been at boot camp; I had a bit more meat on me—but eight or nine months into Farsi, real cold settled in.

In my gauntlet through medical I learned the color changing in my hands was a constriction of blood flow, a condition called Raynaud's disease. First the tips of my fingers turned white. Then my fingers. Then my fists. Standing at attention my hands tingled, then numbed. Like slipping on ice gloves, the numbness crawled upward, until I only had a sense of shoulder to elbow—then nothing.

Then cold infiltrated movement. My hands froze curled when I ran. They could be in supplication. They could be fists. I saw them as claws. At 0500 I ran into hotel lobbies and elbowed the bathroom hand dryer, holding useless hands under heat until they thawed.

Cold settled in my blackened hip. I lurched if I stood still for too long. Fall out, a sergeant bellowed, and I stumbled.

All of it made me mad—weakness!—and all of it made me run more, bloodless limbs be damned.

Cold crept into my organs. I threw up so frequently, the downward current of my digestive tract became confused. Food wasn't digesting right. I threw up food I'd eaten days before. I began to feel as I had after MCT, a weight in my gut, a compact bezoar that refused to budge. It felt sentient, a hostile worm. I tried to evict it by throwing up until I kind of thought I was going to rip myself apart.

One night the worm stirred. I woke gasping. For a second I thought I'd been stabbed.

The ER doctor waived it off as an ulcer or two.

"Try to manage your stress better," he said. "Are you a freshman?"

"I'm a Marine," I said through gritted teeth, which meant, *I feel no stress.*

"Oh," he said, strangely embarrassed. "Watch how much you drink, then."

I missed my own damn race that time, shitting in intestinal exorcism. *No wonder we never win*, I thought heatedly, keeled over in the ER bathroom in a fetal position, *if our captain is such a pansy.* When I left the hospital I hazed further shit out of myself running hills. I was angry and embarrassed to receive medical attention: I was still fat. The stabbing was probably from eating too much.

When I cramped home Gerecht tackled me.

"Are you *trying* to hurt yourself?"

"When the mind fails, the body must pay."

"And when the body fails?"

"I don't know, mind over matter or some shit."

For the first and only time Gerecht pulled rank on me. He ordered me to sit my already perfect ass down and drink a goddamn protein shake.

I shivered on the front step while Gerecht locked the door. He wrapped an arm around me, and we walked to Fisherman's Wharf.

In winter, festive sailors—civilian, Monterey Yacht Club, Sperry-wearing types—decorated their slips for Christmas, bright lights running the length of the masts. Electric lights blessed *PEACE ON EARTH.* Gerecht and I walked through the park walled by Spanish adobe. Civilians passed by laughing, porting plastic bags of carryout. A curly-furred dog ran up to us wagging its tight tail. Its owner called, and the dog sprinted off, panting toward bikers zipping along the recreational trail. The wharf smelled like saltwater and the fish laid on ice under slices of lemon.

It all felt very far away. A cinematic shot of a friendly hometown. A tall and handsome soldier, a woman in a form-agreeing gray overcoat on his arm. But the woman was faded, like she wasn't all the way there.

I felt stupefied. That morning an Army medic's face had changed when he read my blood test results. "Oh," he'd said. "You're right, you do feel shitty." He pointed at a red line on his screen. "There's your problem. You're hella anemic."

My thoughts were heavier, too, wrapped in gauze. Calm hid somewhere I couldn't reach with my hand down my throat. Only sharp things cut through the seafoam gauze. Honor and discipline, motivation by stabbing.

Didn't I know there was a war on? I didn't have time to take off. Did I think al-Qaeda was going to stop being a threat to American peace and prosperity while little Lance Peanut Williams sat down and took a *break*?

Gerecht ordered calamari. We watched the kelp sway under the wharf. For a moment I leaned against him, my eyes closed, and felt the watery reassurance this, too, would pass. His number was called, and Gerecht crunched through a baby squid with gusto, eyes closed appreciatively. He snapped the Styrofoam container shut.

As we walked past the plaza he reached for my hand. I shook my head and shied away. I didn't want to absorb calamari from his hands. What if I forgot, touched my mouth later before I'd washed my hands? What if I transmitted a molecule of God knew what oil they cooked calamari with into my mouth? And what if it were one of the awful chemically ones, and/or I accidentally consumed unsustainably sourced seafood and therefore contributed to the precipitous decline of the oceans, inadvertently participated in the impending collapse of fisheries worldwide?

Gerecht pulled back his hand, a shadow of hurt confusion across his face.

I wrapped my arms around myself. My fingers fit reassuringly into the spaces between my ribs. Despite that bony comfort, I felt like disappearing. I soothed myself by imagining what I would look like once I was thin. I smiled at Gerecht, the flaking plaster I put over not wanting to smile at all, and asked him if he enjoyed his food, in Farsi.

Home. My phone vibrated.

"Hey, gorgeous. You going to be okay tonight?"

I looked down. Guilt burned me as though I held a lover in my arms instead of a bowl of cookie dough. Gerecht hated when I threw up at the apartment. "Yeah. I'm going to be fine."

Hope waded through Gerecht's tired voice. "Please be?"

I swallowed surreptitiously so he wouldn't hear.

Gerecht was on duty in the Army HQ, leaving the apartment under my management overnight. Which meant I'd smashed through the door hours earlier, armfuls of grocery bags dangling in orbit around me, shed my shoes, ripped off my coat, and barricaded myself in the galley kitchen. No point in putting the food away. Cardboard granola boxes relieved of every sickening calorie fell over on the counter.

After splattering the toilet with blood-speckled vomit yet again, I sopped myself up and wobbled to the bedroom. My head spun—the bulimic take on drunken spins. The glass door creaked when I slid it open. I stepped onto the narrow deck. Sea lions barked at the wharf. Bells clanged from sailboats, half muted in the fog.

The seclusion of the bedroom felt hallucinogenic, confined, when I stepped inside. I kept the lights off, welcoming the nuzzling darkness.

Gerecht kept his gun in his sock drawer, half buried under random debris. Ear plugs from the rifle range, stray sheets of Farsi. He used to keep the sidearm on the plastic bin we used as a bedside table, but it freaked me out in a way I couldn't explain, seeing it every time I went in or out of the bedroom. He said it was pointless to keep a loaded gun across the room, and I said it was pointless to keep a loaded gun at our heads, and he said well it wouldn't go boom unless one of us pulled the trigger, and I said that was exactly what I was afraid of, and he didn't understand, but he moved it.

Marines were dying out there, and I was throwing up cookie dough. The word execution stamped across my brain. Weighed (many times each day) and found wanting. I deserved to be taken out and shot for my failure to get my shit together.

I took Gerecht's gun out of the sock drawer. The weight of the 9mm felt awkward when I turned it to myself. Once I'd read an old school Texas military execution was a shot not to the head, but to the chest. Something to do with honor. Probably more pain. The barrel rested left of my sternum. I kept my finger straight and off the trigger until I intended to fire.

I worried I'd fuck it up. I *would* be that idiot who missed at point-blank range. I placed my palm against my chest, trying to feel where my heart was, exactly where to aim.

Under my hand, I felt my heartbeat.

I felt its surprising urgency.

I put the gun away.

CHAPTER 17

MENTAL HEALTH DAY

We take a certain sick pride in the fact that we know the caloric and fat content of every possible food on the planet, and have an understandable disdain for nutritionists who attempt to tell us the caloric content of anything, when we are the gods of caloric content and have delusions of nutritional omniscience, when said nutritionist will attempt to explain that the average woman needs a daily diet of 2,000 or more calories when we ourselves have been doing JUST FUCKING FINE on 500.

—*Marya Hornbacher,* Wasted

Gerecht paused Jon Stewart to watch me cut steamed baby carrots into six bites each. I pronged one bite and rolled it fastidiously through a mountain of salt. "Is that all you're eating for dinner?"

"Yes."

"How far did you run today?"

"Not far."

"And by that do you mean like eight miles?"

"Yes."

"Please talk to someone," my beloved friend said. "Please."

"I'm getting kind of concerned with this, um, eating disorder thing," I told Sergeant Wolf.

"How about spend a few days in an I-love-me jacket?" my squad leader suggested, spitting dip into a Gatorade bottle. "I have a buddy who goes crazy every six months or so, loses his shit for a few days in a padded room, comes back. He's senior enlisted, so obviously it works for him."

Sergeant Wolf was one of the former infantry, now-relaxed-beyond-boot-comprehension types. Dip bulged his lower lip perpetually.

"Look, Williams, you have no good reason to have an eating disorder. First, like, this,"—he indicated the barracks parking lot—"This is nothing compared to deployment."

"Aye, Sergeant."

He gazed over my shoulder. "And second—look, Williams, I don't know how to tell you this, but, like, we—the other NCOs and me—you know, we talk. We think . . . Look, we all agree, we think you're . . . attractive. All of us," he said quickly, defensively. "You really don't need to make yourself throw up."

"Thank you, Sergeant, but that's really not why I have an eating disorder."

He shrugged. "Well, let's get it sorted. Go down to mental. See what they have to say."

The Army psychiatrist pulled out a Rorschach test.

"Ehm, isn't this test sort of considered obsolete?" I asked, trying to meet his eyes over the black-and-white splotched card, which was obviously the pelvic skeleton. "Or at least controversial, sir?"

"Do you think so?"

"Um."

"We don't have to do this," he said, pointedly setting the stack in his lap. He had long gray fingers. "I thought you wanted help. If you're not willing to trust the psychiatric process, however—"

"No," I pleaded, "I apologize. Please go ahead."

"Are you sure? I have Marines and soldiers who need my help."

"I beg your pardon, sir."

He nodded after we went through the stack, satisfied. I hadn't seen a damn thing but dissected body parts. The sacrum, an epiglottis, pelvic organs, a thyroid. "Well, the good news is you're not particularly depressed."

"Yes, sir." Oh, well, thank God. Guess everyone lulls themselves to sleep with thoughts of suicide. I told him so, struggling to be polite, but he shook his head. "Not depressed," he repeated, smug.

A few days later Master Guns called me into his office. The Army psychiatrist had sent his notes. If I were as bulimic as I claimed, it read, it was the professional opinion of the shrink that my teeth would be rotting out of my head. Eating disorders were usually just a stage, he advised. She's not too depressed to come to work in the mornings, is she? So she's fine.

Fortunately Master Guns accepted my furiously hissed argument that I'm in the goddamn Marine Corps, no flippin' shit I come to work in the mornings, Master Guns.

The psychiatrist never even looked at my teeth. As a matter of fact, they wouldn't begin to loosen until the ripe old age of twenty-five.

٢

I told Sergeant Wolf that didn't go so well.

"Try the nutritionist," he advised.

The nutritionist flung straightened blond hair over a bony shoulder. "Okay!" she cheered. She held up a USDA food pyramid. "There are three major kinds of energy. Protein, fat, and carbs, or carbo*hydrates*!"

Oh, really?

"So why don't we come up with a meal plan for you," she asked excitedly. She pulled out a chart. I perked up. "Tell me what you normally eat in a day."

I did. I picked a day where my head wasn't in the toilet.

"That sounds so perfect! You eat even better than I do!" she admired. "All these vegetables! And no processed or animal foods? This doesn't seem disordered at all! Why don't we add yogurt in the mornings, though, hmm? For more calcium? It's especially important for us women."

"Um," I said. "Yes, ma'am."

She beamed. "Most of my clients are overweight," she said confidentially. "It's so good to see someone taking care of themselves before then! Not that you have to worry about *that* if you eat like this! You're going to be just fine, Lance Corporal."

"Thank you, ma'am."

I diagnosed her as a fellow orthorexic and dropped the meal plan in the dumpster outside the barracks.

٣

"Er, Sergeant . . ."

"Try Navy Behavioral Health."

"Aye, Sergeant."

The older gentleman interviewing me made dignified sniffing sounds. "So tell me about yourself before you came in," he asked. "What were you doing?"

Voices and laughter of Marines and sailors in the office carried through the walls of the cubicle. This didn't feel like the place to spill my guts. The gentleman in civilian clothing took notes with a silvery pen.

"I was living in Los Angeles, sir. I worked in a medical office and worked nights at a theater, kinda played around with modeling. Took a few English classes through UCLA."

"Oh?" he raised his eyebrows. "What sort of theater? Was it burlesque?"

"Ummmm. No, sir, just a little one in Hollywood. Called the Elephant."

"What about that modeling? Was it nude?"

"It was not."

"Not even for art classes?"

Seriously?

۴

In class I overheard a senior airmen counsel a younger man with a toothache. "You are the subject matter expert on your own health. Military orders can't overrule that. No one at any point knows more about your own health than you."

Galvanized, I marched back to behavioral health and asked, um, please, for, maybe, a different therapist. They could pencil me in in three weeks for a Skype session.

Over the computer screen, this psychiatrist, a Marine officer, was polite and professional. At the end of our session he said he admired me. He emphasized I was unlike other enlisted Marines because I was intelligent. I wondered if this officer had actually met enlisted Marines.

I remembered angry McCone screaming in fluent French and Harvey throwing down tracts of Christopher Hitchens from memory, a friend in Korean casually picking up Mandarin "as long as I'm here." Admittedly, angry McCone had also flung knives, and Harvey had only gotten rid of that stupid stripper T-shirt after I threatened to clean the urinals with it, and my friend in Korean also had dry-erase chemical equations on his mirror for "explosives we could easily make with field-day supplies," so, yeah, we had our issues, but the crayon-eating trope could honestly go die in a fire. Still, effectively insulting every friend I had was a minor demoralization, relatively. I went to schedule another appointment.

"He's been transferred out of the district."

Of course.

۵

Time to call in my secret weapon: civilian health insurance.

I called my dad.

"Well, the silver lining of that socialist in the White House is you are still on my health insurance," my father said. "Can you handle the co-pay?"

"I'll find a way. What is it?"

"About ten dollars."

"Oh! Definitely yeah then. Sorry, Dad."

Unbelievably freeing, finding my own doctor. The compassionate, tall woman named Joy had warm golden eyes. She welcomed me into her Cass Street office, a sunny attic full of books and ferns curled over textured paintings of the ocean, soft sage candles, sea glass, and absolutely no recruiting posters.

For our first session we simply sat. She sat so calmly, so easily. She was a large woman, but seemed unaware she should be freaked out by it. For most of that first hour I silently stared at the draping plants, the gentle flames of the candles. Every surface was soft. Joy sat across from me and smiled gently whenever I dared look at her. Her golden eyes betrayed no hint of impatience, no worry of our time slipping away like sand in an hourglass. Joy did not mind silence.

And then there was a voice in the attic, and the voice was quiet and tired and angry and sad. The voice surely couldn't be mine—saying all I thought and felt. The voice loved the Marine Corps but hated herself. The voice hated her eating disorder, actually, but had very recently learned she loved things like jade plants and soft-flickering candles.

Joy's eyes never wavered. I often looked away, uncomfortable with prolonged eye contact. But each time I glanced back, Joy looked at me with love—active, bodhisattva love—even when all she knew of me was I was quiet and tired and angry and sad.

I went back every week with militant consistency.

With Joy as witness, what came out was sorrow. Mourning so deep and fluid, I felt again like a whale, but this time in saltwater.

No one knows why some people get PTSD.

Four Marines—a fire team—can be in the same event. A vehicular collision, for instance. Three of them will walk away shook, laugh it off, have a beer when they get home.

One of them will think about it every day for the rest of their life.

There were four of us in the car.

Chad laughed, when the car spun across the intersection, before, I think, its accordion fold. The car seat which held my infant brother Sam fell over on Chad, and Chad held an arm over the startled baby.

The gourds in my lap spilled onto the floor. It was October, and we were coming home from the farmers market. Chad was in the backseat because we had an orange pumpkin in the front seat. He was only six, too small to really sit in the front, but it was 1994 and sometimes our mother let him.

I didn't lose my brother. The orange pumpkin was smashed to pulp. So was the front of the car.

Airbags weren't yet mandatory. My mother's body hit the steering wheel with force. I don't know if it was during the spin, the tornado centrifuge, or when we stopped. Cause of death, internal bleeding.

This is a story I don't know how to tell. The mystical and the mundane wrapped together. My mother stepping out of the car. My mother holding my hand, and holding Sam, and Chad holding her arm, and walking us across the intersection, traffic suspended. A halo around the four of us, all movement stopped but us. I remember that perimeter, the circle of quiet. My mother placing me, and my brothers, to the care of firefighters. I remember being held by the firefighter. I remember the raincoat, plastic smell of his uniform. I remember my mother telling me, "Do whatever this man tells you." I can see her face; I was in his arms, and I must have turned to look at her. Her dark hair like mine. Her thick glasses like mine. My mother.

Then my memory scratches. She's not standing with us. She's clear across the intersection—how did she get over there?—on a stretcher, unmoving.

I remember the smell of burning rubber.

Fun fact, Chad remembers that too. Not the rubber. That last thing our mother told us. *Do whatever this man tells you.*

Our mother didn't get out of the car. She didn't walk us across the intersection. She was smashed into the dashboard, and the firefighters had to use poorly named Jaws of Life to remove her from the mangled car.

Something moved into my body that morning in October, some permanent gasp. Some deep and incredible fear, some knowing: It could happen any time. Brace yourself.

What I remember best is the smell of burning rubber.

We were almost home. The intersection was at the base of the long, steep uphill to our house on the ridge. We passed it, my family and I, almost every day, from the accident when I was four until we left West Virginia when I was twelve. We drove through that intersection en route to school and church and the park. We passed Corridor G for groceries and soccer and the pool and ballet.

I always smelled burning rubber.

I legitimately thought that's just what that intersection smelled like now. In snow, in rain, in summer. In October. I was amazed for years that the accident had left such a permanent imprint, such lasting proof. That a collision between two cars had been enough force to brand concrete with the scent of burning.

Not until years later did I mention this to my family, only to find they had no idea what I was talking about.

Your imagination, they said.

I wasn't dreaming. I never dreamed about the accident. I'm only a few months away from another thing, the church hallway thing. That, I will dream about. The smell of rubber was not in my dreams. In my waking, conscious world, I never again passed that intersection without smelling the snub of a torch, black tire skid marks where another car had slammed into ours and sent my family spiraling into strange orbits. Toward religion. Toward gripping things like church, or school, or standards just a little too hard, like the gripping itself would hold us on Earth. It spun me off, just a little to the left, and I went someplace where mostly I only wanted to be still and left alone. Where I always remembered things a tiny bit differently. Saw things a little closer to where they cast shadows. Where details lasted. Where insignificant wounds left scars. Where sun glinted off the warning smell of burning.

I only realize right now, this second as I write this, that the black tire marks might not have been there either.

No one knows why some people's bodies shake things off.

And some people's bodies do not, cannot, will not, ever forget.

I had about two months.

Maybe less.

I don't remember.

Sometimes I think nothing happened. It's pure neurotic fixation, that this thing followed me for twenty years. Maybe What Happened was innocuous. Maybe an elder grabbed my hand to stop me, and the jolt was enough. I was already shook; the accident had been weeks before. Maybe what changed the world was so simple.

It's all forensics. I don't remember a damn thing of what happened.

My body does. I don't. It's like feeling around in the dark, real dark, coal-mine dark, feeling the bruised edges of shins banged into furniture to know where the real objects are. That's how I feel it anyway, how to hold a memory from before I had language.

I remember after. I curled under a chair outside the bishop's office—my dad's office—and pretended I had a shell, like the tortoises my brothers and I found in the garden. I pulled myself inside the hard carapace and tried very hard to pull it shut. I'd stay until someone told me it was safe to come out. Who needs space? Not me. I don't want to take up space. I don't want to be here at all.

So began the first long tendril root of an eating disorder: I was four, and began to wonder if it was possible to crawl out of one's own body.

Why was I in the hallway alone? After church we waited, my brothers and I, after our mother had died, for Dad's bishopric meetings.

My brother Sam was a baby in my dad's arms. Chad was invited to join the meeting. He beamed at me as the door closed. It was good for him to see what priests did: one day he, too, would be one. I would not. I was a girl.

I sat outside the bishop's office, where earnest men prayed fervently for the good of their families, and I waited alone in the hall.

I didn't have words for it. For any of it.

The words I had were "private parts." Their very unnamable-ness suggested bodies were something we didn't talk about.

I couldn't say it felt like something had closed. That my tailbone had a flat edge to it, like roadkill. That my pelvis had *shifted*. That something was wider that very much did not want to be. Space had been opened, something hidden and mysterious, and now closed like a fist. If it didn't, I kind of thought my insides would drop out between my legs. I felt like I'd been disemboweled; a soft clay bowl at the bottom of my core holding everything in and steady had been upended, shaken out. This was the worst part, and the genesis of my belief a body expanding was a body dissolving.

It's funny. In seminary I learned the holiest place in a Mormon church building is the bishop's office. Not the baptismal fount or the chapel, but the place people go when they need help.

My dad—my bishop when I was a child, my seminary teacher as a teenager—told me, "It's in the bishop's office that the power of the atonement can be called forth. Where that sacrifice has meaning on Earth. It's where people can feel clean again."

When Mormons doubt or fear or know they've fucked up, the counsel is always the same: talk to your bishop. A bishop doesn't make you chant Hail Marys or give you a penance—that isn't a Mormon thing. A bishop reminds you God still loves you.

It was in the bishop's office where someone feeling broken could feel remade.

But not everyone was allowed inside.

CHAPTER 18

ZENAN

Reading does not necessarily lead to direct political action, but it fosters a mindset that questions and doubts; that is not content with the establishment or the established.

—*Azar Nafisi,* Read Dangerously

Hunger drove me into the Monterey Public Library. I read ravenously, especially when I was actually ravenous and couldn't be trusted near food. I stood in muddy running shoes—standing, obviously, because it burned more calories—and read every Persian writer I could find.

To read about the Islamic Republic of Iran in 2010 was inevitably to read about women. I wasn't on a women's rights mission when I stormed the library. I wanted to be a better Marine, a more informed linguist. Still I started to pick up stories that forced me to make room in my stale understanding of what it meant to be a girl.

The Islamic Republic instituted explicitly sexist laws. A woman couldn't work, travel, or leave the country without a husband's permission. A woman's blood money—her value in compensation to her family after fatal accident—was worth one-half of a man's, while his testimony in trial was worth twice hers. The visual representation of putting women in their place was the mandatory veil. I read enough to know there were

Muslim women who chose to wear the veil to honor their faith and that was cool, but also, having taken some Mormon prerequisites in modesty, I empathized with the Iranian women incensed at being told how to dress themselves, who didn't feel inclined to dress by regulation lest their bodies tempt men. The veil's mandate was predicated on the assumption that having a female body was an invitation to violation, and it was the responsibility of the owner of a female body to prevent violation by covering herself appropriately. And who should decide what is appropriate? The male clergy doing the gazing, obviously.

Iranian women weren't silent. They used their voices when doing so endangered themselves and their families. That year a pro-government paramilitary group murdered a young woman as she marched in protest, so it was a woman's face softly smiling from posters carried like flags in marches against the regime. Women activists and journalists were beaten or disappeared to the notorious Evin Prison.

What I read by Iranian and Iranian American women made me blink and jab my finger at the words feeling, *Yes. Yes, exactly. This is real. Not alone.*

Living between the rock of religious rule and the hard place of leaving your family. Practicing silence as a tool. Trying to understand how to walk your own devotion to God while dreading the God who wrapped you in layers, packaged your virginity and modesty in suffocating gauze, the God who simplified your worth to your relationship with men. Men having inborn insight to understand scripture better than you ever can, no matter how devoted your study, and therefore intrinsically being God's chosen leaders. That emptiness, the feeling you've lost some integrity, when anyone who feels empowered to stop you on the street does so and scolds, Your appearance is suggestive, I can see you're a girl through that chador (or through that uniform), square it away, for shame! Figuring out how to play an awful high-stakes game where you won by being desired but lost for desiring. Stories of censorship: captivity by language, for saying the wrong thing, but liberation by it as well, for speaking out.

I was one hungry girl living on one small outpost of the Marine Corps, not an Islamic theocracy. I would hear every argument it was an imperfect comparison. It wouldn't change how deeply Iranian women's stories filled me with fire and awe.

As my Farsi improved, I followed the news obsessively. Iranians marching the streets was the first time I witnessed defiance, the first time I saw women reject judgment by appearance, condemnation by assumption. I needed to see dissent was an option. I needed to see that disagreeing with power instead of accepting what power told you was all wrong with you was (oh, my heretical Lord) an . . . option?

Marines' casual condemnation of women Marines who—grab your Article 15s—wore mascara, joked, laughed, or wore a skirt to a bar off-duty, the way we scolded that we shouldn't do such *suggestive* things lest we be mistaken for whores, and that daring to do such terrible things was reiterated when a female Marine said she'd been sexually harassed or assaulted, that these things *somehow had bearing* on whether we believed her—this sounded painfully parallel to morality police beating women who dared allow an inch of hair peek out underneath veils. *Well, were you asking for it?*

Why in God's name was it the length of our skirts on trial when a woman reported rape?

From Mormons to Marines I'd absorbed a similar message. Be modest, in appearance and temperament. Keep yourself locked down for your own good. *Your own good* concealed an implicit threat: *or something bad will happen to you.* Under *this*, the nasty implication: *and you will have deserved it.* But . . .

Wasn't it the zealot flinging acid in women's faces who was a criminal? Yes? When you didn't bother naming sexual harassment because you kinda knew it wouldn't matter?

And what about those of us to whom the Something Bad had already happened? Did it prove there was something bad about us? Or was the Something Bad actually—this was wild—*not our fault or failure*?

In the cool shelves of the Monterey Public Library, reading began to counter my blind acceptance that fault burrowed in Eve's flesh. It only shifted a sigh, my own sexism against female Marines. But enough to get my head out of the toilet long enough to go, Wait. Hang on . . .

We're *all* kind of unhappy?

CHAPTER 19

HEALTH AND WELLNESS

If the feminine issue is so absurd, is because male arrogance made it "a discussion."

—*Simone de Beauvoir*

Gerecht and I spoke Farsi at home. We waded through stacks of text professors sent home before the sobering final exam.

We sat close to each other as we studied. When his arm brushed mine I wondered again. To give up on a good thing because you're not ready: grace, or cowardice? I stayed awake until I gave up on sleep and rolled out of bed to run. At dawn the sky paled pink over the water. Still I couldn't shake what I knew was true.

I had begun to doubt I was ever going to get my head out of the mathematical wonderland. I had started to think, again, about a path too narrow for more than one to cross.

Wherever I was going, I wanted to be alone.

When our final scores were posted the class stampeded the bulletin board. Professors beamed, congratulating us, shaking hands. Gerecht pumped his fists and bounced on his feet over my head, so he saw it first. We'd both passed. I stared incredulously. We'd both done *well.*

After Farsi, the Marine Corps assigned me to Afghan Dari, "the language you'll actually be using." We called it "the Farsi they speak in Afghanistan." Only airmen and Marines had the six-week conversion course, which meant that while I would stay in Monterey, my laughing soldier would rejoin his combat unit in North Carolina. Things shifted as we knew they would, days boxed into checklists and PCS schedules and acronyms. I carted seabags back to my barracks room one by one.

The last night in the empty apartment we threw a sleeping bag on the living room floor. Everything else had been shipped back to Fort Bragg. *This is the last time I'll brush my teeth next to this person*, I thought dully. All through the night Gerecht ground his teeth in his sleep.

In the morning we stood next to each other and pulled on our blouses. He hugged me at the threshold. "Are you sure?" My hair muffled his voice. "Please change your mind."

I nodded. I meant no.

Full means something different when you are bulimic. It does not mean enough. It means everything. Full is when there is nothing left to eat, when the pantry is empty, shelves scraped bare, trash rummaged for stray crusts. Bulimic enough is grasping, groping fear of not enough. Bulimic full strains and tears.

I did not yet understand relationship was allowed to be gentle. Gerecht was too decent to dream of owning anyone. He never yanked on the reins, never tried to push. So I figured he didn't really give a damn.

A sinking realization, home being the barracks again. The lock beeped at my key card. My room stood inspection-ready as it had for the last year, crisp sheets stretched tight enough to bounce a quarter, folds creased at forty-five-degree angles. I'd stopped in to dust before room inspections.

Bulimia sucked enough living with Gerecht. Now I had no brakes. No one to interrupt hours inspecting flesh in front of the mirror. No one to hammer on the bathroom door.

I closed the door and set my cover down. I dropped to my knees on the carpet. I folded my arms, bowed my head, and closed my eyes, as Mormon children are taught to pray.

I didn't move for hours.

As if by holding myself in the shape of grace, even as my mind reeled off in all directions, I could hold myself together.

Inspections composed minor, if constant, nuisances of life. Uniform and room and barracks and wall locker. Normally on Fridays an NCO walked in the barracks room, glanced around, and left. Notes issued in variations of: "Not on fire. Check." "Excellent gaming console. Check." We Febreze-bombed the oxygen out of the barracks. It wasn't unusual to see someone slamming their barracks door, coughing on chemical lilac mist. "Smell: good. Yup, squared away." Sometimes guys felt sassy and hung borderline pornography on the barracks walls to make the inspecting NCOs grin or grimace, because garrison Marines were pretty much kids with a paycheck.

These were our weekly inspections: a few hours of cleaning, boot banding our blankets flat, a cursory check. Occasional tomfoolery with cleaning supplies. Not a big deal.

Then there were the unfortunate health and wellness inspections. They were battalion-wide shit shows. Like North Korean nuclear preening, they correlated none too subtly with changeover in leadership.

Rumors sank through the lance corporal underground that Higher Ups themselves were under investigation, not only the Marine detachment but across DLI, concerning suspicious suicides at the Presidio. What better way to instill good order and discipline than drilling in the rule of law?

Health and wellnesses were annoying as all get out, which, like most attempts to regulate our private lives, didn't stop them from being kind of hilarious.

Higher Ups announced health and wellness inspections at impromptu all hands, designed to give us no warning. At the order to fall out, stripes of barracks dwellers streamed through the woods. Even if you didn't have anything, some idiot in your platoon probably had a shiv or something. Married Marines, who lived off base, came on hand and whisked away Kabars and gin. Marines who owned cars passed keys around. Something like loyalty informed our frantic smuggling. We believed health and wellnesses were really a will-you-protect-your-guys exercise, because we were boots and therefore ridiculous.

Annoyed senior NCOs who would really much rather not be pawing through junior enlisted underpants combed through our rooms, checking as if for ticks in dark moist places. Drawers overturned, wall lockers rummaged, uniforms thrown on the floor with cargo pockets rifled. We stood in cammies outside our rooms at increasingly slack parade rest until the Presidio was scoured.

The primary captures were expired painkillers from medical, knives longer than three inches, and alcohol. The confiscation of the lattermost often turned into something resembling a speakeasy turnout. Marines underage or with a roommate under twenty-one were allowed no alcohol in their room; Marines above twenty-one were authorized to have a six pack of beer or one bottle of wine. Theoretically, no other alcohol was permissible. In reality we reeked with it. This was why you had to be careful swiping a bottle of grape Gatorade Zero from your alcoholic fire team leader's fridge on the way to a combat fitness test, as I'd long ago learned from Harvey, because it could be heavily spiked with an appealing heady taste your recovering-Mormon self doesn't yet appreciate as vodka and then may the good Lord take mercy on your lightweight ass on the CFT.

NCOs stood with their hands in their pockets grinning, as grumbling SNCOs came out of the barracks with handles clinking in each hand.

They frowned over sometimes literal wheelbarrows of alcohol like police officers in a Prohibition-era bust. The NCOs laughed at us mercilessly, then went about trying to get their guys' shit back to them.

Higher Ups slapped us with a health and wellness shortly after I moved back into the barracks. I was the only non-NCO squad leader in my platoon and I had a question. I was geographically too far removed from another female to holler and ask, and if you are in formation, it'd better be a damn important text. I didn't know who I could ask without wanting to shrivel up and die, anyway; my chain of command was male from my platoon sergeant all the way up to Commandant James T. Conway.

Dismissed to line up in front of our doors. "If anyone's got something, you'd better tell me now," Corporal Kingsley shouted at his squad as they fell out. "I'll try to help your sorry asses, but you'd better tell me now."

I hung back to consult Corporal Sebastian, an Okinawa Marine, who was pompous but essentially alright. "Um, Corporal," I asked. "Um."

I am going to die a thousand deaths. "Um . . . theoretically . . . if . . . I had a . . . vibrator, would it be a . . . problem?"

"Jesus! Williams, why the fuck do you have a . . . ?"

I stayed silent, feeling the question answered itself.

He ran his hand over a quick turn of his mouth and followed me inside.

Corporal Kingsley stormed through mid-orchestration. "Alright, who has a Kabar? There's always one of you island-hopping motherfuckers."

Corporal Sebastian mumbled something. Corporal Kingsley snorted and said something as he stomped over that finished with "Ah for God's sake it's just a dick."

I wished I'd waited to figure it out with my new roommate, Torres. Her eyes turned wide as I showed up to our room with two NCOs looking at me like I'd burned the flag.

Corporals Sebastian and Kingsley and my roommate and I—as well as everyone within earshot, which included my squad—held an impromptu theological council. It turned out absolutely no one had any idea if vibrators are Authorized for Sensitive Unspecified Use in the barracks. There was no way this conversation hadn't been had before, maybe in a military branch where women had more significant representation, but it certainly felt like we were having it for the first time.

"Could it be used as a weapon?" Corporal Kingsley asked curiously. "Could you use it to club someone to death?"

"Maybe?"

"Oh fuck, *really*?"

"It would not be the first thing I grabbed," I said, then heard myself. Kingsley looked delighted and Sebastian horrified. "Oh fuck, God, no . . . I mean as a weapon of opportunity. It would not be the first thing I grabbed if the barracks got broken into, and, like, I had to kill somebody, Corporal."

"Now I'm curious. What would you use?"

"There is a very solid stake by my wall locker, Corporal."

"You've really thought about this."

Yeah, I'd put it there.

Corporal Sebastian coughed. "Can we talk about the *dildo*, please?" His voice dropped to a hissed whisper. "I don't want my Marines looking like they're Just Here to Date."

I bit my lips. "Technically, Corporal, er . . . it could be taken to mean I . . . am not . . . dating . . ."

Corporal Sebastian deepened to maroon, mustache bristling. "Is it allowed or not, devil dog?"

Corporal Kingsley insisted. "But you *could* kill someone with it?"

There was a deep hum under my rib cage. Kingsley was going to break me. If I started laughing I wouldn't be able to stop. If I started laughing I was going to laugh myself into a different human, crack right out of my cold tight tendinous body. I wrestled my shit together.

"Corporal, if I really had to I guess I could probably choke someone out with it."

My roommate broke in. "Gunney Tenner said females *should* get dildos," she pointed out, loyally.

Oh god. DLI's sole female gunnery sergeant, she who denounced us, and I quote, "shitbag taints." When she called a female all hands, I commandeered the run team and ran miles off base. Run team was unusually popular that day. We weren't surprised to hear we'd missed another expletive-punctuated lecture to all us (fucking) females to stop being (fucking) whores, keep it in our (fucking) pants, and get a (fucking) dildo.

"Williams can say she was following orders."

Unexpectedly Kingsley mused poetic on dicks as classic iconography of the art of the Marine Corps. The artistic trope of the phallus was drawn on port-a-shitter walls from Lejeune to Leatherneck. With the medium of Sharpie on polyurethane walls, Marine Corps artists portray the penis with exceptional and detailed artistic commitment. The NCO reminisced fondly on a particularly impressive port-a-shitter fresco in Iraq, featuring a fantastic and fastidiously anatomical Sharpie sketch of dicks in Kevlar riding dick horses into battle, brandishing dick swords against dragons who were, amazingly, also dicks.

"Is it realistic? We can say it's, like, a statuette."

"It is pink, Corporal."

"Fleshy pink?"

"Neon, Corporal."

"Whatever, we can make it work. Williams, get two and cross them on the wall."

I recalled weddings and masses which both (thankfully rarely) went down in the barracks. "Like the arch of steel, or, like, a crucifix?"

"Fucking Christ, warrior," Kingsley sounded inspired. "You're going to need more."

"Will someone please shit me out the regs on this?" Corporal Sebastian shrieked.

In the end the NCOs stood in my door frame and grinned/panicked respectively as a SNCO turned over my clothes. There was no way he didn't see the pink plastic, but I guess he really, really didn't want to talk about it.

Health and wellness. Nice to know they cared.

I didn't live in the barracks long.

A few weeks later I came home from a long salty run and checked my phone, an old flip phone I rarely carried. I opened it to a string of texts from a Marine I vaguely knew, a former infantry guy and the acting barracks NCO.

<I'm in your room. It smells nice. Like you.>

Followed, an hour later, by, <Where are you? I'm worried about you.>

The next day I introduced myself to a female NCO in the S shops and said I'd heard she had a room for rent. She lived out in Fort Ord, a semi-decommissioned Army base twenty minutes north of the Presidio.

I moved in that weekend.

CHAPTER 20

DARI

People take the feeling of full *for granted. They take for granted the feeling of steadiness, of hands that do not shake, heads that do not ache, throats not raw with bile and small rips of fingernails forced in haste to the gag spot. Stomachs that do not begin to wake up in the night, calves and thighs knotting in muscles that are beginning to eat away at themselves. They may or may not be awakened at night by their own inexplicable sobs.*

—*Marya Hornbacher,* Wasted

In southern Afghanistan Harvey manned a machine gun on an MRAP, an armored vehicle designed to withstand IEDs. He sent video of his convoy rattling through Sangin markets. Though a language-enabled analyst, he volunteered for the turret with characteristically dry logic that his teammate had a fiancée, so, more reason to live. He wrote, "Guess who everyone wants to shoot at? The funny-looking MRAP with all the radio antennas sticking out of it. That would be ours."

Elsewhere in Helmand Province, Trom saw a Marine step on a Soviet-era pressure plate explosive. Trom wrote about brushing what he thought was ground hamburger off his notebook, focusing on his job in post-explosion adrenaline. The bits of meat were the Marine's leg.

Meanwhile I sat with my head between my knees in Joy's attic office.

I'd been blacking out daily. Stand up from my sock drawer in the morning, scene fades to black as I storm to the sink to spit toothpaste—never will I sit or be chill when I feel like I'm going to pass out, because fuck me, that's why—and then my hands are on the floor, toothbrush still in my cheek, the bristles chewed flat.

At the end of our hour I stood up and promptly sat back down.

"I feel two-thirds fainting goat," I told the floor irritably.

Joy passed me coconut water. "Maybe you aren't in the right world for you. Maybe you should go somewhere that encourages compassion."

I shook my head and wished I hadn't: it made me horribly dizzy. Marines don't just *leave*. You sign the dotted line to give your body for a war, not the eating disorder you aren't thin enough to have anyway.

Joy serenely dropped into the dark with me, sat cross-legged at my feet. The world was quieter with my hands over my head. Joy illuminated the foxhole. "If you want to leave, you can."

I gathered my knees into my chest. "I mean, okay, yes, bulimia is shitty. Profoundly fucking shitty. This cannot be how I live. But my friends are getting shot at. Marines are getting blown up, like, *on*to my friends. The whole bulimic depression thing isn't *that* bad. Real Marines have it a lot worse."

"The suffering of others doesn't benefit from your suffering."

"But this is nothing compared to what they're going through. *They* deserve compassion."

"Compassion isn't something you earn. It's something you practice. Like mercy."

I didn't want mercy either. I didn't want shit I hadn't earned.

I may have missed something about grace.

September 2010. Lady Gaga wore fifty pounds of raw meat as a dress to raise awareness for LGBTQ+ service members. As a queer, vegan-ish service member, I had absolutely no idea how I was supposed to feel about this.

In Dari a kind professor praised what he called the polite way I observed Ramadan with the teachers. We fasted for a month. Modified Ramadan, which included pots and pots of black coffee. Anything to make my insides less cold. I sat in the back of class and tended the coffeemaker like the Tomb of the Unknown Soldier at Arlington.

During Ramadan devotees fast from sunrise to sunset. I ran until well after dark to be on the safe side. I showered in the barracks and prayed in front of the microwave. I was deliriously excited at the discovery of hot food. I'd unearthed boxed soups at Whole Foods that tasted like *food*, for a divinely acceptable two hundred calories.

My tastes had changed. During Arabic and most of Farsi, it was bread. I wanted carbohydrates so badly I'd drink them like water if I could. The biggest thing I'd needed then was just a whole hell of a lot more calories.

In Dari, though, I craved heat. Wanted every swallow to burn like whiskey. I nuked soups until they congealed in rings around the carton, and still, after a few spoonfuls, microwaved it again. I craved intensity. Nothing could be too sour, too salty, too bitter, too acidic. I poured low-sodium soy sauce into the carton. Anything that scoured the emptiness, how far my spirit had gone out of my jaw.

Fasting, my dad said more than once, was not going without food. It was about thinking on God. Diverting attention inward and upward.

As the little box spun around in the microwave, I prayed this time faith would meet me halfway. If I really occupied hunger with God, if I converted all the lonely silences, those blank spaces when the thoughts in my head went empty, into a meditation, if I fasted with *purpose*, with the intention to just *listen*, this time, I would understand. I would understand how to live without wanting.

I loved studying Dari, its texture a tiny window into Afghanistan. But black edged the autumn weeks. I lived in an Arctic always-night. If I turned my head the world dimmed around my peripheries. I learned I needed to stand carefully between lectures, or a heavy black curtain fell over me and I crumpled to the ground. At my desk I gripped a paper coffee cup with always-cold hands, my face close to the rising heat.

Ramadan ended. A calm lingered. It felt so good to fast. I felt lightheadedness as a gift, a literal lifting up and out of my body by my ears. Such an enormous relief on my head and neck, to not forcibly vomit for hours. Compared to purging, passing out felt rather nice, actually. Like relaxing into oblivion.

Five of us in Dari, two Marines and three airmen. The quiet junior airmen would astound us by killing himself a year later. He laughed with us then, when the two senior airmen told stories of flight crews gone awry in Baghdad. The other Marine, Gunney Neilson, sat in front of me, sleeves thrown up haphazardly. He leaned back in his chair, roaring in laughter.

One bizarre morning I walked into class. The senior airmen were sniggering over a computer screen.

"Williams, you'll appreciate this," one said. "This new fat acceptance movement—can you believe it?"

They were laughing at images of women holding signs saying "beautiful," "beloved," "sexy," "valuable."

"'Fat acceptance," my friends laughed. "Who are they trying to kid?"

"God, is this a convention? How did the plane take off?"

"Another way of shrugging off personal responsibility. This one's in a bikini! This is making my morning. Williams, look at this."

I stared. The Black woman stood grounded as a mountain, a sign held across her hips. Her face was breathtakingly unafraid.

How radical it would be, to stand with that confidence. How incredible, to breathe into your edges. How holy, to claim to have a soul regardless of the shape of one's body.

The woman's sign read, "Worthy."

You could name that . . . for yourself?

I cleared my throat. "Why . . . would I 'appreciate' this?"

"Because you get it. You take care of yourself. If any of these had an ounce of the self-discipline you do, they'd lose two hundred pounds instead of pretending they're healthy as narwhals."

Their words sounded far away, as I heard most things those months. I felt like my words had farther to go to get to them, that theirs came down a long tunnel. I still recognized something about this was kind of wrong.

I said, "I don't think it's funny," so quietly I wasn't sure I'd said it out loud.

"Williams, come on. Would you ever let yourself get like this?"

In a small voice I said, "I think they're brave."

When they finished laughing they subjected me to the lecture people give people who don't hate fat people who don't hate themselves: They're a drain on the healthcare system ("our tax dollars, Williams, the money you make as a US federal employee goes to these women's triple bypasses so they can keep double fisting cheeseburgers"). They're impotently shaking fists in the face of the obvious fact that thin is healthy.

I let it go. At the water fountain I burrowed my fingers between my ribs. I felt like I had a point I could make, if I could find it. A point about thin maybe not being the best indication of health. About having no idea what's going on under anyone else's skin. But I couldn't quite find words. Words blurred under the black coffee and fourteen pounds of Splenda fighting gamely to keep me alive and learning Dari.

It was a landmark day for me, a bizarre split. I was, by Marine Corps Order 6113.0, officially underweight. Incidentally at night I'd started to burst awake as if from underwater. It infuriated me that my shitty body had found another way to shirk. Keep *breathing* through the night, was that asking so much? Sometimes a black demon grinned on my chest, skeletally thin yet dense as marble, and I sucked air like I was starving.

Taking care of myself—ha. Hahahaha. Yeah. I was doing great.

One November night the red barracks door slammed open. Gunney Neilson, my Dari classmate, hauled down the hallway. "Get fifth platoon," he hollered. "I want everyone in the common room ten minutes ago."

I flung down *The Things They Carried* and started banging doors. Marines rushed in with fervor for Gunney Neilson: we all liked him. It was as rare to see him in the barracks as it was to see him angry, face red with blotchy rage.

The gunney spoke low, but his voice shook.

"When I was in Iraq, I was on a helicopter flight crew. One of our jobs was medevac." Medevac—medical evacuation—meant casualties, injured Marines. The common room was quiet.

"I don't know how many times I saw a Marine's face when he realized the last thing he was ever going to see was the ceiling of that bird," the Gunney said softly. "I just spent the last six hours in the ER waiting room with some dumb eighteen-year-old private who decided he's suicidal. He's just sitting there, pleased as punch, and doctors are trying to put together a family who'd come in from a car accident."

I had a funny idea I knew where this was going. I wrapped my arms around my stomach.

"Let me make this clear," Gunney Neilson growled. "If any of you are thinking of getting out of work by claiming you feel like killing yourself because *Monterey* is too hard for you, either just do it, or get your head out of your ass. There are Marines doing a lot harder shit than sitting in class studying a language, I promise you that. I *promise* you that. Shit or get off the pot."

I stared at my boots.

He cooled down. "I'm not going to take up more of your liberty. Have a safe weekend, and remember why you're here." He shook his head. "I needed to tell you all. Every day a good Marine dies because he was in the wrong place at the wrong time. You don't have a right to choose what he didn't."

How badly I wanted to tell someone I dreamt of smashed highway guardrails. I hadn't stopped thinking about killing myself since, basically, I didn't know, last year? I'd developed a fixated awareness on the soft spots on my wrists, conscious of sharp edges. I Googled if I needed to drive up to San Francisco to drop my body off the Golden Gate Bridge or if Bixby would do it.

The night the gunney left I picked up *The Things They Carried*, resumed quietly reading, and tied a black ribbon around the only thoughts left in my blurry noggin that still came in loud and clear. Have a Marine's sense of purpose. Either do it, or get your head out of your ass. No one wants to hear about your agnostic suicidal tendencies.

That was the hardest thing, when I finally started to question things I heard. There were some genuine asshat Marines. But mostly, the worst shit I heard, the things that stuck with me, the things that silenced me, came from men I'd call friends. When men you admired said that kind of shit? Told you whatever you had going on really, truly did not matter?

God almighty. You don't forget it.

The last week of Dari I sat in the classroom, head between my hands, and stared at my workbook. Black, wispy Dari blurred. The long lines of script crawled into an intricate mandala and a rare lucid thought: I can either give in to Joy, who'd been increasingly begging me to seek inpatient treatment, or I can shut the hell up, be the best Marine I can be, and get my ass to Afghanistan.

My eating disorder screamed, *Stop being a little bitch and do your fucking job.* I agreed. Inspired, I snatched my water bottle and sprang up to refill it, planning a long run after class to redeem my doubt. I crashed to the floor.

I pulled myself up by a desk.

"Jesus," said an airman. "I thought you hit your head this time."

"Alright, sunshine," Gunney Neilson said cheerfully. "What the hell is going on?"

I'd passed out in class before but I'd always laughed it off. Clumsy. Whoops, dehydrated. Ah, you know, I run.

That morning the gunney called my platoon sergeant.

So I faced my new platoon sergeant, Staff Sergeant Manning, and admitted I had what I'd personally diagnose as one hell of an eating disorder, Staff Sergeant. There's no way he's going to believe me, I panicked. I'm too fat. He's not going to believe me.

To my astonishment Staff Sergeant Manning nodded. He believed me.

Joy nodded wisely when I told her about my precisely timed face plant. She said, "That sounds like a cosmic bitch slap."

With a sensitivity for which I was deeply grateful, Staff Sergeant Manning figured if I needed to stand in front of men, senior Marines, and talk about my body, I might like a woman beside me. He tapped in a friend of his, a staff sergeant in Indonesian with whom he'd deployed. The two senior NCOs marched me down the hallway. "Don't worry. We're going to Master Guns. Let's see what we can do."

Master Guns asked me my story.

"I'm still bulimic."

"Right," came his response, then paused confusion. "Wasn't this an issue a while back?"

"Yes, Master Gunnery Sergeant."

"You don't look like you've lost much weight since then."

Oh God, kill me now.

Staff Sergeant Carlisle spoke up. "You've been in the Corps twenty years, Master Guns. Haven't you ever seen a Marine get help for an eating disorder?"

"Sure I have. But in that case she was . . . it was clear she wasn't eating enough. Looking at you, I have a hard time believing you're throwing up every last bite of food you eat."

"Master Guns," I said, and wavered. Three senior Marines looked at me, really quite patiently. "People with eating disorders *eat*," I tried, "But we . . . do weird things with food. And we . . ." I sputtered, because Master Guns had leaned back, unimpressed, ". . . we have . . . like, it causes other health problems. It makes you crazy. The body stuff feels like the least of it."

Well, I'm sure now we all rate doctorates on the subject.

I swung for it. "You saying I don't look like I throw up every bite of food I eat, honestly, I hear that as, I should go puke harder."

"But you're not *fat*," Master Guns protested. "You don't need to lose weight, either. You're perfectly healthy, Williams. You don't need an eating disorder."

I opened my mouth and closed it again. I heard, *You're not skinny enough to have an eating disorder*, which I believed, because I had an eating disorder and therefore believed I was roughly the size of a caribou.

Senior NCOs didn't retreat so easily. "Master Guns, she's our Marine. She says she needs help."

"Well, is she ever late?"

"No."

"Skip things?"

"No."

"Complain?"

"No."

"Go on and off chit a lot?"

"No. She's a good little trooper."

"Then why is this a problem?"

Master Guns wasn't being sarcastic or rhetorical. He sounded genuinely confused.

And the fuck was I going to do, open my mouth right there in front of God and everybody? Confess, "I have an eating disorder so completely it's not so much that I have bulimia, it's more like I am bulimia. And if it means anything to anybody or anything, I miss being human. I miss thoughts that aren't food or bone. I'm hearing shit that isn't there, I think my last period was July, and I can't sleep through the night because I can't breathe. Also I am fucking freezing. My eating disorder has gotten so bad it makes the fact that by the way, and also, I think I've maybe very badly injured my hip, which, fun fact, is deeply related to my eating-disorders-make-you-insane theory, and even as I'm trying to figure out how to walk without pain, honestly, that seems like the least of my problems. I am very seriously considering putting an end to my life, and I beg you your help."

I could not possibly say this. To say this would, first, require words, intuition, and guts that were in the pounds I'd lost, over and over again for years. And to speak would admit I was hurting, a deep, all the way down to my bones kind of hurt, and I would not claim that. Because then I'd be a weaker female Marine and honestly fuck that, I'd rather keel over.

"Looking at you," Master Guns concluded, "It doesn't seem like whatever you've got going on with food is interfering with your ability to do your job."

I had the passing sensation I understood a witch trial. If she drowned, she was innocent after all.

That Saturday I came to with my face a few inches above a toilet bowl of puke, crouched in a civilian bathroom in downtown Monterey. Another lonely Saturday passed in the usual manner, wrappers littering my car floorboards, and puking myself clean. I jolted, alarmed by the unknown lapse of time passed out over the toilet. Rainwater had seeped under the door and pooled along my jeans. Had I gotten it all out, before passing out?

Without thought above vague regret I hadn't asphyxiated in my own vomit, I shoved a swollen hand in my mouth and resumed puking.

In my car I slouched over the steering wheel. Rain splattered on the windshield. What if I just drove south? Jerked down hard with my right hand, went off the steep cliffside road into Big Sur? Slipped over a guardrail? The windshield wipers tsked. How long would it take before anyone realized I was gone? It would be so easy, an accident, a watery day like this. Marines don't give up, but maybe they could give out.

I stared at my cover thrown on the dashboard. McCone had been the one to show me how to put a piece of cardboard into the front to make it stand up sharp. Marines liked to use condoms. I used my library card.

My phone vibrated.

<Good afternoon, Lance Corporal. I wanted to confirm we're running at 07 or 08 tomorrow.>

Shit. Stevenson.

Stevenson was one of the females the boys grinned about and said she wouldn't get much attention in the civilian world, so you had to forgive her for going a little nuts. Visibly pregnant, she'd sought me out to say she was turtle slow but liked running, had never run before boot camp, and could I maybe help her? Stony faced, I'd said if she was willing to try I could get her to run a 300 PFT post-baby. I'd wanted to hug her.

My icy hands shook, even in front of the blasting car heaters. <Thank you for following up. Yes, we're still on. Let's do 0700. Meet between the wings, if it's still raining we'll just do a joy run.>

Big Sur and the highway south would be there next weekend.

Harvey was the first person I honestly spoke to about PTAD: permissive temporary absence of duty. A leave of absence, essentially. Could I pull it off? Ask for three months off work, fly across the country to an eating disorder rehab center, learn how to eat like a normal human, come back and do this thing? I'll go quietly, I'll pay, I'll come back ready to fight.

"Do I deserve this?" I emailed him, as he was in Afghanistan. "Am I even sick? I'm still fat."

Harvey replied, "Yes, you actually are sick. Please go."

I said, "I've probably gained weight since whatever picture you've seen of me."

It was the only time his voice was harsh. He said, "Bailey, I'm not fucking around. Go. Now."

I formally requested three months to please get this bulimic lance corporal's head on straight.

Instead I went to ghost platoon.

PART III

WAKING

CHAPTER 21

GHOST PLATOON

The deal with so many chronic illnesses is that most people won't want to believe you. They will tell you that you look great, that it might be in your head only, that it is likely stress, that everything will be okay. None of these are the right things to say to someone whose entire existence is a fairly consistent torture of the body and mind.

—*Porochista Khakpour,* Sick

Every company had a ghost platoon. A part exempt. Marines with Something Going On, fallen out of order. We haunted administrative limbo waiting for some paperwork, somewhere, to go through.

When I reported to the Charlie Company office, Lance Corporal Aoife, shiny raven hair tucked into a heavy bun, sat hacking printer paper into snowflakes for a holiday party.

She announced, "Living in admin limbo is a Kafka whorehouse. They pay you, but they fuck you *inventively.*" She held up a snowflake critically. "This shit is mandatory. I'm trying to get a skull into each one." She handed me heavy scissors. "Wanna play Marine Corps arts and crafts?"

In the linear masculinity of the Marine Corps, Aoife caught me by surprise. She was the first Pagan I'd met in the flesh, for one thing;

she spoke Gaelic, kept an altar, and occasionally hexed Marines who annoyed her, wrapping up little spell bundles with twine.

Like me, Aoife had graduated Farsi; like me, she'd run herself into a diagnosis of a labral tear in her hip. Among many shuffling visits to medical, the clinical roulette of harassed doctors, stern nurses, and condescending E-4 Army medics, I had at one point been examined by the same doctor as Aoife. He'd recommended the same surgery. I figured I was too fat to take time off running for surgery and chose the "grit your teeth and deal with it in your impossibly far removed thirties" option.

Aoife chose surgery. Medical plugged her hip together with metal rods, eight inches more than they'd told her she'd need. They jokingly suggested she bring her X-rays to airports to get through metal detectors. Aoife turned her face to the wall when she pressed herself up from her chair. I rarely showered after a run without first pressing my hands into the walls, bending over to relieve the god-awful pressure in my hip, but watching Aoife's halting movement didn't convince me I'd made the wrong decision.

The other Charlie Company ghost, Koldar, graduated Russian and landed in admin limbo because he was overweight. A second failure to meet weight standards meant administrative discharge. Koldar waited in ghost platoon advocating for the Marine Corps to pay for skin-removal surgery.

"I've lost the weight," he insisted. "You just can't tell because it makes your skin hang off you."

I wondered if I could ask the Marine Corps to arrange for gastric bypass in lieu of rehab. Liposuction, please, feel free to remove any nonessential paired organs while you're at it.

A senior NCO who knew I was bulimic snarled at Koldar, "Maybe you should take a leaf from Williams's book."

"To be clear," I said quietly, when Koldar did indeed sidle up and ask if I had any good dieting tips, "You should do absolutely nothing that I do with food."

My new coworkers: a ghost from botched surgery, a ghost with too much skin. And me, with . . . well, whatever the hell was wrong with me. The hungry ghost.

Week one. You write an introductory Dari course. You ask admin about your PTAD request. Week two. You write the Charlie Company zombie contingency plan. You ask Staff Sergeant Manning to ask admin about your PTAD request. Week three. You translate the Charlie Company zombie contingency plan into Farsi. You are now prepared for the undead in two languages, which is helpful because you wake up feeling like you're being eaten from the inside. Admin tells you both to wait.

You wait.

You find random tasks and do them. Because there are so few female NCOs, a senior NCO strolls into the office one day, announces you are close enough, and voluntells you to monitor piss tests. "Congrats on your promotion. Go watch hairy snatches."

You tutor Farsi and teach your squad to read Dari. Sometimes you float lightheaded and pause mid-swoop of marker across the whiteboard.

"Do you need to sit down, Lance Corporal?"

"No, thank you, King."

Sometimes cramps seize muscles under your cammies. You walk into the head and double over. You spit bile. You puke at work until you tear the lining of your esophagus, and then there is blood in your spit too. Marines with spare time are classically encouraged to work out. You obediently take your gurgling, anemic ass to the gym.

Ghosts were loosely tasked with studying our languages. I read the Farsi translation of *Harry Potter* Dad gave me for Christmas. Aoife translated gory European history. We taught ourselves Tajik.

If Koldar studied Russian, it wasn't obvious. He mostly found reasons to not be in the office and moaned it wasn't his fault skin doesn't just go away. Koldar acted supremely inconvenienced he had to wait for the Marine Corps to deem him worthy of skin-removal surgery.

"I mean, I graduated Russian," he insisted. "I have a top secret security clearance. I'm a valuable asset. Think of the tax dollars that went into my education."

Aoife and I grinned at each other. We felt in on a little secret. We understood our sense of personal value didn't mean shit to the Corps. We weren't Marines with security clearances and critically essential languages. We hadn't proven something when we pushed athleticism to the edge, and pushed until we pushed through: that proved nothing about how badly we wanted to be Marines. We were only ghosts, Marines whose bodies betrayed us one way or another. Aoife was bolted together and I'd gone full fainting goat. Ugly necessity, bulky refuse from high enlistment quotas. Like fish who spawn millions, you kind of expect a few not to make it through.

As for cost on US taxpayers, true, but it didn't matter, we were American. In the vast swells of resources washing over us, money went out, out to make missions happen across the seas. Our national military budget topped the next ten countries combined. The cost of our training was pocket change. I figured we were maybe worth a Hellfire missile. The military had scuttled bigger.

As we waited I felt shaken loose. My body was a broken cog in a giant machine. Spare parts.

CHAPTER 22

BODY OF WATER

When a woman is thin in this culture, she proves her worth. . . . We believe she has done what centuries of a collective unconscious insist that no woman can do—control herself. A woman who can control herself is almost as good as a man.

—*Marya Hornbacher,* Wasted

Dreamlike, everything about that night. My car not starting. Flush of anxiety, turning the keys over and over. Screaming irritation, tow companies closed on New Year's Eve. Lying on my back in the barracks common room.

A torturous dream, space to be human. I had no idea what to do with myself if I couldn't throw up. I had nothing to binge. I'd walk down to a grocery store eventually, but I felt heavy, bones replaced with lead. So I lay inert on the couch.

The heavy red door slammed. Surreal, the entrance of a troop of Marines in Russian marching in. The female among them, a curly haired redhead, grinned. She bore an American eagle tattooed across her chest. "Williams! Come on! New Year's party!"

"Thanks, but I'm running a 10k in the morning. I don't want to stay out late."

"Come out and leave early?"

"My car's not starting."

"*Ni vaj na, vodka yeest*!" one shouted. Russian's contribution to DLI's multilingual oaths—It's nothing, there's vodka! They'd rented a hotel suite so no one had to drive. There'd be a female-only room. "Come have a drink and rack out early as you like. It's New Year's. Besides, this way someone can drive you to your race in the morning, you crazy motivator."

I didn't know what else to do with myself so I fell in. Surreal, marching with a group of American kids jabbering in Russian. The New Year's revelers combed the barracks deck to deck, wringing out Marines watching TV alone.

Surreal, that I thought, *Maybe this won't be so bad.*

The hotel lights sprawled through the oak trees above Asilomar State Beach. The suite was close enough to hear the wheel of the ocean. The quiet party balanced on alcohol and comfort with strangers. I cared for neither. I hovered awkwardly by Koldar, the only person I sort of knew. He handed me a vodka Sprite. I sipped at it to be polite, but there wasn't diet Sprite and this bulimic did *not* drink regular.

Dreamlike, crossing the room. How far away the conversation, muffled, underwater. The door passing though my hands. I floated through the dark trees down to the ocean. The night air soothed me, relief for this contusion in my skull. I sat in the sand squaring myself against the wind as long as I could take the cold—an hour before midnight.

I returned to the hotel with salt on my cheeks and hair wind wild. I kicked off sandy Converse, tread directly into the female-only room, and closed the door. A spoken commitment, a party house rule: no males in the female room. Surreal, that I thought it was cute the Russian Marines believed in the rule of law.

Why did I think that? What reason did I already have for doubt?

The party murmured on the other side of the door, a thin crack of light into the dark room. I wove myself into a ball, into the briny ocean smell of my clothes, and fell asleep. Surreal, that I slipped asleep telling myself everything would be different in the morning.

Soft fingertips traced my collarbone in the dark.

Wait.

Humid breath wet on my shoulder.

I couldn't roll away. Something heavy.

Wake up. Wake up now.

My body shot awake before I did. She waited, heart pounding, while I stroked anemically from sleep.

I surfaced and understood what had hauled me up: a stranger's mouth on my throat.

Awkwardly I said, "Um. Hi. Can you please . . . not?"

Strange, to hear my first name. But he would know. We worked together and saw each other's IDs all the time. The ghost with too much skin slowed down, content with kissing my neck more softly.

"I am uncomfortable," I muttered into the dark. I could barely hear myself. I cleared my throat and repeated myself, louder. "Please stop."

"I'm sorry," he breathed into my ear. "I don't want to make you do anything you're *uncomfortable* with." His last words were heat in my ear. His breath tasted like alcohol. He ground against me. I heard rather than felt it, rustle of sheets. His hand ran between my thighs.

I shrieked at my pathetic ass to *do* something.

I couldn't move.

Petrified. If I unrolled from this ball, if I moved at all, I might pull every ligament in my body. I felt conscious, body-wide panic: *Don't move. Don't move, or you'll make it MUCH WORSE.*

I was on my own, with only my long-stifled voice.

"I need to wake up early." This was what I heard myself say, as if what I wanted may have been a matter of interest to him. "I'm running in a . . . look . . . can you leave, please?"

Stop fucking humping me. Get your fucking hands off of me. Where were these words? I didn't even think them. I didn't have them to think.

He circled his hands under my clothes. I hated myself for reflexively sucking in my stomach. I didn't want to feel fat, even to him, even now, even as my skin tried to crawl away in protest.

"Hey, Zach? Will you *please* leave me alone, man?"

I shouldn't have said his first name. At the intimacy he groaned, looped a heavy leg over my hip and rolled himself over me, kissing my neck, pulling at my jeans. I was pinned. I gritted my teeth and balled cracked fists. My fingernails bit crescents into my palms. Inward, direct your implosive fury inward. Don't be rude. "Please. *Go away.*"

I thought I had a shell. I thought I had three feet of blubber. All at once I was a skinny holed-up mammal, soft-skinned, and he found me easily. His hand wormed into my jeans and shoved into me.

Dreamlike, the thing he said. The thing I always feared.

"You're saying no, but your body is saying yes."

Remember this.

Every mile was a prayer. When I ignored pain, ran on clicking hip, there'd been a supplication. When I let my stomach growl, when I wouldn't quit vomiting until bile and blood, I gripped a prayer in my hand. Turning it over and over again like worry could render this ugly question smooth, plead with God to meet me halfway.

If I had complete mastery over my own body; if I could overrule what she said; if I could be stronger than my own physical being, hold my desires at arm's distance; if I could be cold and severe; if I could run away my hips and breasts and soft tissue, cork my laughter and secure my anger, would I earn the free will to exist, to be, to speak as my own damn self? To be only me, not me-as-a-girl? If I held my gender as far away from myself as I could, did I get to be fully human?

At what point, weight, rank, or cost could I transcend my girlhood? If I hammered myself skinny could I eradicate whatever soft thing sounded like *yes* even when *I* said no, because I would have full choice over my body?

That's why I had an eating disorder. Self-sovereignty. I wanted to be my own.

When Koldar said, "Your body is saying yes," I heard, *You are fat.*

Not enough. You haven't done enough.

I thought all this while he touched me. I could feel him inside me, but I couldn't feel him too. I retreated to my head, abandoning body. Save yourself. She clenched in her protective ball, pinned by weight and alcoholic breath and assured hands and his penis against my skin. He pressed my jeans down.

"Please stop," I whispered.

He groped my underwear aside and pressed into me. I felt him inside me, but I couldn't feel him too.

My haywire brain rioted. Sparks fizzled. The stability of a grenade with the pin pulled. Reaching for something, anything, that wasn't paralysis.

The bullring.

"When you're grabbed," the instructor had stated, "You'll want to seize up. But what you're doing is carrying some of your own body weight for him. That makes it easier for him. Go limp. Dead weight. Williams, relax."

I couldn't shove him off or barrel my way out of my petrified bind, but God knew I'd practiced disintegration. I melted. My body slid away from him. I flowed out of his grip and poured to the floor, a body of water. Blood pounded in my ears like the crash of waves at Asilomar. I pulled my jeans up. I hated exposing skin.

Koldar reached down and touched my shoulder. It jerked away of its own accord. Flammable, the guilt I felt: I didn't want to hurt his feelings. That I felt guilty disorientated me. Made me stay instead of bolt.

Made me feel like I owed him something, the decency of an apology or explanation. I wanted to scream.

"I'm sorry, Williams." Still he slid his hand over my shoulder, down over my breast. I shuddered away. "C'mon, I thought you wanted it." He massaged my neck instead. "I'm sorry. Hey, come back in bed. I won't touch you. I promise. Just what you like."

"I would really, *really,* like to go to sleep," I said through gritted teeth. What I wanted was secondary. I had to convince him he wanted to leave me alone. He had to want to stop.

Go the fuck away. Who the fuck do you think you are? Back off now.

Nope. Didn't have them.

"Okay. C'mon. We can just go to sleep."

I sank my teeth into my knee so deeply it would bruise. "*Go. Away.*"

Can't you tell I meant it? I dropped "please."

He curled over me, his mouth back to my neck. "You're just so beautiful."

The door slammed open with a bolt of light, my deus ex machina, driven into the hotel doorstop by a pack of female Marines. Koldar jerked upright. It was midnight.

They pulled up abruptly when they saw Koldar. "What are you doing here?"

Blood in my ears. Muffled words. I stayed curled on the floor, my back to the bed, my knees in my face.

". . . checking on her."

"Is she okay?"

"Drank too much . . ."

"New Year's resolution?"

A square of light crossed the carpet. The door closed. He was gone.

The females changed into pajamas, giggling alcoholically about New Year's resolutions. They didn't suspect anything. Why would they? I hadn't said shit. I was clothed. It was dark. He could have covered himself. Nothing happened.

When I stood my knees buckled. The narrow hotel hall twisted. My shoulder thumped against the wall. I careened into the bathroom, clicked flimsy brass lock. I about-faced and shoved my fist down my throat. I coughed up a thin spit of Sprite. I didn't even have enough in me to puke. I dropped to my knees on the tile.

Come on. Wash your hands. Check your pockets. Phone, ID, room key. Go lace up your Converse. You always wear shoes you can run in. Leave the party quietly. Just go. Storm across the suite. Walk past the Marines smoking outside. Do not stop. Do not say hello to anyone. Do not turn if anyone says hello to you. Then run. Tear straight, churn down the windy corridor to the ocean. Sprint, jeans be damned. When you hit the ocean turn right: Bolio Gate is closed, but Franklin Gate will let you in.

Get up. Why won't you move? Fat fuck.

C'mon, the good NCO encouraged. Breathe. *Smell the salt. Wills, it's Asilomar Beach—it's right* there. *You can run it in the dark. You have, many, many times. You've run that trail back up to base a hundred times. Hundreds of times. There is starlight. You can do this.*

So get up and go. Get up, God damn you, you fat, lazy, fucking lazy, fuck . . .

But my adrenals were done. I'd short-circuited. It took the last surge of adrenaline I had to barricade behind this flimsy—fucking flimsy—locked door, willing my weight to mean all I feared it did, placing my—God, was it mine?—body between me and everything I'd have to face on the other side, chiefly my own cowardice.

Get up, I silently screamed. Tears burned in my eyes at this new revolt. I didn't know I could hate my body more than I already did. *Get up. Get up. Fuck you. FUCK YOU. WEAK.*

She stayed on the bathroom tile.

Ok, the quiet thought came later. *Can we maybe just stand up?*

I slouched back to the female room and curled in the corner of the closet, my back to the wall.

The females laughed in the dark. I didn't know them. They looked up when I lobbed past. Cheerfully shouted, Do you want a pillow?

No thanks, I mumbled.

A minute later I lashed out and grabbed a pillow.

What's wrong with you?

Hold your breath and count until you see stars. Don't breathe. Hold in your emptiness until you feel like your head is lifting off your body. As if maybe, if you lay very still and don't breathe, you won't have a body at all.

When I awoke in the closet the next morning the suite was silent. Koldar had managed to sleep in the female-only room—I wasn't terribly surprised to see—cuddled up with another Marine. Had she been more amenable than I was? I extracted his keys from a jangle on the counter and commandeered his Buick to run my race in Carmel-by-the-Sea.

My stomach churned empty through the New Year's run. I ignored the food at the finish line.

I texted Gerecht.

<Things weren't awesome last night.>

A pause. I saw the weariness behind his words. <Will, I can't handle this right now.>

I couldn't blame him. I'd been far more dramatic over far less. He probably thought I'd eaten french fries or something.

I emailed Harvey. <So, this guy tried to get in bed with me last night.>

Immediate. <What? Did anything happen?>

I considered this.

<No.>

<Oh. I'm sorry, lady. Glad nothing happened.>

<Yeah. No big deal. Happy New Year.>

Gripping a tray in the chow hall, I stared as steam lightened the heat guards, confounded by the entire concept. Food seemed more optional than ever. I set the tray down and left.

I bought sleeping pills. I trudged to the barracks after work, kicked off my boots, tore off the plastic. I downed most of the bottle, indiscriminate. Unconsciousness floored me until 0600. I struggled awake, buttoned my blouse over yesterday's skivvy shirt, and tread another day in the office, blearily semiconscious. After work I'd finish the bottle. Dully I hoped I'd lose weight if I went full comatose between work.

Like every Marine who ever was, I'd privately wanted to know, when the time came, whether I'd go down swinging. I felt I knew the answer now. I did not like what I felt.

<Hey, Williams?>

Fuck. Koldar. I clicked the Facebook private message like yanking off a bandage.

He was sorry, he said.

I wanted, savagely, for this to be no big deal. I savagely wanted it to be nothing at all. So I typed, <It's okay.>

<Did i hurt u?>

It was the grammar that got me. The fucking "u." You're apologizing for something you know was wrong, and you can't spare the millisecond for two more letters? No shred, no trace of dignity, *tarof*? You, sir, can call me thee.

Again. <It's okay.> I didn't know I'd been sexually assaulted. I was the dumbass who put her female body in a bed and left it unsecured.

<I feel bad. i was pushy.>

I needed him to shut up now. I needed him to not take one more sliver of me, the slightest anything. I needed him to shut the fuck up and get the fuck away from me. So I said, <Don't worry about it. I'm fine.>

I said, <Can we please keep this between us? I don't think it would be professional to bring to work.>

If it got out I'd messed around with him I'd never live it down.

A Commander's Cup staggered around. I asked Duryea to pace. I'd run in formation. I didn't want to be distinct, to stand out. Duryea was smart, and I saw the doubt in her eyes: she'd never paced before. To even think about winning we needed every shred of tactics we had. I'd surrendered, and she knew it. She said only, aye, Lance Corporal.

The starting pistol. Hallucinogenic, running through a cheering tunnel of uniforms. Faces blurred, the effect of camouflage, making it harder to tell one from another. Among them, somewhere, Koldar.

I didn't want anyone to look at me. I couldn't do it again, try to lead, not on this small hilltop track on which I had by conservative estimate run the length of the country, sea to shining sea.

A clean second behind the Air Force. Men's faces blurred, congratulating me. "You're getting so much better. Such a good time. High-five, Williams." My team looked happy, relieved, as ever, a little sad. The new girl looked elated. Good luck, babe.

The commanding officer ordered the male run team captain and me forward. He shook our hands and had us stand beside him as he shouted about motivation to the Marine detachment. "Above and beyond is only the baseline. Be like these motivators," he bellowed. "Samuels, Williams, well done."

Please don't look at me.

I let myself into my room. I dropped to my rack and curled into a ball, my back against the wall.

If anyone asked me why I stopped running, I couldn't have said.

I never officially surrendered my billet. When my alarm went off, I still sat up. I stared at my phone, then texted Panno or Burkhart to run practices. Sometimes I showed up, sent them somewhere, nodded curtly, then went to puke in the pinecones.

The stuffed otter on Joy's bookshelf stared back unhelpfully. "It's not a big deal," I told the otter. "I deserved it for pretty much sucking at not being a woman."

Joy's golden eyes darkened. "Actually, this is a big deal."

I shrugged, cementing shoulders one micrometer higher. "Nothing happened."

"He had no business getting in your bed when you were asleep. You have a right to be upset."

"It's fine. It's fine. It just sucked."

"He penetrated you without your consent. Would have continued to, from what it sounds like, if you hadn't had the insight to use something you learned from martial arts. What does that tell you?"

"That I'm a shitty Marine?"

"No. *That he was attacking you.* What you're describing is absolutely sexual assault."

The otter and I stared.

I'd forgotten innocence. I'd been desensitized by language, "cunts" and "dicks" slashed off and bandied about the barracks like a body could be ripped apart without consequences. I'd forgotten my body had rights, if only animal rights, a small stalwart mammal steadily picking her way through lean years. I honestly wasn't sure my body was mine, not actual government property. Bodies were just things. Bones and meat and a little electricity. They didn't fucking matter.

In the Mormon story, before birth all of us existed only in spirit. We pleaded with God to be born. We wanted physical bodies, like He had, to be more like Him.

I'd forgotten that in my earliest bedtime stories, the first fairytales I'd ever heard, to have a body made us more like the gods.

Joy answered my silence. "I don't know what of this you can hear right now, but I want you to hear this from someone. He had no idea who you are. He had no idea what you've lived through. He scared you, and you froze because you've been powerless in that situation before. He had no right to touch you without your consent."

"He didn't . . . get . . . that far."

"How far is far enough to be upset?"

I didn't answer. I felt a longing that shattered me once a decade or so. I missed my mom.

"Did you want him to so much as kiss you?"

"Fuck no."

"How's your eating disorder been since then?"

I made a fist. My knuckles were tooth torn.

"I've never seen you sit so still."

My knees shuddered against my chest. "I'm cold is all."

Her kindness held a firm edge. "I'm writing you a prescription to the public library."

Joy instructed me to check out every book on feminism I could get my hands on. "You need to be . . . *introduced* to the idea of equality."

Cradling my head in my palm, I read the provocatively titled *Full Frontal Feminism* in the barracks common room.

A passing sergeant barked, "Williams! Stop reading smut in the barracks!"

I closed my book and said aye, Sergeant, because he had been to Iraq.

CHAPTER 23

THE OTHER F-WORD

I believe any woman for whom the feminist breaking of silence has been a transforming force can also look back to a time when the faint, improbable outlines of unaskable questions, curling her brain cells, triggered a shock of recognition at certain lines, phrases, images, in the work of this or that woman, long dead, whose life and experience she could only dimly try to imagine.

—*Adrienne Rich,* On Lies, Secrets, and Silence

I slipped library books into the barracks with covers turned toward my body.

So, said feminism, Y*ou realize it's problematic to worship bone and distrust flesh?*

I mean, is there any other option?

Oh, friend. Sit down.

To feminism my eating disorder was real in a way I had never heard acknowledged. I didn't have to weigh eighty-two pounds. The thing itself, feminism warned, the very willingness to enact violence against my own body, was, in and of itself, enough cause for pause, consideration, even concern. There was context to this war beyond myself.

Why had I learned to treat girls as I had? Why had I learned to judge and police and suspect? I had learned to erect impossible standards of sleek composure. I had, and only ever would have, this one woman that was mine, my body, and I did hate her. I starved her, isolated her, tore into her, didn't listen to her, didn't trust her, told her she was shit, found violence against her tolerable, even preferable, to bridle her unruly disobedience. I was a practicing misogynist.

Feminism urged me to understand: You weren't born hating yourself. You learned.

It was weirdly freeing, even if I didn't quite believe it, to try context on for size. I was mired in my own story, but also part of a larger story I hadn't known existed.

And in that story I wasn't alone.

I started to hear female Marines. Just to take a pulse. I had to consciously shut up that part of me so conditioned to inject female voices with a mainline of *Well they're not real Marines, they haven't been in combat, what do they know about suffering, they're probably exaggerating, can't hack it, nothing compared to what He is going through, did you see that Facebook photo of her in a bikini with the duck lips, she just wants attention—*

When I set aside skepticism I heard a continuous whisper of just one thing: we are having trouble with boys.

Be careful around that staff sergeant.

Oh god, that guy.

That guy cheated on his wife, and I never told anyone. I mean, he's my best friend, he was going through some shit. I went home with somebody, he's the only one I told, and suddenly I'm hearing about it from battalion. What the fuck?

If you're on duty with him, drink more Red Bull than you think you need. Stay wired.

Sorry, I've got to go—my boyfriend doesn't like it when I stay to talk after formation. He always thinks I'm cheating on him because his ex-wife did. She was a civilian but he says he can't trust girls now.

He doesn't like female Marines, females whispered. We were always apologetic. Eager to support one another not to be like those females.

We never said, *He's a bully*. We would never say, *He bullies women*. We said, *We can be better.*

We stayed silent because we were goddamn Marines. We could take it. We wouldn't be quelled by words. We wouldn't complain, like those *other* little female Marines. No, we would starve ourselves instead, work ourselves out half to death. We would take it and take it and take it and wonder why we felt hollow inside. God knew I'd taken it until my pelvic bones imploded.

We'd distrust other women, too, to be more like the guys.

We were far too conditioned to believe female judgment was acceptable. Not even judgment at all, simple undeniable fact. Women are weaker, amen. Anything suggesting that, in every context or without any at all, is just science, amen. And females only report to destroy men's lives, and it's really not fair to judge someone over a few minutes of indiscretion; it's really a war on men, amen. And suggesting men like to look at women (and we should be okay with being reminded of that seventeen hundred times a day) is also just biology, amen. And if we're not comfortable with hard fact, well we're the irrational ones, AMEN.

We were judged guilty until proven, through disintegrating cartilage from overuse injuries (so common in us females), innocent of charges that our injuries were fantastical, our fears and concerns about male colleagues irrational batshit, our promotions preferential treatment for sexual acts or their suggestion, our very presence a distraction or even threat to national security and a righteous American civilization. *IRAQ*, we screamed in the face of any female who spoke up. *AFGHANISTAN*. Always a reason not to listen, to make simple bullying a worthless issue, to make our speaking up seem petty or small. Like there could only be one battle. As if the United States had never fought in plural theaters.

Dimly I began to get it. I could listen to whatever the lowest common denominator told me I was. Or I could question my internal narrative. I could petition my own worth.

There are miles between knowing and understanding. This call to self-worth was fire I had no place to tend. My insides were all wormy with bulimia. Nevertheless I felt traces of reintegration.

For example.

One NCO hovered around the company office. I didn't particularly dislike this NCO. I didn't particularly like him. He seemed low-key enough. Occasionally he'd take a pen and prod the back of my head with it, pumping it in and out of my sock bun. "I'm bun-raping you, Williams," he'd laugh, "Do you like it, or are ya gonna report me for sexual assault?" I generally waited until he got bored of poking my head with a pen then ran down to the ocean, sometimes considering throwing myself in and swimming for Honolulu.

One day this NCO seized my wrist, pulled my arm above my head and shook the shit out of me for disagreeing with him, which I'd done I thought politely, reciting the memorized regulations in question. This NCO was rather taller than me. For a moment I flailed like a rag doll. Then I had the horrifying realization being shaken like said rag doll would cause my fat to wobble, and I ripped my arm away. This wasn't exactly a self-compassionate or empowering thought, but yanking free was an unprecedented act that aligned with the radical women I'd been reading who believed I had a right for my body not to be touched any damn way I didn't want it to be, by anyone. The action set me up for defiance. The force behind it, maybe. For once I didn't pop to parade rest, hands respectfully folded behind my sacrum. For once I didn't humbly lower my gaze. I caught his eyes and stared. I stood arms by my sides, my hands loose but ready for fists, my feet planted through my boots and ready to take on sudden weight. I said nothing. But the thought must have glared through my eyeballs: What the fuck, Sergeant.

To my amazement he didn't read me the riot act. He gave me a strange look—surprise?—and walked away.

"*That* horse face picked up corporal before me? There's no way she didn't suck dick for that one."

That horse face was a woman on the run team. I looked up from my book. "Russian has a way lower cutting score than we do. And she's strong and motivated as all hell."

As always. "Williams, you're so fucking sensitive. Grow a thicker skin and take a joke."

For some reason my skin stayed soft. Bite my female ass.

CHAPTER 24

ADMIN ASSAULT TEAM

To unravel life's cloth is to scorn a gift. . . . We discard the gift in favor of a self-created world that we know is incoherent and cannot be sustained.

—*David George Haskell,* The Forest Unseen

I'd asked for three months of PTAD. After five months sitting in administrative limbo I regretted asking.

By winter all I wanted, all the time, was to lie on the floor and cover my head with my hands. I layered wool socks and thermals under my cammies. Still my hands froze to fists. My bones wanted . . . *more* to me, a shade of heft. My weight stepped back into Order 6110.3.

Koldar continued to work—or at least exist—next to me in the office.

By April my senior NCOs were ready to murder someone on my behalf, but didn't know who. No one knew what to do with my PTAD request.

An eating disorder? She doesn't look *that* thin. It's affecting her health? Is she medically unwell? Not that we can see? Then she's malingering? No? Then . . . what is it? She's depressed? Ah! Head case. Why didn't you say so! Psychiatric discharge. Wait, she's not crazy? She's polite and composed? Then . . . what's *wrong* with her?

"We're trying to say, *she* says something's wrong," Staff Sergeant Carlisle confided to me. "And we trust *her*. But that seems weird to Higher Ups because you're still coming into work and doing your job."

I wondered if I'd get help if I barreled down the hall shrieking and actively projectile vomiting—and I wasn't above it—but then severance would be swift and permanent. I wanted to finish my enlistment. I wanted to be a Marine for twenty years. I had to hope Higher Ups decided I was both legitimately unwell and *also* valuable enough to help.

Military bearing. I nodded politely.

One of the most maddening aspects was the ceaseless game of telephone. No matter how carefully I laid out my thoughts to my NCOs, they had to run it up the chain. Weeks were spent over who would *fund* treatment, when I had explicitly stated I would pay for it myself. After another attempt to prod Higher Ups toward a decision, Staff Sergeant Manning came into the office swearing. "You might need to fund treatment yourself, Marine."

"That's fine," I choked. "I didn't expect the Marine Corps to pay. I just need permission to go."

Civilian eating disorder residential facilities were thousands of dollars a day. I told my staff sergeants about my secret weapon: Obamacare had just come into effect. Under it, I was still covered by my father's health insurance until I turned twenty-six. (Dad: "Alright, that socialist in the White House might actually have done just this one thing right.")

Staff Sergeant Manning asked what was I even doing, trying to get help through the military. Lines were long, continuity of care nonexistent. I had Real People health insurance. I agreed. All I needed was permission. Three months. Give me three months, and I can get myself help.

Thanks, Obama.

I didn't understand why we were all acting like mine was a unique case, like I was the sole bulimic to infiltrate the Marine Corps. I wasn't even the only bulimic Marine in Monterey. When you spend long enough staring at a toilet bowl, you do start to recognize vomit tracks. I was saddened but not surprised when I puked in the barracks and saw tell-tale traces of other women's disdain for their bodies in the porcelain.

Nowhere could anyone camouflage an eating disorder better than in the Marines. Competitive, dualistic, driven, perfectionistic, body-centric, too fiercely loyal to those who have it worse to ask for help: these things make admirable Marines and/or eating disorders. Across the five military branches, 66 percent of reported anorexics are Marines. One study reports not only are eating disorders rampant in the military, higher than civilian rates, they occur most frequently in the Marines, affecting, overwhelmingly, junior enlisted female Marines. To which I say, *No shit.*[3]

Yet we had no standard operating procedure for malnourishment. None of my senior leadership—Marines with ten and twenty years under their belts—knew how to respond to a Marine with an eating disorder. What the fuck, actually? Never mind no care: how was there no record, no precedent, no trace for me to follow?

Had we so consistently been ignored?

I dreamed of PTAD. I always pictured the AFTER. I gazed at my reflection, imagining current pudgy-faced-me (my thyroid had swollen) on the left, the chagrin-filled BEFORE. Then on the right AFTER treatment, somehow sharper about the jaw.

In my AFTER fantasy I was always a corporal. I'd paid attention in Goodfellow, gotten through the program in one good shot. I'd caught up with my friends. I wasn't emaciated, but leaner now that I never binged. I had a rifle in my hands again. I was going overseas. How badly I wanted that AFTER, to come back and finally use Dari where it mattered. I still wanted so badly to deploy, what I'd set out to do three years ago. It was all on the other side of rehab and losing a modest ten pounds or so, I knew it.

With rare clairvoyance the lance corporal underground figured something was awry with Run Team Williams. Someone placed a report on my desk about alcoholic Marines receiving PTAD for rehab. I wished I was an alcoholic. The Marine Corps understood that. The Marine Corps knew all about alcohol. You drank yourself stupid when you were junior enlisted, deserved a drink when you got back from deployment as an NCO, and then senior NCOs kept saying they'd probably better quit drinking for a while.

I turned twenty-one. I tried drinking instead of bingeing, hoping if I transferred my addiction from food to alcohol I'd have a problem the Marine Corps accredited. I vaguely recall a spinning night studying Judaism at the bottom of a rum bottle, but it didn't stick.

One morning I didn't hear back from Harvey. Through a clamor on his Facebook wall, I heard he'd been medevaced. Word had gotten so far as "amputation."

I paced my workdays in a state of quietly contained panic, marching a useless stack of files up and down the hall.

Finally Harvey himself posted to Facebook. His toe had been severed by the heavy door of an MRAP. Hanging by a bit of sinew, he'd asked field medics to cut the damn thing off. They'd insisted on flying him to Leatherneck, the principal Afghan Marine base. He posted a picture of himself giving a thumbs-up, tanned and dirty and thin and sporting a ridiculous handlebar mustache. Other than earning the nickname Nine

Toes, he would be fine. Mortified to be medevaced for such a trivial injury and supremely embarrassed by the attention, he informed us he was great. He sarcastically reported British nurses were performing fellatio in lieu of painkillers.

Well then.

A boot Marine disinterested in throwing elbows, a boot Marine not foaming at the mouth to jostle to the front of the pack, incurs suspicion. I had a brief flirtation with legal punishment around the next Commander's Cup. Burkhart assumed captaincy of the female run team and called a time trial. I told her I'd be there but didn't show, defeated in a way I couldn't explain. Brush scratched my legs on a solitary trail run at Fort Ord instead.

The morning after the ignored time trial, a female staff sergeant came into the Charlie Company office. I'd never seen her before; she was new to DLI.

"You're Lance Corporal Williams?"

I stood. "Yes, I am. Good morning, Staff Sergeant."

She narrowed her eyes. "I don't think it is. I'm going to be helping Burkhart with the female run team."

A golden beam, a sudden window in a dark room. "I am delighted to hear that, Staff Sergeant," I gushed. I couldn't wait to see what could happen with staff sergeant, with real rank, real leadership, giving it a go.

"Why weren't you at the time trial yesterday?"

"I know I'll be running in the Cup, Staff Sergeant. I didn't think Burkhart needed to see me run."

And, Staff Sergeant, because leading that team for the last two years with neither support nor supervision led me to believe no one would give a flying fuck.

She answered coolly, "I'm going to take this seriously. I want you to know, I don't have a lot of patience for females who aren't willing to take their obligation to the team seriously."

The window slammed shut.

"I sincerely apologize, Staff Sergeant. I really didn't think it was going to be an issue if I wasn't there."

"Well," Her nostrils flared, "I'll be talking to your chain of command, Lance Corporal Williams, about the appropriate disciplinary action. As far as I'm concerned you were AWOL."

As a god, the Marine Corps is a heartless bitch.

I knew damn well an NJP on my record killed any chance I had at PTAD. The risk of losing my chance at treatment spring-loaded me. I sprinted and held planks in the sauna and anxiously threw up until I spat acid and took nothing but salt water and laxatives, losing something like twelve pounds in five days, so I wouldn't look like a fat-ass, ergo predetermined to moral shortcoming, at my disciplinary board.

I waited for my NJP, but it never came. Staff Sergeant Manning texted me not to worry. When he'd heard the female staff sergeant report I ought to be NJPed for skipping run team, he texted me that he'd laughed aloud.

"If you actually took a day off running, I'll get you a medal."

Mostly the ghost months blurred as my body quietly began shutting down.

CHAPTER 25

COSTS

Eating disorders linger so long undetected, eroding the body in silence, and then they strike. The secret is out. You're dying.
—*Marya Hornbacher,* Wasted

One morning I spat a mouthful of blood into a sink. I didn't know where it came from.

At this point I realized I might actually die in the Marines. My frenzied response to this was to starve myself as quickly as possible, so when I died from an eating disorder I'd be thin enough for it to be believable.

The thing my eating disorder failed to tell me when I married her was, it wasn't skinniness that was going to kill me. There are so many tremendously awful ways eating disorders savage you long before you would call yourself thin. Bulimics don't delicately fade away. Our cheeks balloon over swollen lymph nodes. We don't sigh our lasts looking waifish and artistic in hospital gowns. We asphyxiate in back alleys on our own vomit. A bulimic's stomach can hold seven times the amount of food as a healthy adult. Think of the fullest you have ever been, remember the weight of your stomach when fully stretched like a canvas bag, and imagine six more of those hanging in there. Our stomachs swell until they hinder breathing and inhibit blood flow to the intestines. Our breath becomes shallow and superficial, the mechanics of hyperventilation and perpetual stress, the muscular pump of the diaphragm compromised to cascading deleterious effect on immune and lymph and nervous systems. The whole body has to work harder all the goddamn time, to which, with bulimic derangement, we say: *Good.* Because working harder burns more calories. We're wrong, and more than in simple factual terms. We think we are machines, governed by calculus. We do not understand and to some degree despise the aliveness of our bodies. We believe to a cellular level not a single iota of body deserves compassion. We love the space around our bodies—the space we don't take, gaps between ribs and light between bowing thighs—more than we tolerate our own physical presence.

Bulimic hearts take high casualties. Vomiting is corrosive cardio.

Electrolyte imbalances feel like stars going supernova.

I stood at attention one morning formation in April. My stomach shot breakfast up, flooding my mouth with acidic oatmeal. I stared straight ahead and swallowed it. My stomach pressed it up. I swallowed. We debated this for a while.

Malnourishment takes different forms, not all of them the desirable rib cages, oh-so-elegant shadow-casting hip bones. Malnourishment looked like a calm blue sky, the baffled moment I stopped walking home, gazed upward, and couldn't remember where I lived.

Once someone asked my first name. Took me a second.

You go into an eating disorder thinking it'll be mutually beneficial. You'll give her your body and she'll make you who you want to be. Competent. Protected. Powerful. You think she'll weld your body into an armored shell. But she is a parasite. An eating disorder eats you.

Still my command had no idea what to do with me. They shipped me to Balboa, where the trend continued. I spent a few days in the Wounded Warrior barracks studiously avoiding the no-shit amputee and Purple Heart Marines. ("Yeah, I'm here because I make myself puke . . . sorry about your leg.") I was supposed to be meeting a specialist but I highly doubted they existed. The command had no idea who I was or why I was there. I took an eighty-five dollar cab ride to a twenty-minute appointment with a counselor's aide, who also had no idea who I was or why I was there. When I said I had an eating disorder, she asked why it bothered me. When I said it castrated my ability to stand up for myself and sabotaged personal relationships, she diagnosed me with borderline personality disorder. I flew back to Monterey unsure of what just happened. From the plane, watching San Diego get smaller along the turquoise shore, I thought, *Yeah. Like the Marine Corps is going to buy* that.

I went back to mental to receive the okay for PTAD. I prayed I was thin enough for the same Army psychiatrist—he of the Rorschach test—to believe me. I wasn't.

He looked at me a bit longer. "Maybe," he said at last, with a deep shrug of resignation, "this is one of those *rare* cases where perhaps you need more help than we can give you." He said, "Maybe we should talk to your command about getting you out."

Yes. For three months, please. Return ticket.

"You know," he intoned, "You're not as depressed as you say you are."

"Oh?"

"If you were that depressed you would have killed yourself already."

A black hole opened behind his shoulder, and his face dissolved into it.

"So let me ask you: why haven't you?"

I felt my face dissolving too. I ran my thumb over my left wrist. My tiny shield, my Jewish star. The Shield of David. Why had I gotten that tattoo? Oh, yeah. I was a daughter, once. Someone had wanted me to be. I had been called into being by parents who loved me. Both my Jewish and Mormon ancestry—Scottish converts to the new religion—emigrated to the country stitched into my uniform to escape being harassed or killed for their faith. For God knew how many generations, my life—my existential call to *be*—had been fought for. Sacrificed for. I came from somewhere, and to throw that away did not come easily.

"Sometimes things feel like they might be okay, sir. Sometimes I feel like being alive is a divine gift. I think it honors its Giver to . . . kind of try and hold on, if you can. Sir."

The sallow psychologist blinked. "So some days you're sad, and some days you're happy?"

"Er, yes, sir."

"Suicidally unhappy?"

"Yes, sir."

"And *divinely* happy?"

I considered this. I thought of golden light streaming through the long shadows of cypress across the running path beside the ocean. Yeah, I'd call that divine.

"Yes, sir."

"Well, you have bipolar," he announced, leaning back in his chair. "The Marine Corps can't help you with that."

I mulled this medical opinion as I trudged up the hill back to work, assisting my right leg with my hand, a pinch and pull to my trousers every step. I felt unconvinced gratitude was manic, diagnostically speaking. I still kind of believed in hope as like . . . a human birthright.

One Army doctor seemed genuinely concerned when I said I had an eating disorder and needed to extend my prescription of iron pills, please. The uniformed doctor told me the Army sent their females with eating disorders to Germany. He described a mystical facility to me, a place where I'd get help from people who could at least define purging orthorexia.

"Occult bleeding means you're starting to hack into real damage," the doctor warned. "Lasting damage. Talk to your command. Self-advocate. Get orders to Germany."

There wasn't a chance in hell. Junior enlisted female Marines do not "get themselves orders" anywhere—are you serious? But the potential reward of Germany gleamed, so I tried, this one time, to self-advocate.

I squared my shoulders and raised my head and marched down the hall. I'd knock on Master Guns's door and just fucking ask. Could he follow up? Could I follow up? Could this maybe be my job, as I sat in admin limbo? Could I be trusted to figure out a plan? What needs to be done, and can I do it? You need my records from Balboa? Sir, I have a car and a vengeance. I'll grab a new kid to take the wheel if I pass out. I will go right now. No Marine on hand cares more about Mission Get-Williams's-Head-Out-Her-Ass than me.

Master Guns had pinned a news article outside his door. I stared at it as I waited. For the first time in those hallways adorned with male faces, I saw a woman, and one I knew. Her name was Audrey Dorion. She'd been in Pashto with Trom. When I came into their platoon, she'd had tight friendships with the other girls, and they were working together now in Afghanistan. Months ago she'd knocked on my door and invited me to her room for microwave brownies and a Pixar movie with the other girls. I'd hung for a minute, but I was mid-vomiting, and anyway, what was this? Chocolate and whimsy? She even had colorful Tibetan prayer flags draped across her cinderblock. The familiar anxious pulse in my neck softened. For like a whole three minutes, I hadn't even felt like I was in the world's proudest gun club.

What had I achieved by fighting so hard not to be like other girls? Like the actual, real, girls around me? What hollow point had I made?

In the newsprint, Audrey sat with her Kevlar at her side, legs crossed, laughing and having tea with Afghan women and curious children. Another shot showed her on patrol, speaking Pashto in a Talib-held village, her finger straight and off the trigger.

I hadn't eaten dinner last night. That's what I accomplished, trying so damn hard not to be like Her. Great.

This was She. This was the real female Marine. The fuck was I doing?

Deep down in my twisted pelvis I felt aware there had always been a different kind of female Marine. I'd known that. I'd seen Her from the beginning. I'd seen Her in the women around me. I felt ashamed I'd believed the shit we said. I wished I'd eaten that damn brownie. What had I done instead? Shuffled out to puke and probably text another round of fighting with Trom. What had the boys been doing that Friday night? Almost certainly drinking and playing video games. Why had I turned my nose up at girls creating space for themselves? Why had it seemed softer, weaker?

Maybe if I'd stopped listening to the language around the disembodied Her I'd been so afraid of becoming and opened my eyes to the real life women around me, I wouldn't have wandered so far from reality.

I heard other Marines say Dorion was top of her class in Pashto, even better than Trom. Trom had called her "kind of a whore." God, I'd been brutal in who I was willing to believe.

As I waited outside Master Guns' office, I ducked my head to pray. Please God, *Kyrie eleison.* Mercy, just this once.

A staff sergeant approached me. I liked this staff sergeant. I'd've called him a friend. He was waiting to start Farsi, and I tutored him now and again when he asked. He was a good guy. His weird act of post-combat rebellion was refusing to ever wear a skivvy shirt, so his cammie blouse showed a bare breast, and daring us to ask why. He asked why I was speaking to Master Guns.

"He told me to come to him if I really needed it."

This senior NCO exploded in front of my eyes.

"Who the *fuck* are you to break chain of command?"

I realized I was about to receive an ass chewing. I tucked my shoulders and stepped respectfully into parade rest, but my eyes did not leave his. Yes. What can I do for you, Staff Sergeant?

"Who makes decisions in the Marine Corps, Williams?"

His jaw clenched.

"I . . ."

His rage was astounding. I knew his face, but I didn't know the man inside it.

I didn't know what answer he sought. I didn't know this riddle.

"I . . ." I repeated slowly. "Higher Ups, Staff Sergeant?"

"Williams." He clamped down his rage and stepped very close to me then. He would do me the courtesy of not screaming at me in the bustling hallway.

"*What the fuck do you think you are doing*? If he didn't pass down word to you that he had word to pass, he has nothing to say to you, Williams. Your staff sergeants don't know about this? Why the fuck is a fifth platoon lance corporal standing in front of the detachment Master Guns right now? *Who makes decisions in the Marine Corps, Williams?*"

God, I was hanging on to every word, listening desperately for an answer. What the hell did he want me to say?

"I . . . don't know, Staff Sergeant," I said. "I . . ."

They fell. The tears stashed behind my eyes for so long. God, fucking damnit, this, again. I didn't know what he wanted me to say. Anyone you like can make decisions in the Marine Corps, Staff Sergeant. Whatever the fuck you say. Whatever you need to hear right now to see me as a respectful, trying-her-best lance corporal, that is absolutely what the fuck I will say, Staff Sergeant. But then, God, please, what next? Is it really so above my paygrade, my life? Is this really so officious, and behind-closed-doors that I couldn't possibly weigh in, report back on my own eating disorder? My heart's stopping now, man. I got to drive three hours to Travis Air Force Base—freaking out I was going to pass out and crash in Bay Area traffic the whole time—to get a heart monitor, because when I stand up too fast, friend, my heart doesn't stand up with me. My blood pressure is hella low, and I understand we've accepted me blacking out multiple times a day as a nonemergency situation, but . . . maybe I have . . . some right, maybe even some responsibility, to follow up with this? Am I not the subject matter expert of my own disorder? Do I truly have no ownership in this question of what will happen to me?

I did not, of course, say this. I chewed my lips into my mouth to keep them from trembling and cursed the hot tears that fell smoothly onto my collar.

The staff sergeant marched me back to the Charlie Company office. He ordered me to sit down and closed the door.

"Okay, Williams," he said, and suddenly he was friendly again, a man I looked up to. "Take a breather. Don't ever fucking break chain of command again. Just calm down. Trust your NCOs."

Who makes decisions in the Marine Corps? Not me.

I should have known better. Who did I think I was, to speak directly to Higher Up? In Mormonland, too, I'd required better, sanctified men to intervene on my behalf.

I so looked forward to my follow up with the sole Army doctor who'd voiced concern, who'd sent me to Travis AFB in the first place. When I came back with a heart monitor taped over my chest but bearing no news from my command (I never did talk to the Master Guns, and my staff sergeants had no idea what I was talking about. *Treatment in Germany? We'll have to talk to Master Guns*), the Army doctor was curt, empathy worn out.

"You're a Marine," he said sharply. "You need to figure out a way to get yourself help, and soon."

A bizarre interface, Marine Corps to rehab. Two very different worlds butting into each other, and I stood like Alice with one foot in the rabbit hole, unsure which was real.

I paced the barracks talking to an intake counselor on the phone. I chose the treatment center I did because my father's insurance covered it and it was in the woods. That was the extent of my research: How far into the woods could I go while learning how not to be a bulimic shit show? This one's in a forest? Perfect, I'm living there.

I didn't know I'd gotten very lucky. This treatment center was known for treating chronic cases at the estuary of disorder and sexual trauma. It had real heart, art, a resident Buddhist, and was, as advertised, in the woods.

It was odd to speak to a soft voice, someone like Joy who clearly lived in an alternate universe where there wasn't a war happening *right now and you need to be ready to GO holy shit.* I wasn't sure what made the counselor's world different than mine, but I knew my whole body felt like weeping when she spoke to me kindly. I'd once felt relief to be yelled at, because it was familiar. That it made me feel like weeping alarmed me more than the gobs of bodily tissue in my puke or blood in my shit: I was cracking.

"How often do you vomit on a bad day?"

"Ten times."

"How often do you vomit on a normal day?"

I paused. "Ten times."

I was astounded when I got the results back from my intake. They'd placed my name at the top of their list. I called them up, embarrassed, to make sure they hadn't gotten my weight wrong.

"I'm not that thin," I apologized. "Most people don't believe I even have an eating disorder."

The kind voice. "Your weight doesn't matter. We're worried about your heart."

I wasn't sure if she meant my literal heart or, like, my emotional one. But after I thanked her and hung up, I felt a warmth in my chest, a brief sense of softening.

It took me a second to recognize the sensation.

That one was relief.

Why would a wild animal ever run as hard, as fast, as long as they could on an injury that made them limp? Only if they were running from something, only if they were running for their life.

I knew the path I was on went nowhere good. I was lost among other humans. I tried to be kind and polite but I was so hangry and anxious I didn't have anything like integrity, only feral eagerness to please.

If I carried on this path I was going to slip out of my body one way or another. The persistent whisper towards suicide was chiseling me down.

I couldn't see another path, but my body sure as shit did. She knew an animal running madly on adrenaline and fear was a wounded creature, yes, but one fighting to live. That meant some intact part had not given up and was sure as hell not going down without a fight.

Hope was the small part of me that watched me hurl myself forward and thought, *Hey, I might make it.* Find cover, dig some quiet shelter to curl up, draw my leg into my chest and be very, very still for a while. And if it was an eating disorder facility, I could hand over the problematic reins of food. Surrender control, yes, but also my whip.

I couldn't see further along the path than that faint trailhead, couldn't imagine a life without choking my body, but I knew I needed help if I wanted to find out.

And for that, I needed the men above me to decide my eating disorder was real.

All that mattered while my command decided amongst themselves if I had an eating disorder or not was the fact that my weight fell within Marine Corps Order 6110.3. She's not underweight, they repeated. It can't be *that* bad. I did not volunteer the information I shat black coal, aware I could be bleeding in my intestinal tract. Ulcers in my stomach and small intestine made me feel less like I digested food than ran it through a gizzard like a bird. Christ, was I fucked all the way through? I didn't disclose that blue veins crisscrossed my stomach, internal pressure straining veins to the surface, that I stared at what looked like a hydrological map across my abdomen every time I showered.

I was never in the room, so they never saw the cracked red skin around my mouth like broken parenthesis, or knuckles that looked like I was a member of a really shitty fight club. None of that weighed in. Because ulcers are just ulcers and maybe manage your stress better, Marine. Why are you even stressed anyway, don't you know there's a war on? There are suppositories for the shit situation, Williams, you can deal with this yourself, and make sure you hydrate before PT, devil dog, and none of these things will actually kill you.

I was beginning to feel not entirely human. Maybe I really was a ghost, only loosely bound to earth through a deadweight of a body I didn't inhabit, just shielded in camouflage and hauled from sleep to obliterating sleep.

I opened the office calendar to May and dashed a red line across the third week so violently the pen ripped the paper. Either I got my ass to treatment, I weighed under 110 pounds, or I killed myself. One way or another, I would not be here by the end of May.

I had friends who feared for their lives in the Marine Corps, but we had very different experiences of it. And because Marines were still being medevaced from combat zones, I didn't tell anyone about my stupid red line. Shit or get off the pot.

Byzantine, the administration of an empire. Every few weeks my name reached someone else in the detachment. He'd call me in. I'd check my teeth for puke, pat foundation over the torn skin around my mouth, and start over.

"What's the situation, Williams?"

He would respond the same way (he would always be a he). "An *eating disorder*?" Sometimes kindly, sometimes angry, most often very confused: "You don't look sick," and the dreaded, "You don't look too skinny."

These were the men who'd held Fallujah. They'd never felt the size of their thighs was tied to their intrinsic worth as a human. The general response was . . . what?

Higher Ups finally sent word. Tell her not to puke. Order her, if necessary.

Staff Sergeant Manning considered this. "Would that work? What if, as your platoon sergeant and a staff noncommissioned officer of the United States Marine Corps, I order you to stop throwing up?"

"I think I would commit hara-kiri, Staff Sergeant," I said quietly. I meant it. Ripping out my stomach struck me as a fairly appropriate course of action.

He laughed. "What if I order you not to do that either?"

"Then my last thoughts would be highly conflicted, Staff Sergeant."

No one felt empowered to agree to my PTAD plan. Probably too much liability, sending a girl across the country, still an active duty Marine who'd pass out over bloody puke in some civilian airport. If anyone believed I was sick in the first place. No one seemed to believe how I blacked out was anything but psychological. But like . . . what if she is as sick as she says she is? Too bad, bro, it's not our fault the Marines lets in teenage girls. What did they say behind closed doors?

Maybe they were kinder. Maybe they said, She's alright. She's trying too hard. But she's a respectful female. Maybe we just let her go.

Maybe the hang-up was the counter: Now tell me. Do we pay this girl three months of vacation to fly across the country and take a mental health break?

I don't know.

I think most likely I wasn't discussed at all.

Maybe it went like this:

Anything else, Master Guns would say, after a briefing. The platoon commanders, the men with heavy rank, would be pressed into his office, leaning against the walls.

Ah, yes, Staff Sergeant Manning would say. He'd be seated easily, but drum his pen on his notepad, betraying a hint of severity. My Marine, who—

The one who we—

Yes, the one who still—

—the one we talked about, roger. Hang out after.

The Master Guns would tell him, Well, I haven't heard anything. Maybe I'll talk to the first sergeant and get him to weigh in on this. I'll tell you, the CO himself knows about this, we're trying to find a solution. Just tell her to sit tight.

That seems most likely. Because every week I received my orders, as my red line stalked closer: sit tight.

Too easily things fell through administrative cracks. My file could always be handed off. Let someone else make the call. Then another man—a combat veteran, a warrior—this man was staring at me blankly. I felt untethered, like I'd done something I shouldn't have. Shame ate me. To admit to men I would follow crawling if I damn well had to, if I could only get this knotted, gnawing thing *off of me* that I am maybe not . . . totally okay. And another man who had stood in places few could imagine and pulled a resisting trigger stared at me and did not try to hide his skepticism. Bulimia was my cursed reality, constant and private. I swore for exposing its underside to prodding and doubt.

In the dark barracks I burst out of nightmares, sure someone was in bed with me. As my heart slowed, I felt profoundly grateful I kept *that* to myself. If I wasn't skinny enough to have an eating disorder, I probably wasn't pretty enough to have been sexually assaulted.

The Kafka whorehouse was a powerless hell. I began to doubt the integrity of my own experience.

No one noticed I'd dropped out of running like a deranged husky, so I doubted anyone noticed when I threw myself back into it. Forty miles a week felt pitiful. I ran under a lead blanket I berated as laziness. I didn't recognize the heaviness I felt for what it was: I was discouraged.

I drove farther and farther away from base. Tiptoed out-of-bounds to run in the Santa Cruz Mountains, where towering redwoods made me feel like a small, held creature. Toeing the line into Big Sur, where sometimes I ran the steep climb up the coastal peak Garrapata and watched the sunset over the Pacific and passingly didn't feel so afraid.

I ran to savor this beautiful land where mountains met ocean. To smell the redwoods and live oaks and feel the soft trails under my feet. One way or another I was leaving Monterey soon. I didn't know if I'd be back.

No one asked why I started running again. But if anyone had, I would've looked at him dumbly. I would've indicated my bruised and scarred shins and hoped they spoke for me.

Somewhere high above me mystical Higher Ups counseled, trying to decide what to do with Bulimic Run Team Williams. The junior female who looked fine but admitted imminent collapse. "Lance Corporal Williams complains of bulimia," read my medical file testily, which killed me. I didn't want to complain. I wanted to stop hurting. I was low priority. I understood that. There was a war on.

Deep underwater, beneath undulating kelp, I felt pinned. An anchor compressed me to the coarse sediment. Higher Ups had finally seen air bubbles rising to the surface. I ran waiting for some creaking mechanism to haul the great weight off me from above.

I ran because it was the only way on God's good green earth I knew to try to push *up*.

Finally one morning at 0700, the new XO—second in command to the commanding officer—dropped into the Charlie Company office.

"What's your story, Williams?"

I rose to attention and swayed, but met his eyes through the black daze. "I'm bulimic, sir."

"Hmm." He squinted, then glanced at my desk. "What're you reading, Williams?"

I held up the paperback flayed open by my keyboard. The major knew enough Dari to read the title. "You're reading Ahmed Rashid in Dari?"

He sat down, stretched out his legs. His combat boots looked twice the size of mine. "Have a seat."

I sank.

"Bulimia, huh? Now, what do you think caused that, Lance Corporal?"

"I don't know, sir."

"I'm not asking you as an officer. I'm asking you as a human. Why do you think you have bulimia?"

He was so kind I wished I knew.

"I want . . . to be better. I don't think . . . I'm enough."

The XO waved this off. "You mean, you don't think you're attractive enough? I can tell you this as a happily married man, you're fine." He smiled genially. "Matter of fact, you're pretty easy on the eyes."

"Thank you, sir, but, no. I mean, yes, I do think I'm fat—" because I am fat "—but that's not really the problem. I could say I came from a bad place, and that's true but it also . . . isn't. May I . . . Permission to speak plainly, sir?"

"Off the record."

"I know I definitely brought neurosis into the Marines. I think a lot of people brought insecurities and things they want to prove they're stronger than, but mine happened to clash with—I mean it met what there was so much of here. How people talk about how bodies define your motivation and who you are. The standard of what 'good' is, is so . . . physically prescribed. I know it's like that for men too, sir. It's . . . what people say about females."

"All that bull about being weaker?"

"Yes, sir, but more than that." What we cut out of ourselves to fit in. Original sin, still female. "Like . . . our default state is still Eve and the fucking apple."

Oh god. I'd sworn in front of an officer. I froze.

But he said merely, "Have you eaten breakfast, Williams? Have you eaten anything today?"

"Yes, sir."

"Are you sure?"

No, I wasn't. I wasn't sure what day it was. I had to think harder and harder to recall the events of more than an hour ago. I ate breakfast or that was yesterday.

"Yes, sir."

"So why are you getting PTAD? This might be a years-long process. Shouldn't you be getting out?"

"I am afraid I am malingering," I said quietly. "Bulimia . . . I mean, I do it to myself. I don't want to leave for . . ."

For making myself sick. In a time of war, how was bulimia anything other than cowardice? How was this different from shooting my own foot like some kind of . . . dissenter?

"My sister has bulimia," the XO said conversationally. "I don't think it's a matter of making yourself sick. You're sick, and it's finding a way to come out of you."

It was the closest a Marine appointed over me came to seeing me, and it shot me full of iron. The wild permission to give a shit about my own life.

That afternoon I went to Staff Sergeant Manning.

I chose my words with care. I said, "I am running out of time."

I saw the question in his eyes. I don't know what he saw in mine, but he nodded. "Alright, Williams," he said at last. "Let's get you out."

Much easier to toss me out than get me help. The mechanics of discharge were better-oiled than individualized PTAD. Fair, I figured sadly. I hadn't done fuck all for my country anyway.

The moaning separation paperwork meandered up and down the chain of command half a dozen times. It stopped along the way to rest on a desk under coffee, rejected for an imperfectly sized margin, rejected again for inconsistently indented paragraphs. Admin debated if "bulimia nervosa" was supposed to be capitalized. They decided no and sent it up. The CO said yes and sent it back down.

I vomited until I was hoarse and tried to be polite to everyone.

The new Charlie Company commander, a young captain, considered my forehead while I briefed him on his new company, including ghost platoon. I braced myself to endure the Williams Head Case Briefing again.

"Bulimia?" He continued to address my forehead. He sniffed. "That sounds like fraudulent enlistment to me. I'm referring your separation be under Other Than Honorable conditions."

Fleeting, the regret that I'd just lost all veteran's benefits, including the GI Bill, my access to a free college education. If I didn't get out soon I'd be dead before I got to college anyway.

A few hours later Staff Sergeant Manning stuck his head in the door.

"Williams," he said sternly. "You're getting Honorable."

"Captain Ja—"

"Yeah. I know. Don't worry about him." The NCO's disgust wasn't toward me. "As soon as I heard I went straight to the XO. He had a little chat with him."

I grinned. I knew what a little chat with a Higher Up looked like.

He paused. "Personally, Williams, I don't think it's your fault none of your leaders know what to do. I probably shouldn't say this but . . . it's asinine, the way this has been handled. In my opinion, the Marine Corps is failing you."

The last question: should I be separated administratively (AdminSep) or medically (MedSep)?

In the land of AdminSep dwelt fat Marines or Marines with mental disorders deemed preexisting or faked or Marines who did something ponderously stupid but not strictly illegal. Marines who hadn't done anything wrong but were horribly unhappy could be AdminSepped for Failure to Adapt. Sometimes raped Marines slipped out that way. Sometimes their rapists did. AdminSep was there to blot out the messiness of human error. No harm, no foul, but you're on your own.

A MedSep implied whatever was wrong with me was related to my military service. MedSeps came with certain legal protections, potential for disability benefits, and VA medical care.

Staff Sergeant Carlisle insisted I get MedSepped. I heard her shouting behind Master Guns's door. "She is bleeding into her eyeballs. This is *medical.*"

I was mortified. I flatly refused to jump in line for VA benefits before a goddamn war hero. MedSeps were for Purple Hearts, not bulimics in garrison. We scoffed at Marines who took medical care liberally. NCOs bitterly called out non-deployed POGs who claimed VA benefits because their backs hurt after sitting at a desk for four years.

Okay, yes, walking hurt. Every damn day. My hip clicked with the snap of an M16 ejection port cover. But could I walk? I could walk. Some Marines couldn't. So shut up.

Anyway, Aoife, waiting on her MedSep with visible furrows of surgical scars and bones bolted together, would sit in the Charlie Company office for another entire year.

My body sent out an emergency flare, something that flamed hot and quiet and true. *I don't have time for this.*

Administrative separation it was.

Getting out had as much paperwork as going in. I signed a stack of affidavits super promising I didn't have PTSD or a TBI, that I wouldn't claim to have PTSD or TBI in the future. The acronyms sternly reminded me real Marines did.

I would've confessed to witchcraft.

The sheer mass of the US military exerted gravitational pull on time. My file waded through copious sublevels of bureaucracy, manned by the many ghosts there because of the bureaucracy, mentally or physically ill Marines waiting for endless offices to bestow a required signature.

Eventually my file was passed to Karlsen, the sole junior enlisted female in admin, and with her it stopped. The copper-haired lance corporal followed up on wait-and-sees, tracked down forms, pounced on signatures, calmly insisted senior enlisted sign. She chased officers down the hall. She bent over her desk, writing *Williams—Needs HELP* on fax covers. She emailed me even if she had no word, making me feel less insanely alone. At the close of the work day she'd pad into the first sergeant's office, extract my file, and move it to the top. Stick a Post-it. *Urgent.*

Karlsen, a very pregnant Marine, did not let up on her admin Jenga until things moved.

The first sergeant called me in.

He glanced up and did a double take. "Are your eyes okay?"

The strain of constant vomiting burst blood vessels in my eyes and stained the whites of my eyes red. It freaked me out the first time I saw it too.

"I'm fine, First Sergeant, thank you."

The first sergeant sounded genuinely concerned. "Did that just happen? Are you okay?"

"Sometimes my contacts irritate me, First Sergeant. I'm alright." I wondered what he'd heard about me. Lance Corporal Williams does not *willingly* complain of bulimia, damnit.

He looked unconvinced but placed his fingertips on my file. "This can go two ways, Williams. I can make this go away, or I can push it through. PTAD isn't an option."

Black worms across my vision. Something tried to speak, a depleted whisper. *Keep me. Let me stay. I can do better. Please don't send me away.*

"What is your position, Williams?"

You have potential, but you need to eat.

There are Marines in war zones, and y'all are lying around the barracks eating fat-kid food.

You don't need to run to prove you're hard.

Fucking fat-ass always-broken females.

Breaking yourself isn't going to help anybody.

Marines, I expect you to have the self-discipline to PT above and beyond what's asked of you.

You could take a few days off.

I see you running all the time, so you can't be too much of a shitbag.

Waking up inches above vomit shot with blood.

You're not thin enough to have an eating disorder.

"Do you want to get out?"

You're saying no, but your body is saying yes.

"I think I probably should, First Sergeant."

April disintegrated into May. I zombied to S-1 for Karlsen's update. "We need one more thing. A signature from that counselor's aide you saw in Balboa. I've left about a dozen messages in their office, but I think she's been transferred."

"I talked to her for twenty minutes."

Karlsen nodded. "I know. But Higher Ups want documentation that proves the Marines tried to help you."

While hiding in my room in the Wounded Warrior barracks, I had felt such shame for taking up that hallowed space that I'd vomited until I clogged the toilet *and* backed up the shower, then spent a feverish night unclogging the drain with a wire hanger. This weekend proved the Marines tried to help me?

I couldn't believe what I said. I didn't know where it came from. Maybe it was because Karlsen looked at me like she believed me. I cracked, a hairline fracture, the closest I came to admitting my red line. A whisper pushed past frayed vocal chords: "Lady, I don't mean to bother you. But if I don't get help soon, I am going to die."

Her serious eyes did not leave my bloodshot ones. "I will get this done. Hang on, Williams."

On May 12th, three years to the day since I stood on the yellow footprints at Parris Island and one week before my red line, she did.

"Aoife?"

"Hmm?"

I stared at the Charlie Company office ceiling, or more accurately watched black spots drift between my eyes and the ceiling. Two of the circles intersected, a phantom Venn diagram. I was the CO's signature away from no longer being a Marine.

"Do you think I fraudulently enlisted?"

The black-haired beauty set down the battery she was carving open with a knife for reasons I didn't know. "Do you know the shit people have done to serve in the military? Kids have lied about their age and sometimes their nationality. American women have served in combat dressed as men since the Revolutionary War. People lie about medical conditions and drugs they've been on. That's just how we are, Williams: you want to serve so badly, you find a way. You've followed the legacy of every dumb kid who maybe shouldn't have but wanted to serve anyway." Aoife smiled. "We're all mad here. Think about the times NCOs have gone absolute apeshit."

"Yeah."

"Tell me there's any way in hell they don't blur lines to keep post-traumatic stress off their reenlistment papers. It's what we do. Shit, the highest compliment we give is being hard. But all guts are squishy, Will. We are *all* soft and fucked inside."

Staring at the ceiling, I recognized a stray thread hanging off the last three years. I took it and pulled.

At Parris Island, each of my drill instructors pulled me aside to say something strange. Accentuated with varying profanity, they'd said, You could be good. But you need to eat.

Arabic. McCone looked at me and said, Stop this now. You could do better. Artigas shared a bunk without wringing my weepy bulimic neck. Harvey told me Artigas charged down Marines who talked about my body behind my back, told them to shut right the hell up, Williams doesn't need your shit. Tucson advocated for my sanity, remarkably compassionately. Williams, if you throw up, don't come to run team.

When I passed out in Farsi Gerecht walked right by. He couldn't be seen showing me preferential treatment, that is, showing concern for a junior enlisted woman. By the time my vision cleared there was a female soldier on my right and a female airman on my left. These classmates pushed crackers into my hands and scolded, saying they saw how I worked out at lunch and I probably needed to eat something.

The women of the run team followed me to the brink of breaking myself, conferred with one another, and sat down on a dark track. They tried to pull me back. They had shown up for one another, and they had shown up for me. When I dropped out of life after New Year's, fellow female Marines—my teammates—picked up my slack without a single accusative word.

The competent women studying Pashto, all now deployed and actually doing our job in Afghanistan, invited me to dinners I declined, offered hands of friendship I shrugged away, determined to be one of the guys. They'd still reached out.

Dari. Washing vomit off our wall, my annoyed roommate Torres still found the grace to say, It's not your fault you're sick. Keep trying to get help.

Ghost platoon. Fiery Staff Sergeant Carlisle spent her afternoons terrorizing S-1 to "get her help or get her out." Untamed Aoife sat next to me with a wide smile and bracketed hip offering her own enthusiasm. She turned her face to the wall when she stood up while the ghost with too much skin complained of unfairness. I credited Karlsen, the pregnant lance corporal in admin, with getting me out alive.

There were others. There were many others. There. I'd pulled the thread as far as it went.

I stared at the ceiling.

Almost every woman I'd worked with for the last three years tried to help me. The weakest, most fucked up, head-up-her-ass Marine in the most POG-ass enlistment in the history of the Marine Corps: the response of the women around me had been to grab on and haul me up. Marines had consistently encouraged and defended me, followed me and cheered me on, people who were competent, trustworthy, and brave, and I'd totally missed it because so many of them had been disguised as female Marines.

Surreally I remembered the sensation of hands on my head. By some tear in all logic, a sliver of truth slipped into my Patriarchal Blessing. The patriarch said I would be protected by the sweetness of women. He never said it would be mine. He hadn't said it would be soft or weak. I couldn't have known the "sweetness inherent to my gender" could be the grit that weighted smaller boots striding hallways adorned with men.

Perhaps the patriarch himself hadn't known a much older definition of the word sweetness: nobility. That which forbears when there is every reason to be harsh.

I really wished I'd noticed the women Marines around me were there to help. I might've given them a chance.

On my last day in the Marine Corps, I closed my eyes and decided for the first time in my enlistment to be still and listen to a woman.

Aoife spoke calmly. "Williams, I don't know if you've seen yourself lately, but you look like you've gone somewhere you shouldn't go alone. Believe me, I know depression is a bitch. A total fucking bitch. It doesn't care where you are or what you're doing or if you don't have it as bad as someone else. Forgive me for saying this, babe, but you do not look okay. You need help. Fuck everything else. I know we all want to save lives, but if the only Marine you ever save is you . . . babe . . . that's what you need to do."

My DD-214 stated Honorably Discharged for the Convenience of the Government for a Condition Not a Disability. This confused two male Marines passing through admin.

The sergeant asked me, "Did you fuck an officer?"

"She wouldn't get kicked out for that," the corporal speculated. "She'd get promoted. Are you *knocked up* by an officer?"

I'll miss you too.

The red doors clanged behind me. I accepted a congratulatory cigarette from a beaming friend, who was sure I was elated. I said, thank you, Sergeant. Then I paused, looked at her, and said, Thank you, Sarah.

I watched the smoke trail rise against the barracks on Rifle Range Road. For the first moment in three long years, I was accountable to no one. Just like that, I was out.

Sort of.

CHAPTER 26

ABOUT FACE

What do sad people have in common?
It seems they have all built a shrine to the past, And often they go there and do a strange wail and worship.
What is the beginning of happiness?
It is to stop being so religious
Like
That.

—*Hafez*

The first thing No-Longer-Lance-Corporal Williams did was drive to the ocean.

I pulled over to the sandy shoulder and swore lightly as I untangled myself from seatbelt and blouse. I folded my blouse neatly on the passenger seat. I paused, then unlaced my boots and set them next to my blouse.

Then I did a very odd thing. I stepped out of my car.

I'd never so openly broken rules before. It was out of regs as a Marine to be off base in cammies, and illegal for a civilian to wear a Marine's uniform. I added it to the tally of all the ways I sucked and got over it.

I walked down to the water.

The ocean unfurled in a long gray expanse. Its surf stung my skin with salt. I'd chosen this beach because it was tucked into a quieter side of the peninsula. I was the only one in the sand. I sat and wrapped my arms around my knees.

Part of the reason I hadn't killed myself was because I was a Marine. I'd gotten a lot from that identity, arguably more than was good for me. But now I wasn't. I had nowhere I needed to be. I was without orders. Untethered. Free to answer the insistent call that had been circling my mind recursive as a snake eating its own tail.

Just go. You don't have to live like this.

This was a ridiculous way to kill myself. I was a strong swimmer. I swam competitively for years. I hadn't set records, but I was hardly afraid of drowning.

Which was why I was here.

I felt so heavy. I looked at my hands. They were already white, the cold wind off the Pacific sweeping away the blood. They would yellow and deepen to blue, and if I sat long enough, black, like the night I'd sat on the beach to see how long I could take it, the New Year's shit got fucked. I wouldn't be able to put my blouse or boots on now, even if I wanted to. If I went back, I'd swear, fumble with my keys, swear some more, and finally blast the heater, hold my useless claws in front of the vents until they thawed enough to manage a steering wheel.

The water of Monterey Bay is good for whales because it gets very deep, very quickly. I knew nothing of the ocean but felt vaguely optimistic the known riptide might work in my favor, wrestle me out.

If I swam out far enough . . . I knew this one thing about myself. I knew I would swim as far as I could, strike out in a forward stroke. I knew I'd doggy paddle beyond that. I'd side stroke when my hip froze and I couldn't kick. Maybe this was the best way to kill myself, actually. I could override the gradual disintegration of my body. That was the space I'd lived in for the last three years. I knew this one thing of myself: I would keep going.

I was mildly hypothermic sitting with my ass in the sand. My feet numbed through wool socks. I only had to swim far enough to let the cold take me. Cold would seep up my limbs until I could feel nothing of them. I knew I'd keep my face turned up as long as I could. She'd always been so stubborn, this body. She'd fight until she couldn't.

If No-Longer-Lance Corporal Williams could see ahead, if the gray rolling sheaths of ocean waves turned into white pages with a hint of the future would have been in a language she couldn't yet read.

I didn't know I'd come back to Monterey for college, and again for graduate school. That I'd sit on this beach many times, with friends and fire and cocoa and laughter and music.

I didn't know that things will change with an email from Harvey. That he'll be the one to tell me McCone had been raped. It will shatter the delusion that set order to my world, that if we were just good enough, we'd be safe. If we did everything right, we'd be okay.

The word will unhinge me, and some part of me will revolt, scream that she *mattered*, her torture *fucking mattered,* even in a Marine command that turned a blind eye to whispers, encouraged us to feel glee at the prospect of destroying bodies, indulged sexual bullying as boyish misdemeanor, natural expulsions of pent-up sexual frustration—these are warfighters (as if their victims aren't) it's really not that big a deal, females whine so easily—

The word will be a harsh light on my silent complicity. I'd given away power I didn't even know I had. The priests had not intervened, but neither had I. Could I have?

Could I yet?

I didn't know I'd live.

I didn't know the suicide attempt will crack me open, let in space. I didn't know I'll try to starve myself to death for real, drop into double digits on the scale, and get so cold I can't read before I finally start eating. I didn't know my own body will demand it, march me out of bed with the surprising ferocity of ninety-seven pounds of pure will to the fridge, to the pantry, set out apples, set out peanut butter, will eat the entire jar and flatly refuse to do anything but go back upstairs and go back to bed. I had no idea that in the end, it will be my body who insists we live.

I probably would've known that if I'd been paying attention.

I didn't know recovery will be harder than being sick for a long time, until all at once it wasn't, finally working with my body instead of against her. I didn't know she'd kick in as a powerhouse ally, someone whose hungers and needs and feelings, when met, made me a saner, calmer person. I didn't know recovery will look like laughing until my stomach hurt and being curious about things again and sobbing sometimes.

I didn't know in a few short years I'll limp into a yoga studio, begin practicing, and grow two inches in six months. I didn't know I'll live in my body again, feel her unfurling, finally taking her birthright, the space I'd conceded when I started starving myself at seven. I will feel my crown reach up and claim the space above my own head. I will give myself this private blessing.

My right leg will never be the same. I didn't know this, too, will be a gift. What will help is walking, and so I will learn to carry what I need and walk under the open sky. I will backpack alone thousands of miles. It will cultivate a quiet confidence that would seep into bones made strong again.

I didn't know I will fall in love with climbing, that a shrug of muscle will reclaim the bony desert of my ribbed back. I didn't know only a few miles from where I sat above the water wondering if I should write a note to my dad in case my body never washed up, I'll find a place called Sanctuary.

Sanctuary is the climbing gym where I'll do something life changing: I'll make friends with girls. A group of hilarious, loving, powerful climbing babes will swallow my lonely being into their brilliant embrace. We will climb in Yosemite and Shuteye Ridge and Red Rock and Joshua

Tree and Bishop and backpack all over California. We will laugh and share beds and sandy cars and a revolving cast of happy dogs and plants as we take turns squaring off on some new adventure. We'll make fire and ceremony and deliver one another's babies and marry one another's roommates and cheer one another on and witness one another be strong. We'll have the kind of group text that would, when I come out of the Sierra mountains from a solo trek and drive back into service, vibrate my phone off the dashboard with 119 ecstatic messages.

I will be so deeply loved, so entirely forgiven, and I will so deeply love. I'll understand how much I missed by failing to cultivate female friendship while I was a Marine. It might have made all the difference. I was so hung up on brotherhood I missed fellowship.

I will have so, so many friends and lovers and teachers along the way. I only needed to survive the next few years. I will. Because even as I sat on the edge of the water, no longer a Marine and not yet fully human, I wasn't alone. I sat beside my body, and she was so much more than hunger. She was earth and fire, heritage and dreams, and she was determined to live.

That girl on the sand knew none of this. I only knew, with a resigned groan, there was a pretty good chance I wouldn't drown. I knew my body might struggle until she attracted attention or washed ashore dizzy but intact or she might just fight her way back, will to self-destruct be damned. I knew there was a pretty damn good chance this ornery body would fight me hard enough to win.

I'd been a sturdy enough teenager to do just fine in boot camp on starvation rations, to keep it together in the world's most miserable private bulk-up session in combat training, and to settle into quasi-adulthood as someone who enjoyed a ten-mile run after dinner when dinner had been hopefully dropping a lemon into my water bottle.

The sweet, arrogant girl in the sand didn't yet recognize what she hated so much about her body wasn't its weakness, but its strength.

I don't remember walking back to the car, but there was certainly profanity as I numbed my way in. As I left the ocean to pack and buy a ticket to a city named after a saint, the blue vein under the shield at my wrist pulsed.

Arguably the Marine Corps had chewed me up and spat me out. Still I stood differently because I'd been in the Marines. I walked differently. I would always walk differently. My relationship to heaven and earth had shifted; my center of gravity had changed. I carried ten thousand miles in my bones. There was a story in my body that hadn't been there before.

She said, Keep going. Whispered, We will find another way.

Finally I heard.

CHAPTER 27

WE WHO ARE MARINES

This sky
Where we live
Is no place to lose your wings
So love, love
Love.

—*Hafez*

TWO YEARS AFTER THE MARINES

I always knew how far he was from me. An eleven-hour drive when he said alright.

Eleven hours later I knocked. A bearded giant flung open the door. I went airborne as he enveloped me in a bone-crushing hug.

"Welcome home," murmured Harvey.

Incentivized by six figures a year and repurpose, some cunning linguists of the United States Marine Corps regrouped as civilian contractors at Fort Gordon (now Eisenhower) in Augusta, Georgia. Scott Harvey grew a beard. Kate Artigas came charging. Jane McCone emerged, drawn and stern. While they stressed over polygraphs and bought civilian dress pants, I bid a cheerful to hell with my security clearance and made coffee for seven dollars an hour.

Harvey took in a puppy abandoned on the highway. We named her Honey, after an American whiskey.

We who were Marines figured out how not to be.

At home Harvey screamed. He grabbed Honey by the scruff and threw her in the closet. He punched a hole in the wall and buried his head between his hands. The young dog had chewed through the pack he'd carried in Sangin. It was the only thing he'd brought back from Afghanistan. That and this new thing of slamming doors.

His friend Luke, the only Mormon Marine I knew, was killed two weeks into their deployment. Latter-day Saints don't use the sign of the cross, so they'd put the angel Moroni on his gravestone at Arlington. Higher Ups would name a barracks after him at the Defense Language Institute. I found it a dubious honor.

Artigas confirmed it. "It sucked. Afghanistan sucked. I had a fuck-all comfortable mattress, but otherwise, I was stuck in the same five hundred feet for eight months." She'd worked with the Jordanian army in Kandahar.

She'd had the opportunity to lead a female engagement team, and turned it over to a junior Marine. "She was dying to get some experience. She wasn't ever going to get promoted without it." Artigas shook her head. "Remember Patz?" Vaguely. She'd been in a Pashto while I was in Farsi. "She was leading a FET. They heard gunfire, way across the valley. She told her team if they fired into the bushes, they'd get their combat action ribbons. It's too bad. She was the best Pashto linguist we had, but all anyone remembers her for is that."

Ah, how we'd envied that ribbon. *Engage in enemy fire.* That ribbon, stapled onto a crisp uniformed chest, broadcast credibility. That ribbon